COBOL
by
Command

COBOL by Command

Bernard V. Liengme

Department of Mathematics and Computing Sciences
St Francis Xavier University
CANADA

A member of the Hodder Headline Group
LONDON • SYDNEY • AUCKLAND

First published in Great Britain 1996 by
Arnold, a member of the Hodder Headline Group
338 Euston Road, London NW1 3BH

Whilst the advice and information in this book is believed to be true and
accurate at the date of going to press, neither the author nor the publisher
can accept any legal responsibility or liability for any errors or omissions
that may be made.

British Library Cataloguing in Publication Data
A catalogue record for this book is available from the British Library

ISBN 0 340 65292 6

Printed and bound in Great Britain by The Bath Press, Avon.

Contents

Preface

This is a book on the language of COBOL 85. It is intended for a course at the beginner or intermediate level in which the instructor has her/his own plans for the programs the students will write and what programming style will be used. The book concentrates on syntax.

My main objective is to provide the student with a concise and readable reference source. The sample programs are purposely not "real life" programs. Such programs require long narratives to describe the problems and result in lengthy code. This book gives either complete programs or program segments to demonstrate topics. The complete programs are short; each is designed to exemplify one language concept. For example, the student who wishes to see how a SORT statement is used is ill served by a 300 line program. What is needed is a simple example of how a file can be sorted; the reason for performing the sort is not relevant. The concepts in each program are readily adapted to whatever task in which the reader is engaged.

Syntax diagrams are given as each topic is introduced. In most cases the full syntax of the ANSI specification X3.23-1985 is used. I have tried to avoid making COBOL appear to be a limited language. To avoid overload, a few clauses or phrases have been omitted. In particular, it is assumed that the reader will be interested in disk and printer files but not in files stored on magnetic tape and that these files will be of fixed length. Syntax options for these topics are not shown in the diagrams. Certain elements marked in the standard have been omitted (for example, Report Writer). Others such as the paragraphs in IDENTIFICATION DIVISION other than PROGRAM-ID are mentioned only briefly.

While COBOL is a standardized language, it is impractical to avoid mentioning the implementor-defined elements such as how to reference an external file. It is assumed that the reader will be using either Micro Focus COBOL (or Micro Focus Personal COBOL) or Liant's RM/COBOL-85. The enhanced versions of the ACCEPT and DISPLAY verbs, which will be part of the COBOL 9x standard, are demonstrated for each implementation together with how to use the SCREEN DIVISION. I mention these implementations in other parts of the book where knowing how they behave is important. Clearly, there is not space to discuss other enhancements provided by them. When comparing a sample program provided by one of the vendors with the rules set down in this book, the reader should be aware that these implementations relax some of the standard's rules. For example, Micro Focus does not require the first paragraph in the PROCEDURE DIVISION to be named in a paragraph-header. To avoid repetition in the text, I sometimes use the phrase "most compilers". This should be taken to include Micro Focus COBOL and RM/COBOL-85 unless the text states otherwise.

Each chapter begins with a statement of its major objectives. The student should endeavour to master these before moving on. The selection of the more advanced topics is left to the instructor. Most chapters end with review questions: answers to starred questions are provided in Appendix D.

Whilst I have taken every care to ensure that the information is correct, there may be a few errors. If any of these cause you to spend unnecessary debugging time please accept my sincere apologies. Please let me know if you find a serious error. My Internet address is *bliengme@stfx.ca.*

Acknowledgements

At the request of the American National Standards Institute (ANSI), the following acknowledgement is reproduced from *American National Standard Programming Language COBOL, X3.23-1985:*

Any organization interested in reproducing the COBOL standard and specifications in whole or in part, using ideas from this document as the basis for an instruction manual or for any other purpose is free to do so. However, all such organizations are requested to reproduce the following acknowledgement paragraphs in their entirety as part of the preface to any such publication (any organization using a short passage from this document, such as a book review, is requested to mention "COBOL" in acknowledgement of the source, but need not quote the acknowledgement):

COBOL is an industry language and is not the property of any company or group of companies, or of any organization or group of organizations.

No warranty, expressed or implied, is made by any contributor or by the CODASYL Programming Language Committee as to the accuracy and functioning of the programming system and language. Moreover, no responsibility is assumed by any contributor, or by the committee, in connection therewith.

The authors and copyright holders of the copyrighted materials herein have specifically authorized the use of this material in whole or in part, in the COBOL specifications. Such authorization extends to the reproduction and use of COBOL specifications in programming manuals or similar publications.

FLOW-MATIC (trademark of Sperry Rand Corporation), Programming for the Univac++ I and II, Data Automation Systems copyrighted 1958, 1959, by Sperry Rand Corporation; IBM Commercial Translator Form No. F 28-8013, copyrighted 1959 by IBM, FACT, DSI 27A5260-2760, copyrighted 1960 by Minneapolis-Honeywell.

Micro Focus® is a registered trademark of Micro Focus Limited.

Micro Focus Personal COBOL™ is a trademark of Micro Focus Limited.

RM/COBOL-85® is a registered trademark of Liant Software Corporation.

RM/CO★® is a registered trademark of Liant Software Corporation.

Other registered trademarks and trademarks are acknowledged as the property of their respective owners.

Source Code and Other Files

To obtain files containing the programs discussed in this book:
1) With your Internet WWW browser download the files from
   http://juliet.stfx.ca/people/fac/bliengme/c-by-c.html.
2) Send an e-mail message to *bliengme@stfx.ca* requesting an e-mail reply with the files attached. Please state if you wish to have the Micro Focus or the RM/COBOL-85 files. Your e-mail reader must be able to handle binary files as MIME attachments.
3) Send an e-mail message to *bliengme@stfx.ca* or write me at *Department of Mathematics and Computing Science, St Francis Xavier University, Antigonish, Nova Scotia, Canada, B2G 2W5* requesting the files be mailed on disk. Please state if you wish to have the Micro Focus or the RM/COBOL-85 files, and the disk size required.

Throughout the book the term "the disk" is used for convenience to refer to the source of these files. The collection of files, which will be sent in self-extracting compressed format, includes:
1) The COBOL source code files of programs discussed in the book. These files have the extension .CBL.
2) Data files required to run the sample programs. Sequential files have the extension .DAT; indexed files .INX (together with corresponding IDX index files in the case of Micro Focus); relative files have the extension .REL. This naming convention is used so that the reader will know the organization of each file and not try to load anything but .DAT files into an editor.

   It will be necessary to make minor adjustments to the programs if your default directory is not the directory in which you have stored the data files. If you place them in the directory D:\SAMPLE, you will need to change the SELECT entries.
   Change `SELECT file-name ASSIGN TO DISK "external-name"`
   To   `SELECT file-name ASSIGN TO DISK "D:\SAMPLE\external-name"`
3) A file in Adobe Acrobat format containing information on the use of the Micro Focus Personal COBOL or the educational version of Liant's RM/COBOL-85 software. These are called MFCOBOL.PDF and RMCOBOL.PDF, respectively.
4) The Adobe Acrobat Reader (ACROREAD.EXE), to enable you to print the files referred to in 3) above. Adobe Systems Inc. permits this program to be distributed freely.
5) A data file (PEOPLE.DAT) of names and addresses together with some numeric fields. This line sequential file may be used for class assignments. The Micro Focus version contains 5000 records, the RM/COBOL-85 version contains 1000 records.

Instructors are free to distribute these files and/or photocopies of printed files to their classes.

1
Introduction to COBOL

Objectives

- Know what is meant by "COBOL is a standardized language".
- Know what is meant by enhancements.
- Know the advantages and disadvantages of COBOL.

1.1 The Evolution of COBOL

COBOL = COmmon
        Business
        Oriented
        Language

The first computers were programmed in machine language in which all instructions were strings of binary numbers. Next came assembler languages with mnemonics like ADD and MOV. Third-generation languages were introduced to make program code closer to "natural" languages such as English, French, etc. The first of these was FORTRAN, introduced in 1957. It was designed for scientific and engineering applications. It was followed in 1959 by COBOL. It was developed by the Conference on Data System Languages (CODASYL), a U.S. Government committee with representatives from industry, universities and computer manufacturers. The committee's objective was to develop a programming language for business use. In 1968 the American National Standards Institute developed a standard form of the language to avoid incompatibility between different versions used by various computer vendors. The standard was revised in 1974 and again in 1985. The latest version, called COBOL 85, is ANSI number x3.23-85. The language is upwards compatible; a program written using the 1974 syntax will compile and run on a computer using the 1985 version. A new standard (temporarily called COBOL 9x) is currently being developed by a committee of the International Standards Organization (ISO). COBOL 9x will include Object Orientation.

The ANSI standard states that "*COBOL is a language standard and is not the property of any organization or groups of organizations...*". Although it is standardized, there are some differences in the COBOL supplied by the various vendors. Many versions contain some components that are not part of the ANSI standard. These components are called extensions or enhancements. For example, RM/COBOL-85, Micro Focus COBOL and most microcomputer implementations of COBOL have enhancements for the DISPLAY and

ACCEPT statements that allow us to write user-friendly interactive programs. In this book we will generally stay with the ANSI standard. The major exception will be the DISPLAY and ACCEPT enhancements since these are very useful and will be part of the COBOL 9x standard.

The COBOL 85 standard includes some items marked as obsolete; these will not appear in the next standard. In this book we omit reference to most of these items.

1.2   A Preview of COBOL

The mandate of the CODASYL Committee was to develop a standardized language for business applications. The members, very wisely, agreed to make COBOL very English-like. Instructions use English words rather than complex code. There are several advantages to this: the language is relatively easy to learn; it is easy for users, who are generally not programmers, to understand what a COBOL program does; and the programs are self-documenting; this is a boon for the programmer who must modify a program written by someone else.

To give the reader a preview of COBOL, we shall see how some of the more common programming elements are implemented in COBOL. Comparisons with other languages are made to aid the reader with programming experience.

DATA
DECLARATION

COBOL is a structured language and requires all identifiers to be declared before they are used.

Most languages require each identifier to be assigned a "type". For example, the types STRING, INTEGER, SINGLE, LONG and DOUBLE are used in Microsoft QuickBASIC. COBOL does not refer to "types" but uses the more-or-less equivalent term "categories". The five identifier categories are: alphabetic, alphanumeric, alphanumeric-edited, numeric-edited and numeric. The size and category of an identifier are defined by a PICTURE clause.

`ITEM-A   PIC A(4)`	Alphabetic: this item may contain up to 4 characters taken from the set: A-Z , a-z and blank.
`ITEM-B   PIC X(10)`	Alphanumeric: this item may contain up to 10 characters; these may be letters, digits or symbols such as *,), ?, etc.
`ITEM-C   PIC 999`	Numeric: ITEM-C may hold 3 digits.
`ITEM-D   PIC S9V99`	Numeric: ITEM-D may contain values in the range -9.99 to +9.99
`ITEM-E   PIC 999` `  OCCURS 10 TIMES`	This defines a table (generally called an "array" in other languages) with 10 elements each of which is a 3-digit integer.

COBOL programs generally read and/or write to files. Consequently, the record structure may be thought of as the primary data structure in COBOL. A record is defined by level numbers that precede the identifier names. A record begins with a level 01 identifier and ends immediately before the next 01 level identifier.

In the following example two records are defined.

```
01 HEADING-RECORD.
      02  HEAD-ITEM             PIC X(20).
      02  HEAD-DATE             PIC 99/99/99.

01 CUSTOMER-RECORD.
      02 CUST-NAME.
         03 CUST-LAST-NAME      PIC X(20).
         03 CUST-GIVEN-NAME     PIC X(20).
      02 CUST-STREET            PIC X(30).
         ....
```

Compare COBOL record definitions with an example from Pascal:

```
TYPE  myrecord =
   RECORD
      name-one : PACKED ARRAY [1..20] OF char;
      name-two : PACKED ARRAY [1..20] OF char;
         ...
      END;
   VAR customerrec : myrecord;
```

ASSIGNMENT Assignments are made in BASIC with the equal (=) sign, while Pascal uses := as the assignment symbol.

```
         BASIC:    X = 3     X = Y
         Pascal:   X:= 3     X:= Y
```

In keeping with its philosophy of using English-like structures, COBOL makes an assignment with the MOVE verb:

```
MOVE 3 TO X   MOVE Y TO X
```

It should be noted that few programmers would use X or Y for identifier names. Rather, they tend to use names that reflect the meaning of the identifier; for example, DISCOUNT-RATE, CUSTOMER-BALANCE. The use of meaningful names aids in program coding and can prevent logic errors that can easily arise with names like X and A3$, which give the programmer no hint as to their purpose. Furthermore, in COBOL, the meaningful names, together with the English-like verbs, make the program self-documenting to a large extent.

Most languages allow the programmer to initialize identifiers in the data declarations. COBOL does this with the VALUE clause:

```
ITEM-X PIC 99 VALUE 23.
```

PROCEDURES

In Modula-2/Pascal, a line of code such as THIS_PROCEDURE causes the procedure to be executed. In QuickBASIC a CALL statement is used (e.g. CALL THIS_PROCEDURE). In COBOL a procedure consists of one or more paragraphs and is executed using a PERFORM statement (e.g. PERFORM THIS-PARA).

Unlike Modula-2/Pascal, COBOL does not require the procedure coding to be located in the program before a call to it. COBOL does not permit recursive procedure calls.

REPETITION

To repeat a section of program code BASIC uses the FOR...NEXT, DO...WHILE and DO...UNTIL constructions; Pascal's constructions are WHILE...DO and REPEAT...UNTIL; COBOL uses PERFORM statements. For example, PERFORM...UNTIL and PERFORM...TIMES.

CONDITIONS

The IF-ELSE conditional statement of other languages is constructed very similarly in COBOL. The EVALUATE statement in COBOL is equivalent to the CASE statement of Pascal and QuickBASIC.

ARITHMETIC

Most languages allow the programmer to code arithmetic expressions in much the same way as one writes them by hand.

BASIC: X = X + 1   Y = X + 3   Y = X**2 + 6*X + 9

The preferred method in COBOL for simple calculations is to use the ADD, SUBTRACT, DIVIDE and MULTIPLY verbs:

```
ADD 1 TO X        ADD 3 TO X GIVING Y.
```

The COMPUTE verb may also be used:

```
COMPUTE Y ROUNDED = X**2 + 6*X + 9.
```

A recent addition to COBOL is the introduction of functions. Modern compilers now include functions to compute logarithms, trigonometric functions, statistical data, and financial data such as present-value. See Chapter 31 for details.

STRING OPERATIONS

Since COBOL was designed for business operations that must frequently handle strings, such as names and addresses of customers and suppliers, it is not surprising that it offers several string operations. Concatenation is performed with the STRING verb, while the reverse operation uses UNSTRING. COBOL also allows one to address sub-strings. The INSPECT verb permits one to examine a string, look for a specific character, or to change some characters to others. Modern compilers include functions (see Chapter 31) which also enable the program to convert strings from upper-case to lower and from lower to upper-case, etc.

FILE OPERATIONS
The input-output (read and write) file operations are implemented very similarly in all languages; there are, of course, differences in the syntax of the statements. COBOL offers additional build-it file operations like SORT and MERGE. COBOL supports three file formats: sequential, indexed and relative.

1.3 Summary

With this preview, the reader will have thought of many advantages and some disadvantages of COBOL compared with other languages. These may be summarized below.

Advantages
Relatively easy to learn.
English-like statements with code that is:
  self-documenting, and
  easy for the author and others to read.
Rich language with many internal procedures, such as:
  SORT, MERGE, INSPECT, SEARCH.
Good file handling facilities.
Structured programs.
Standardized

Disadvantages
Verbose, long source files.
Longer compilation times compared with other languages.

To quote the *Encyclopaedia Britannica* (4:1055 1975 edition):

> *The advantages of COBOL can be summarized as follows: COBOL programs are stated in precise, easily learned, natural words and phrases: they can be read and understood by non-technical people with minimal background in data processing; programs written for one computer can be run on another ...; training time is negligible...; and program testing is simplified and can be completed by someone other than the original programmer.*

The self-documentation feature of COBOL should not be undervalued. In the business world, few computer programs remain unmodified. Some 80% of all programming costs are incurred in updating programs to meet changing needs. The structured nature of COBOL and its use of readily understood words makes modification a less arduous task than with programs written in other, more cryptic, languages. It is estimated that some 75% of all business computer programs are in COBOL. These amount to many billions of lines of code. With this large investment, it seems unlikely that COBOL will be superseded by one or more of the fourth-generation languages for some time.

2
Structure of a COBOL Program

Objectives

▸ Know the names and functions of the four COBOL Divisions.
▸ Be able to define: section, paragraph, sentence, statement and entry.
▸ Be able to define, and give examples of, user-defined word, reserved word and figurative constant.
▸ Know the COBOL character set.

2.1 Program Components

A COBOL program has a defined structure:

```
COBOL program
    DIVISION (there are 4 Divisions)
        SECTION
            PARAGRAPH
                Entry (in first three divisions)
                Sentence (in the Procedure Division)
                    Statement (Procedure Division only)
                        Word
                            Character.
```

It will be helpful for the reader to refer to the sample program at the end of this chapter.

DIVISION   There are four *divisions*.

                   The first is the IDENTIFICATION division, the main purpose of which is to name the program.

                   The ENVIRONMENT division specifies the environment for the program; of major interest to us will be the specifications of files used by the program.

                   The DATA division describes the data structures to be used.

Finally, the PROCEDURE division contains the coding to execute the purpose of the program.

Note that the word DIVISION (and a terminating period) follows the name of the division; for example, IDENTIFICATION DIVISION. This is called the *division heading*.

SECTION
Divisions may be divided into *sections*. The ENVIRONMENT and DATA DIVISIONS have predefined SECTIONS; for example: CONFIGURATION SECTION. When sections are used in the PROCEDURE DIVISION, the programmer provides the names. In most programs the procedure division has one, unnamed, section.

PARAGRAPH
Sections are divided into *paragraphs*. The paragraph names in the first three divisions are predefined — see Chapters 4, 5 and 6. Paragraph names are programmer-defined in the Procedure Division. Note that, whereas divisions contain the word *DIVISION* and section headings the word *SECTION*, the word *paragraph* is not used with paragraph names. For example, in the IDENTIFICATION DIVISION we find: PROGRAM-ID. This is the paragraph name; note the terminating period. A paragraph name must not contain spaces; the paragraph name COMPUTE TAX is not valid; COMPUTE-TAX is a valid name. A maximum of 30 characters is allowed in a paragraph name.

SENTENCE and
ENTRY
The PROCEDURE DIVISION paragraphs contain *sentences*; all other divisions contain *entries*. A paragraph may contain one or more entries or sentences.

ENTRY and
CLAUSE
An *entry* is a descriptive or declaratory item. In the sample program that follows, the FILE-CONTROL paragraph contains two SELECT entries. Note that each entry is terminated with a period. The first entry contains three *clauses*: a SELECT clause, an ASSIGN clause and an ORGANIZATION clause.

SENTENCE
A *sentence* is a sequence of *statements* terminating with a period.

STATEMENT
A *statement* is a group of words in the PROCEDURE DIVISION beginning with a COBOL verb. In Chapter 15 we shall learn that statements are classified as declarative, imperative, conditional or delimited scope.

PHRASE
A *phrase* is part of a *statement* or *clause*. The two READ statements in the following program contain the conditional AT END phrase.

WORD
A *word* is a series of *characters* terminating with a space. The maximum number of characters allowed in a word is 30. There are three types of words: *user-defined*, *reserved* and *system names*.

USER-DEFINED

User-defined words are generally the names of identifiers, paragraphs and files. They are formed from the digits, letters, and the hyphen (-) symbol. There must be at least one letter in the name. The hyphen cannot be the first character. There can be no spaces in a word. It is poor style to start a word with a digit. Examples of user-defined words: STUDENT-NAME, ITEM25.

Remember the 30-character limit on identifier-names, paragraph-names, and file-names.

RESERVED WORD

Words which have special meaning in COBOL are called *reserved words* and may not be used as user-defined words. Examples; ADD, MOVE, SUM, ALL, IF, END, OPEN, CLOSE, COUNT, LAST, FIRST. See Appendix A for a complete list of reserved words. If a reserved word is used as a user-defined word, a compiler error will result. Chapter 6 offers suggestions for avoiding reserved words.

FIGURATIVE
CONSTANTS

There is a special class of reserved words called *figurative constants*. These provide the programmer a set of predefined items. They include:

SPACE, SPACES	Has a value of one or more spaces.
QUOTE(S)	Has a value of the quotation mark (").
ALL literal	Used to fill an item with the specified literal.
ZERO, ZERO(E)S	Has a value of zero.
LOW-VALUE(S)	The lowest value in the computer's collating sequence.
HIGH-VALUE(S)	The highest value in the computer's collating sequence.

SYSTEM NAMES

When a program needs to reference the computer's operating system (for example the printer), a *system name* is used. The rules for forming system names depend on the computer being used.

CHARACTER

A *character* is the smallest component of a program. The COBOL character set consists of:

Digits:	0 to 9
Letters:	A to Z and a to z
Blank or space	
Special characters:	+ - * / = $, ; . ( ) < > " '

LITERAL

A *literal* is a word with a value defined by the characters that form the word. The term constant is used in other programming languages. A nonnumeric literal is a character-string delimited by single or double quotation marks. A literal may contain up to 160 characters. A numeric literal is series of digits (1 to 18) with an optional decimal point, which may not be the rightmost character, and an optional algebraic sign as the first character. Examples:

```
                    MOVE "Acme Manufacturing" TO HEAD-NAME
                    MOVE 12.5 TO VAT-RATE
```

Traditionally in ANSI COBOL, all coding, except nonnumeric literals, had to be in uppercase and nonnumeric literals had to be delimited by double quotation marks. Modern compilers accept lowercase coding and single quotes (`move 'Canada' to city-name`). If an identifier is coded in lowercase in one place and in uppercase in another in the program, the compiler will consider both to refer to the same item. Some programmers use uppercase to code with lowercase coding to show changes during the testing stage of a program development. Comments in lowercase are often easier to find.

2.2 Sample COBOL Program

This sample program, which reads a file, displaying and printing each record, illustrates the structure of a COBOL program. Material within brackets, <...>, is not part of the program code but is provided here for explanation. A COBOL program file cannot contain comments of this type.

For RM/COBOL-85 the second entry in FILE-CONTROL should read:
```
    SELECT PRINT-FILE ASSIGN TO PRINTER "PRINTER".
```

```
    IDENTIFICATION DIVISION.                         <A division header>
    PROGRAM-ID.   CHAP02-1.                           <Paragraph name entry>
    AUTHOR.    B. V. LIENGME.
    ********************************************************
    * Program to read, display and print file records   <comment, * in column 7>
    ********************************************************
                                                 <A blank line to aid readability>
    ENVIRONMENT DIVISION.
    INPUT-OUTPUT SECTION.                            <A section header>
    FILE-CONTROL.                                    <Paragraph name>
        SELECT DATAFILE ASSIGN TO DISK "CHAP02-1.DAT"    <first entry>
           ORGANIZATION IS LINE SEQUENTIAL.
        SELECT PRINT-FILE ASSIGN TO PRINTER             <second entry>
           ORGANIZATION IS LINE SEQUENTIAL.

    DATA DIVISION.
    FILE SECTION.
    FD DATAFILE.
    01 DATA-REC   PICTURE X(72).
    FD PRINT-FILE.
    01 PRINT-REC   PICTURE X(80).

    WORKING-STORAGE SECTION.
    01 WORK-ITEMS.
        02 END-OF-FILE   PIC X VALUE "N".

    PROCEDURE DIVISION.
    MAIN-PARA.                              <Programmer-defined paragraph name>
        OPEN INPUT DATAFILE                         <a statement>
```

```
        OPEN OUTPUT PRINT-FILE
        PERFORM  READ-WRITE UNTIL END-OF-FILE = "Y"
        CLOSE DATAFILE PRINT-FILE
        STOP RUN.          <a program must have at least one STOP RUN statement>

 READ-WRITE.
        READ DATAFILE
             AT END       MOVE "Y" TO END-OF-FILE <Indentation for readability>
             NOT AT END   DISPLAY DATA-REC
                          WRITE PRINT-REC FROM DATA-REC
        END-READ.                         <period required at end of paragraph>
 *................. END OF CHAP02-1 .....................    <a comment>
```

2.3 Program Skeleton

The reader may find it useful to memorize the following skeleton of a program. It includes
only those items that are commonly found in a program. To accentuate them, periods have
been show as ● in this outline. The comments within brackets are not part of the program.

```
IDENTIFICATION DIVISION●

PROGRAM-ID●   program-name●                          <names the program>
AUTHOR●       author-name●<optional, but useful for instructors when marking>

ENVIRONMENT DIVISION●

INPUT-OUTPUT SECTION●                          <specifies files to be used>
FILE-CONTROL●
    SELECT logical-filename ASSIGN TO physical-filename●

DATA DIVISION●                                 <specifies data structures>

FILE SECTION●                                  <data in file records>
FD logical-filename●
01 record-name          PIC X(n)●

WORKING-STORAGE SECTION●                             <other data>
01 record-identifier●
   02 group-identifier●
     05 elementary-identifier  PIC picture-string●

PROCEDURE DIVISION●                               <program logic>
first-paragraph-name●
    statement beginning with COBOL verb
    ...


    STOP RUN●

second-paragraph-name●
```

```
statement-1
statement-2
...
statement-n•
```

2.4 Review Questions

[handwritten: IDENTIFICATION DIVISION / ENVIRONMENT DIVISION / DATA DIVISION / PROCEDURE DIVISION]

1. Name the divisions in a COBOL program.

2* Divisions are divided into _____SECTIONS_____, which, in turn, are divided into _PARAGRAPHS_.

3* This line appears in the Identification Division of a program:
   PROGRAM-ID.   PROG-X.   *[handwritten: RESERVED WORD]*
   The word PROGRAM-ID is a _PARAGRAPH_.
   The word PROG-X is a _ENTRY   USER DEFINED WORD_

4* Paragraphs in the Procedure Division are composed of _SENTENCES_, which, in turn, are composed of _STATEMENTS_.

5. A statement always begins with a _COBOL verb_.

6. A word may contain a maximum of _30_ characters.

7. The words which have special meanings in COBOL are called _RESERVED_ words.

3
Coding a COBOL Program

Objectives

▸ Know the position and use of: Indicator Area, Area A and Area B.
▸ Know all the punctuation rules.
▸ Be able to read a COBOL syntax diagram.

3.1 The Areas of a COBOL Program Line

The standard ANSI line has five areas:

1	2	3	4	5	6	7	8	9	10	11	12	13	14	...	72	
Sequence number area						I	Area A				Area B					
Indicator area →								Identification area →								

Sequence area: This is used for line numbers which are used only for diagnostic references. Most applications generate these line numbers in the compiler listing; they are not coded by the programmer.

Indicator area: This area is column 7. It is used primarily for the comment symbol but the following symbols are legal in the indicator area:
     * denotes a comment in the program.
     - (hyphen) used to continue a nonnumeric literal value.
     / forces a new page when the program is listed.
     D to denote a debugging line.

Area A: This area is four columns wide; positions 8 to 11. The division headers, section headers, paragraph-names must *begin* in Area A. The FD and SD level-indicators, and 01 and 77 level-numbers must also begin in Area A.

Area B: This area starts in position 12. All other COBOL text must begin in Area B. For example, all statements in the Procedure Division must be in area B; i.e. they must start at or after position 12. The length of the area is implementor-defined. Usually the right margin (R) is in position 72.

Identification area: This area is not used by Micro Focus COBOL. It is used by RM/COBOL-85 to reference COPY files.

The ANSI rules defining the columns in which each area starts were formulated in the days of punched cards. Some compilers relax these rules and allow free format coding. Micro Focus does not enforce the Area A and B rules — items which ANSI requires to begin in Area A may start in Area B, and visa versa.

 There are several ways the programmer can make the program more readable. One of these is the use of line indentation, especially in multi-statement sentences. Another is to put documentation at the top or end of the program rather than using too many comments within the paragraphs. An obvious method is to use blank lines to separate different parts. Formerly, such lines needed an asterisk (*) in the Indicator Area; this is no longer the case and omitting the asterisk makes for tidier and easier to read code.

3.2 Punctuation in a COBOL Program

1) Words must be separated by at least one space.

2) Arithmetic symbols (= + - / * **) must have a space each side.

3) A space is required before a left parenthesis '(' and following a right parenthesis ')'. Most compilers relax the rule requiring a space before a left parenthesis.

4) Periods must not be preceded by a space but must be followed by a space.

5) Where a space is required, more than one may be used to make the program more readable.

6) Periods must be used:

   — after all division, section and paragraph headers,
   — at the end of each sentence.

The scope terminators (END-IF, END-PERFORM, etc.) of COBOL 85 have greatly reduced the number of *required* periods in the procedure division. If these are always used and the program does not use the NEXT SENTENCE construction, the only required termination periods in the procedure division are those at the end of each paragraph name and at the end of the last word in a paragraph.

NOTE: To emphasize periods in some examples, a large dot (●) has been used.

7) Commas may be used to separate item-names in a list. They are optional and are ignored by the compiler. Some programmers think commas make the code more readable. Others advise that, being readily confused with required periods, commas should be avoided. If commas are used, Rule 4 applies.

8) Semi-colons are used optionally to separate clauses. Rule 4 applies to semicolons.

9) An opening quotation mark (" or ') must be preceded by a space. A closing quotation mark must be followed by a space.

3.3 COBOL Syntax Specifications

The syntax of each element of COBOL may be displayed in one of two ways. The classical method is to use a Format Specification consisting of a series of words and the symbols: braces { }, brackets [ ] and ellipses ... (three periods).

The convention used is:

1) Each uppercase word is a *reserved* word.

2) Each underlined word is a *keyword* and is required. An uppercase word that is not underlined is optional and may be used to improve the readability of the code.

3) Each lowercase word indicates a word (file name, data name, condition, statement, etc.) to be supplied by the programmer.

4) Braces { } indicate that one of the enclosed entries must be selected.

5) Brackets, [ ] indicate an optional part of the format. When two or more stacked entries are enclosed in brackets, only one may be selected. An optional clause changes the way in which the statement functions.

6) Choice indicators, {| |} indicate that one or more of the enclosed entries may be selected but a single option may be specified only once.

7) An ellipse, ..., following an entry in braces or in brackets indicates that the entry may be repeated as often as required.

In some places in this text we have used a less formal specification. For example:

{ *identifier*−1 / *literal*−1 } is used to represent $\left\{ \begin{array}{l} identifier-1 \\ literal \ -1 \end{array} \right\}$

[*identifier*−1 / *literal*−1] is used to represent $\left[\begin{array}{l} identifier-1 \\ literal-1 \end{array} \right]$

Example: One format for the ADD verb is:

$$\underline{ADD} \quad \begin{Bmatrix} identifier\text{-}1 \\ literal\text{-}1 \end{Bmatrix} \quad ... \quad \underline{TO} \quad identifier\text{-}3 \quad [\text{ ROUNDED }]$$

```
[ ON SIZE ERROR imperative-statement-1 ]
[ NOT ON SIZE ERROR imperative-statement-2 ]
[ END-ADD ]
```

Examples of three statements using the ADD verb are shown below.

1) Adding one identifier to another:

```
ADD ITEM-A  TO ITEM-C
```

2) Adding a nonnumeric literal to an identifier with rounding — an optional clause in the
    syntax:
```
ADD 3.3 TO ITEM-B ROUNDED
```

3) Adding two identifiers to a third with rounding; optional phrase used:

```
ADD ITEM-A ITEM-B 8 TO ITEM-C
   ON SIZE ERROR DISPLAY "ITEM-C is too small"
END-ADD
```

Note the END-ADD scope terminator used to end the statement because it contains a
conditional phrase.

The second method of showing syntax uses "railroad track" diagrams. This method is used
in the on-line help facility of Micro Focus COBOL. In this convention:

1) The diagram begins with a pair of right pointing arrowheads ▸▸ and ends with ▸◂

2) If more than one line is required to show the syntax, the first line ends with ▸and the
    continuation lines begin with ▸. If more than one track is continued they are numbered.

3) The track forks to show alternatives and rejoins after the alternatives.

4) When an item may be repeated the track contains a loop with an arrowhead.

5) Reserved words are shown in uppercase and user-defined words in lowercase.

6) Reserved words that are optional but which alter the sense of the statement are indicated
    by a "drop-out" with wide sides. Reserved words which are optional and have no effect
    on the sense of the statement (i.e. words which are not underlined in the classical
    diagrams) are shown in "drop-outs" with narrow sides.

The syntax for the ADD verb given above in the classical form is shown in "railroad track" form below.

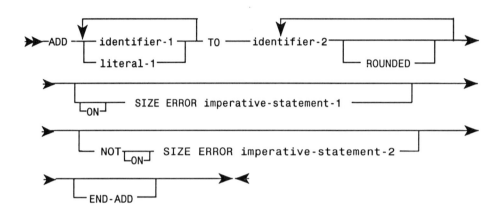

3.4 Review Questions

1. In a line of COBOL code, Area A begins in column __8__, and Area B begins in column __12__.

2* The __*__ character is used to denote a comment; it must be in column __7__.

3* Statements must begin in Area __B__.

4* The last word in a paragraph must be followed by a __Full Stop__. *PERIOD*

5* In a syntax diagram, some words in uppercase are underlined; others are not. What is the difference? *UNDERLINED - must use* *NOT UNDERLINED - optional use*

6* In part, the syntax of one format of the SUBTRACT verb reads

$$\text{SUBTRACT} \begin{Bmatrix} identifier\text{-}1 \\ literal\text{-}1 \end{Bmatrix} \dots \text{FROM} \begin{Bmatrix} identifier\text{-}2 \\ literal\text{-}2 \end{Bmatrix}$$
$$\text{GIVING} \{ identifier\text{-}3 \, [\, \underline{ROUNDED} \,] \, \} \dots$$

a) What is the meaning of the braces after the word SUBTRACT? *Either id-1 or a literal must be used*

b) In the syntax diagram above, the word FROM may be omitted with no effect on the result; true or false? *FALSE*

c) The word ROUNDED is optional and will have no effect on the result; true or false? *TRUE ·FALSE* *TRUE*

4
The Identification Division

Objectives

▸ Know how to code the division header.
▸ Know that the PROGRAM-ID paragraph is required.

4.1 Purpose and Syntax

This division names the program and, optionally, provides other documentation. The syntax of this division is shown in the figure below.

```
IDENTIFICATION DIVISION•

PROGRAM-ID•   program-name  [ IS {| COMMON  |} PROGRAM ] •
                                 {| INITIAL |}

[ AUTHOR•          [ comment-entry• ]…     ]
[ INSTALLATION•    [ comment-entry• ]…     ]
[ DATE-WRITTEN•    [ comment-entry• ]…     ]
[ DATE-COMPILED•   [ comment-entry• ]…     ]
```

4.2 The PROGRAM-ID Paragraph

The first paragraph is the only required paragraph in the division. It is used to name the program.

Syntax	Example
PROGRAM-ID. program-name.	PROGRAM-ID. PROG505.

Most compilers use this entry to name the object and executable program files. This is also the name used when one program CALLs another. The name used must comply with the file naming rules of the system being used. Thus, on a PC the maximum is eight. Extensions, such as .CBL, are not used in program names.

It is strongly recommended that the *program-name* and the name of the source file (without the extension) be the same. Thus the source code for a program called PROG001 will be kept in the file PROG001.CBL. The Micro Focus and RM/COBOL-85 compilers use the extension .CBL for source code files; other compilers may use .COB.

The use of the optional clause IS INITIAL/COMMON PROGRAM, is discussed in Chapter 29.

4.3 Optional Paragraphs

The other paragraphs in the division are optional; they may be used for documentation. They are marked as obsolete (i.e. they will not appear in the next version of COBOL). The AUTHOR paragraph is useful in course work to let the instructor know whose program he/she is marking.

Syntax		Example	
AUTHOR.	comment-entry.	AUTHOR.	B.V.Liengme.
INSTALLATION.	comment-entry.	INSTALLATION.	ST.F.X.U.
DATE-WRITTEN.	comment-entry.	DATE-WRITTEN.	Mar 31, 1995.
DATE-COMPILED.	comment-entry.	DATE-COMPILED.	

The comment-entry for DATE-COMPILED is generally left blank in the source file; the compiler will fill in the current date on its listing output but will not update the source file.

4.4 Review Questions

1. What paragraph is required in the Identification Division? PROGRAM ID.

2. The other paragraphs may be used for DOCUMENTATION.

3* The program-name should be the same as the SOURCE FILE.

5
The Environment Division

Objectives

- ▸ Know how to code the division header.
- ▸ Know the section and paragraph required to code a SELECT entry.
- ▸ Understand the difference between logical-file-name and external-file-name.
- ▸ Know how to code the SELECT statement to reference a disk and a printer file.

5.1 Purpose and Syntax

The Environment Division provides the program with information about the hardware to be used. The simplified syntax of this division is shown below. The two sections, and all paragraphs within them, are optional in ANSI COBOL. We shall be interested mostly in the Input-Output Section that specifies the names and locations of files used by the program.

```
ENVIRONMENT DIVISION.
CONFIGURATION SECTION.
SOURCE-COMPUTER.      source-computer-entries
OBJECT-COMPUTER.      object-computer-entries
SPECIAL-NAMES.        special-names-entries

INPUT-OUTPUT SECTION.
FILE-CONTROL.
file-control-entries

I-O-CONTROL.
I-O-control-entries

              Each entry must be terminated with a period.
```

5.2 The Configuration Section

Notwithstanding the fact that COBOL is highly standardized, there are differences between various compilers. Therefore, the SOURCE-COMPUTER and the OBJECT-COMPUTER entries can provide useful documentation.

The source-computer entry specifies the computer on which the program is to be compiled. A SOURCE-COMPUTER entry such as PC WITH DEBUGGING MODE, may be used to compile those lines marked as debugging lines by coding a "D" in the Indicator Area. We shall not investigate this further.

The object-computer entry specifies the computer on which the program is to be run. Refer to Appendix B (Defining Alphabets) to see how an entry here may be used to specify a nonstandard collating sequence.

5.2.1 SPECIAL-NAMES paragraph

The SPECIAL-NAMES paragraph enables the programmer to use several advanced features such as: (a) relating implementor-names to user-defined names, (b) relating alphabet-names to character sets, (c) specifying symbolic characters, (d) defining class-names, and (e) redefining the symbol for currency (default is $ or £), and for the decimal point and thousands-separator in numbers (defaults are period and comma). We shall not be exploring this paragraph any further except to show an example of redefining the comma and currency symbol.

```
SPECIAL-NAMES.
    CURRENCY SIGN IS "F".
    DECIMAL-POINT IS COMMA.
```

The first entry will change the currency symbol to "F"(Franc) rather than "$". The literal may contain only one, uppercase, character; it may not be A to D, P ,R, S, V, X or Z. When the second entry is used, the number that COBOL would normally display as 1,234.56 is displayed as 1.234,56, where the comma and decimal have been interchanged, as is the convention in some European countries.

Other special-names entries include:
    defining "switches" — not covered in this text
    defining symbolic characters — see Chapter 6
    defining class-names — see Chapter 21
    specifying or defining alphabets — see Appendix B

5.3 Input-Output Section

This section provides the information needed for the program to exchange data with external devices such as disks and printers. Since the majority of COBOL programs interact with files on disk it is somewhat academic to say that the INPUT-OUTPUT SECTION and its FILE-CONTROL paragraph are optional.

5.3.1 FILE-CONTROL paragraph

The FILE-CONTROL paragraph defines which files are to be used and the names they are given within the program. Most programs will therefore require this paragraph. The FILE-CONTROL paragraph has the form:

```
FILE-CONTROL.
    SELECT logical-file-name ASSIGN TO external-file-name.
```

Later in this chapter we will see how to name files when using the Personal COBOL and the RM/COBOL-85 applications. There are several optional clauses in the FILE-CONTROL entry that we shall examine in Chapters 20, 26 and 27.

5.3.2 I-O-CONTROL paragraph

The I-O-CONTROL paragraph allows different files to share the same memory space; this can be valuable with programs using many files. One type of entry in the I-O-CONTROL paragraph allows the programmer to specify the sharing of a memory storage area by more than one file.

```
I-O-CONTROL.
    SAME AREA FOR FILE-X, FILE-Y, FILE-Z.
```

We shall not discuss the use of this paragraph further.

5.4 Example of Environment Division

The names following the "ASSIGN" keyword are the *physical* file names; the names used by the computer system to refer to the files. These are also called the *external-file-names* or *implementor-names*. These are the names of system devices or the names of disk or tape files. Each computer system has it own way of defining physical file names, that is why we speak of implementor names. The system name SYS$PRINT is how Digital refers to the printer on the VAX computer. On a Hewlett-Packard HP/3000 computer, one directs the file to the printer by adding LP to the file name as in "OUTFILE,,,LP". On an IBM mainframe yet another convention is used. We need to know how to identify a file using either the Personal COBOL or the RM/COBOL-85 application.

The first file in each example is the system printer; the second is a disk file. The identifiers following the "SELECT" keyword (OUTFILE and INFILE) are the *logical* file-name; the names by which the files will be referred to within the program. Since these are identifiers, the normal COBOL rules for naming identifiers apply.

Code for the Micro Focus compiler:

```
ENVIRONMENT DIVISION.
CONFIGURATION SECTION.
SOURCE-COMPUTER. PC-using-MICRO-FOCUS.
OBJECT-COMPUTER. PC-using-MICRO-FOCUS.

INPUT-OUTPUT SECTION.
FILE-CONTROL.
    SELECT OUTFILE ASSIGN TO PRINTER
       ORGANIZATION LINE SEQUENTIAL.
    SELECT INFILE  ASSIGN TO "D:\DATA\PROGX.DAT"
       ORGANIZATION LINE SEQUENTIAL.
```

Code for the RM/COBOL-85 compiler:

```
ENVIRONMENT DIVISION•
CONFIGURATION SECTION•
SOURCE-COMPUTER• PC-using-RM-COBOL•
OBJECT-COMPUTER• PC-using-RM-COBOL•

INPUT-OUTPUT SECTION•
FILE-CONTROL•
    SELECT OUTFILE ASSIGN TO PRINTER  "PRINTER"•
    SELECT INFILE  ASSIGN TO DISK "D:\DATA\PROGX.DAT"
      ORGANIZATION LINE SEQUENTIAL•
```

a) Carefully note the periods (shown as •) at the end of each heading and each entry.

b) Generally, the entries for SOURCE- and OBJECT-COMPUTER are only for documentation. Entries are shown here for completeness but we shall not use them in the rest of the book.

c) The FILE-CONTROL paragraph is of most interest to us. We shall examine the ORGANIZATION clause in the SELECT entry in Chapters 20, 26 and 27. In Chapter 20 we also discuss the OPTIONAL clause.

d) In this book, as in the sample programs provided by Micro Focus COBOL, we have specified ORGANIZATION LINE SEQUENTIAL for printer files. Your programs may work without this but could behave differently from the descriptions in the text.

5.4.1 External-filename in Micro Focus COBOL

We begin by looking at disk files. In the examples below, please assume that the entries each contain the ORGANIZATION LINE SEQUENTIAL clause. We discuss this fully in Chapter 20. For now, we note that this clause denotes that the file has the format that text editors generate. Consider the following FILE-CONTROL entries:

```
1   SELECT DATAFILE ASSIGN TO DISK "D:\DATA\SALES.DAT"
2   SELECT DATAFILE ASSIGN TO DISK "\DATA\SALES.DAT"
3   SELECT DATAFILE ASSIGN TO DISK "DATA\SALES.DAT"
4   SELECT DATAFILE ASSIGN TO DISK "SALES.DAT"
5   SELECT DATAFILE ASSIGN TO DISK
```

In the first example, the full path and name of the file has been given. If our program attempts to OPEN the file which the program called "DATAFILE", it will look in the directory DATA on the D drive for a file called "SALES.DAT". In the second example, the file is assumed to be in the sub-directory DATA of the default directory. If, for example, your current directory is F:\HOME\A123, the file will be in the subdirectory F:\HOME\A123\DATA. Example 3 requires the file to be in the directory DATA of the default drive. In example 4, the file must be in the current directory. Finally, in the last example, the file must be in the current directory and have the name "DATAFILE". If the identifer is more than eight characters the physical file will have a name equal to the first eight characters. Note that in examples 1 to 4 the word "DISK", or "DISC", is optional.

We could also code a printer file as:
```
      SELECT OUTPUT ASSIGN TO "PRN:"
          ORGANIZATION LINE SEQUENTIAL.
```

During testing stages we may wish to see the output data on the screen using the code:
```
      SELECT OUTPUT ASSIGN TO "CON:"
          ORGANIZATION LINE SEQUENTIAL.
```

5.4.2 External-filename in RM/COBOL-85

The comments about disk files in the above section for Micro Focus COBOL apply equally
to the RM/COBOL-85 application. The entry for a printer file is slightly different:
```
          SELECT OUTPUT ASSIGN TO PRINTER "PRINTER".
```
Note that we must include the literal "PRINTER". If it is omitted, a disk file called OUTPUT
will be generated in the default directory. Also note that in RM/COBOL-85 a printer file is
automatically of type LINE SEQUENTIAL so the ORGANIZATION clause is not needed.

NOTE: When running one of the sample programs on the disk provided with this text, you
may see one of the following errors:
```
      FILE NOT FOUND (ERROR 013)    Micro Focus Personal COBOL,
or    COBOL I/O ERROR 35            RM/COBOL-85
```
The problem is caused by the fact that the required file is not in your current directory. To
rectify this either (1) change your current directory to that in which you have installed the
sample files, or (2) modify the program to include the full path-name in the SELECT entry
as in example 1 in 5.4.1 above.

5.5 Review Questions

1. What is the purpose of the Environment Division? *To provide program with info on hardware being used.*

2. Name the section in this division which must be coded when a program uses files. *INPUT-OUTPUT SECTION*

3. The SELECT entry appears in the _FILE-CONTROL_ paragraph.

4* A program contains the entry;
```
      SELECT INFILE ASSIGN TO DISK "PROG-A".
```
    Which is the correct statement to open the file?
    a) `OPEN INPUT INFILE` ✓
    b) `OPEN INPUT PROG-A`

6
The Data Division

Objectives

- ▸ Know how to code the division header.
- ▸ Understand the purposes of the FILE, WORKING-STORAGE and LINKAGE SECTION, and the order in which they must appear.
- ▸ Understand the terms: data-name, identifier, alphanumeric and numeric.
- ▸ Understand the purpose of FILLER.
- ▸ Understand the purpose of the figurative constants: SPACES, ZERO and ALL.
- ▸ Know how to code the FILE SECTION for a sequential file.
- ▸ Know that all data-names used in the Procedure Division must be defined in one of the sections.

6.1 Purpose and Syntax

The purpose of the DATA DIVISION is to describe the data structures used by the program. In ANSI COBOL 85 each section in this division, and the division itself, are optional. The components of this division are shown below.

```
DATA DIVISION●

FILE SECTION●                    file-section-entries

WORKING-STORAGE SECTION●         working-storage-entries

LINKAGE SECTION●                 linkage-entries

COMMUNICATION SECTION●           communication-entries

REPORT SECTION●                  report-section-entries

SCREEN SECTION●                  screen-section-entries
```

Each entry must be terminated with a period.

6.2 Sections in the Data Division

The FILE SECTION reserves memory for the records in the files used by the program and specifies their structure. We shall examine this section in more detail when we study sequential, indexed, and relative files in Chapters 20, 26 and 27, respectively.

The WORKING-STORAGE SECTION reserves memory for, and specifies the structure of, data items that are not part of input-output records.

The LINKAGE SECTION appears only in subprograms, i.e. programs that are not run independently but are called from another program. This section reserves memory for the called program to hold the data passed between it and the calling program. The Linkage Section is covered in Chapter 29.

The COMMUNICATION SECTION is used to pass data to a program running on another computer. An example of this would be a program running in a branch office and updating the database in head office. Not all compilers support this feature.

The REPORT SECTION is part of the COBOL Report Writer designed to enable the programmer to produce complex reports. It handles such things as headers, footers, subtotals and totals. Not all compilers include the Report Writer although it is in the ANSI standard. The 1985 standard indicates that this section is "obsolete" and will be removed in future versions.

The SCREEN SECTION enables formatted data to be sent to, and received from, the screen. This section is discussed in Chapter 16. The SCREEN SECTION is not part of the current ANSI standard but is an enhancement provided by most COBOL dialects; it will be part of COBOL 9x.

6.3 Data-names and Identifiers

Each item of data referred to in the Procedure Division of a program must be named and its type defined in the appropriate section in the Data Division. Many programming languages refer to data-names as *variables*. As we will see in this and the next two chapters, COBOL also uses the term *identifier*. There are some fairly simple rules for naming data items. A data-name:

a) May not be a reserved word. This rules out some very useful words such as COUNT, FIRST, LAST, END. Some "tricks" which avoid using reserved words but keep some of their meanings include:
    — using misspellings as in KOUNT
    — using nonEnglish words such as FIN for END
    — using hyphens as in LAST-ONE.

b) May be up to 30 characters long. Avoid the use of single letter names; especially the letter I that is so easily confused with the digit 1.

c)   May be composed of letters, digits and hyphens (-). It may not begin or end with a hyphen. If the compiler allows the use of the non-ANSI underline (_), the symbol will be treated as a hyphen. Thus, ITEM_A and ITEM-A would refer to the same identifier.

d)   Must contain at least one alphabetic character. It is considered poor style to begin a name with a digit. Since rule (c) precludes the hyphen as the first character and a digit would be frowned upon, this rule almost implies that the first character must be a letter character.

e)   A word may not contain imbedded spaces (blanks); it would then not be a single word.

f)   Must be unique within a group. There are occasions when it is helpful to use the same data-name in different records or groups. We will learn the meaning of *record* and *group* in Chapter 7.

The data-name should reflect the data item's function. A college registration system might use STUDENT-LAST-NAME to name the item used to hold a student's last name. It is more likely that an abbreviation such as STU-LNAME would be used; it just as clearly states the purpose of the identifier but gives the programmer less to type. Some programmers use names with most vowels omitted; an example would be STU-LNM. The author finds that names that can be readily vocalized (STU-LNAME = stu-l-name) are easier to remember. This helps with the coding and more readily allows two programmers to discuss a program.

We will see in the next two chapters that there are times when a data-name alone is not sufficient to uniquely specify a particular data item. Data-names that are uniquely identified by using qualifiers, subscripts or indexes, or reference modifiers are called *identifiers*. There are three cases when qualification is needed to identify a particular data item:

1)   When a data item is part of a table (array) we need to use a subscript or index to state which occurrence of the item is being referenced. For example: X-ITEM (2)

2)   When the same name is used for two different items we need to use *qualification*. For example if X-ITEM is the name of a data item in GROUP-A and in GROUP-B, we could refer to a specific one using:
        X-ITEM IN GROUP-A   or   X-ITEM OF GROUP-A

3)   When we wish to reference part of a data item we may use *reference modification*. For example to reference the first three characters of data item X-ITEM we could use X-ITEM (1:3). The reader is cautioned not to use reference modification as a substitute for properly defining data into groups and elementary items.

These notes will become more meaningful when the next two chapters have been read.

The full syntax for an identifier is:

$$\textit{data-name-1} \left[\begin{Bmatrix} \underline{IN} \\ \underline{OF} \end{Bmatrix} \textit{data-name-2} \right] \dots \left[\begin{Bmatrix} \underline{IN} \\ \underline{OF} \end{Bmatrix} \textit{file-name-1} \right]$$

$$[\ (\ \{ \ \textit{subscript} \ \} \dots \ ) \ ] \qquad [\ (\ \textit{leftmost-character-position}: \ [\ \textit{length} \ ] \ ) \ ]$$

In the syntax diagrams throughout this book you will find both *data-name* and *identifier*. When *data-name* appears, the programmer must supply a simple, unqualified data-name. When *identifier* appears the program may use either a simple data-name or an identifier (a data-name with qualification, subscript or index, and/or reference modification).

6.4 The Data-name FILLER

Suppose we are writing a program to print a report. We will have one or more heading-records. These will contain various elementary items, such as the company name, title of the report, etc. Most likely we will (a) give values to these items using VALUE clauses in the data-description-entries and (b) never reference the elementary items again. What a chore it would be if all such identifiers had to be named! Fortunately, the designers of COBOL have come to our rescue. An identifier that is never referred to in the program, other than in the DATA DIVISION, may be called FILLER, or given no name by leaving a space between the level-number and the picture clause. We will examine the use of FILLER in subsequent chapters but here is one simple example.

```
01 HEAD-REC.
    02 FILLER     PIC X(50)   VALUE "Acme Manufacturing".
    02 FILLER     PIC X(22)   VALUE "Sales Report".
    02 FILLER     PIC X(6)    VALUE "Page".
    02 HEAD-PAGE  PIC 99      VALUE 0.
```

6.5 Figurative Constants

The COBOL language has a number of build-it identifiers with predefined values which cannot be changed. Figurative constants are the only identifiers that are not declared in the Data Division. Here are some examples of the use of figurative constants:

```
MOVE SPACES TO STUDENT-NAME.        MOVE QUOTE TO ITEM-A
MOVE ZERO TO MATH-MARK.             IF ITEM-N = ZERO …
IF ITEM-A > SPACES …                MOVE ALL "*" TO ITEM-J
```

The examples show that figurative constants may be used to assign values to identifiers and to test the values of identifiers. Figurative constants will be more closely examined when we look at the VALUE clause, and later at the MOVE verb.

SPACES
: Figurative constants may be used in a VALUE clause or in a MOVE statement to give a data item the value of the figurative constant. The statement MOVE SPACES TO ITEM-X fills the alphanumeric receiving item with spaces or blanks. The figurative constant SPACES (or its equivalent SPACE) may be used in a program in place of an alphanumeric literal consisting of a single space enclosed in quotation marks.

ZERO
: ZERO (or ZEROS or ZEROES) gives a numeric item the value of zero. The figurative constant ZERO (or its equivalent ZEROS or ZEROES) may be used in a program in place of the numeric literal 0. Thus, MOVE ZERO

TO ITEM-N is equivalent to MOVE 0 TO ITEM-N.

QUOTE   QUOTE (or QUOTES) places a quotation mark in the receiving alphanumeric identifier. It is usually found in the DATA DIVISION:
```
02 FILLER PIC X VALUE QUOTE.
```

ALL   The ALL figurative constant fills an alphanumeric item with a nonnumeric literal. Example: 02 UNDERLINE PIC X(72) VALUE ALL "_".

LOW-VALUE   LOW-VALUE fills an alphanumeric identifier with a value equal to the computer's lowest collating sequence.

HIGH-VALUE   HIGH-VALUE is similar to LOW-VALUE but has the value of the computer's highest collating sequence.

Generally LOW-VALUE is a series of binary zeros. If the computer uses ASCII, LOW-VALUE has a hexadecimal value of 00. Conversely, HIGH-VALUE is generally a series of binary ones, or hexadecimal FF in ASCII. These two figurative constants may be used only with identifiers having alphanumeric pictures.

USER-
DEFINED   The programmer may define one or more figurative constants by using the SYMBOLIC CHARACTERS clause in the SPECIAL-NAMES. This is particularly useful when we wish to use characters that are not part of the COBOL character set. For example, suppose we need to display (or print) the half symbol (½). The ½ character has the ASCII value of 171. In the SYMBOLIC clause we need to define the *ordinal* position of the character in the ASCII character set; since the first character has a value of 0, the character with a value of 171 is the 172nd character. We make this definition using:
```
SPECIAL-NAMES.
        SYMBOLIC CHARACTERS  HALF-SYMBOL IS 172.
```

We have now defined our own figurative constant that we have called HALF-SYMBOL. We may use it in the same way as any other figurative constant; for example, in a VALUE clause, a MOVE statement, etc.
The next example defines two figurative constants for the frequently used fractions ½ and ¼.
```
SPECIAL-NAMES.
    SYMBOLIC CHARACTERS
        HALF-SYMBOL, QUARTER-SYMBOL ARE 172, 173.
```

6.6 File Section

The FILE SECTION will be briefly examined here so that we may have a complete overview of the structure of a COBOL program. In later chapters the File Section will be more closely examined to show how it is used with different types of files. The abbreviated syntax of this section for a sequential file is:

```
FILE SECTION●
FD file-name
    [ BLOCK CONTAINS integer-1  {RECORDS/CHARACTERS} ]
    [ RECORD CONTAINS integer-2 CHARACTERS ]●
    data-description-entry●
```

The beginning of the file description entry is identified by the FD that must be in Area A of the code line. In a later chapter we shall see that temporary files used by the SORT verb have a description beginning with SD.

The BLOCK clause can be very useful in improving I/O operations in a program working with large files. For a discussion of this clause, the reader should consult the system manual or an advanced text book such as *Advanced COBOL*, second edition, A.S. Philippakis and Leonard Kazmier, McGraw-Hill Book Company, 1987.

The optional RECORD clause can provide useful documentation. An expanded version of the RECORD clause may be used with files having variable length records.

We have omitted the EXTERNAL and GLOBAL clauses that may be used with subprograms — see Chapter 29. The CODE-SET clause is also omitted — see Chapter 20. The clauses LABEL RECORD, VALUE OF, and DATA RECORD have been omitted since these have been declared obsolete features and are not expected to be included in the next COBOL standard. The omitted LINAGE clause, used with printer files, is discussed in Chapter 20. The data-description-entry is fully covered in the remainder of this chapter and in following chapters.

An example of a FILE SECTION:

```
FD OUTFILE
    RECORD CONTAINS 80 CHARACTERS                         < optional>
01 OUT-REC.                              <data description begins>
    02 STUDENT-LAST-NAME      PIC X(20).
    02 STUDENT-GIVEN-NAMES    PIC X(20).
    02 STUDENT-ADDRESS        PIC X(40).
```

6.7 Working-Storage Section

The WORKING-STORAGE SECTION contains a description of all identifiers that are not input-output records, or subordinate items of such records. The syntax is:

```
WORKING-STORAGE SECTION●

data-description-entry-1● [data-description-entry-2●] …
```

There are three formats for the data-description-entry, two of which are illustrated in this example:

```
WORKING-STORAGE SECTION.

01 HEAD-RECORD.
      03 FILLER         PIC X(30) VALUE "Classlist for".
      03 HEAD-COURSE    PIC X(30).
      03 FILLER         PIC X(6)  VALUE "Date:".
      03 HEAD-DATE      PIC 99/99/99.

01 CLASS-RECORD.
      03 CR-STU-ID      PIC 9(6).
      03 FILLER         PIC XX    VALUE SPACES.
      03 CR-STU-NAME    PIC X(40).
      03 CR-STU-GRADE   PIC 99.
         88 GRADE-A     VALUE 80 THRU 99.
         88 GRADE-B     VALUE 65 THRU 79.
         88 GRADE-C     VALUE 55 THRU 64.
         88 GRADE-D     VALUE 50 THRU 54.
         88 GRADE-E     VALUE 0  THRU 49.

77 STUDENT-COUNT       PIC 9(3)  VALUE ZERO.
77 STUDENT-GRADE-AVG   PIC 99V9.
```

6.8 Data-Description-Entries

There are three formats for the data-description-entries: Format-1 is used for general data items, Format-2 is used with RENAMES and Format-3 is used to define *condition-names*.

```
             Format-1,the general data-description-entry

                              ⎧ data-name ⎫
           level-number       ⎨   FILLER  ⎬   [optional-clause ]…
                              ⎩           ⎭
```

This format, which is discussed in the next chapter, is used for data items with level numbers of 77 or in the range 01 to 49.

```
                   Format-2, used for RENAMES

                              ⎧ data-name ⎫
           level-number       ⎨   FILLER  ⎬   [optional-clause ]…
                              ⎩           ⎭
```

Level 66 may be used to give alternate names to one or more items in a record. All 66 level identifiers must be placed after the last elementary item in the record. We shall not consider the level 66 item or the RENAMES clause further. The interested reader should consult his/her system manual. Generally, one can achieve the same effect, and more, using the REDEFINES clause discussed in Chapter 10.

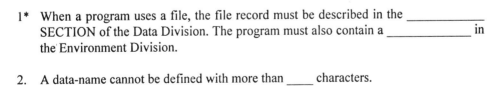

A class of identifiers called *condition-names* are coded at the 88 level using format-3 shown above. Where appropriate, figurative constants such as ZERO, SPACES, HIGH-VALUE and LOW-VALUE may be used in place of the literals. As with data-names, a condition-name may be qualified and/or subscripted. It may not use reference modification. The 88 level will be examined more closely in Chapter 21.

```
05 STUDENT-LEVEL     PIC 9.
   88 FRESHMAN       VALUE 1.
   88 SOPHOMORE      VALUE 2.
   88 JUNIOR         VALUE 3.
   88 SENIOR         VALUE 4.
   88 UPPER-CLASS    VALUES 3 THRU 4.
   88 NON-JUNIOR     VALUES 1, 2, 4.
```

In this example all the items at the 88 level are *condition-names* while the item to which they refer, STUDENT-LEVEL, is called a *conditional-variable*.

In the Procedure division we may test the value of STUDENT-LEVEL using, for example, either of these equivalent statements:

```
        IF STUDENT-LEVEL = 3 OR 4 THEN ...
or      IF UPPER-CLASS THEN ...
```

6.9   Review Questions

1* When a program uses a file, the file record must be described in the _____ SECTION of the Data Division. The program must also contain a _____ in the Environment Division.

2. A data-name cannot be defined with more than ____ characters.

3* Which of these are valid data-names?
   a. ITEM-A,   b. ITEM_B,   c. 9COUNT,   d. BANK BALANCE

4*   What would be displayed by these statements?
   a) `DISPLAY    "Hello, world"`
   b) `DISPLAY    QUOTE "Hello, world" QUOTE`

7
The Record and Level Numbers

Objectives

- ▸ Understand the concept of a record.
- ▸ Know how to use level numbers 01 - 49 to establish the hierarchy of a record.
- ▸ Know what is meant by a group, an elementary item and an independent item.

7.1 Introduction

We saw in the last chapter that every user-defined *data-name* referenced in the Procedure
Division must first be declared in one of the sections of the Data Division. These declarations
are made through data-description-entries, which may have one of three formats. The general
format for a data description is shown below.

```
                        Format-1:
            Format for the general data-description-entry


                        ⎧ data-name ⎫
      level-number      ⎨  FILLER   ⎬
                        ⎩           ⎭


              [ REDEFINES clause]
              [ EXTERNAL clause]
              [ GLOBAL clause]
              [ PICTURE clause]
              [ USAGE clause]
              [ SIGN clause]
              [ OCCURS clause]
              [ SYNCHRONIZED clause]
              [ JUSTIFIED clause]
              [ VALUE clause]
              [ BLANK WHEN ZERO clause]●

      In format-1, the level-number is either 77 or in the range 01 to 49.
                The keyword FILLER may be omitted.
```

In this chapter we introduce *level-numbers* and the concepts of *record, group* and *elementary* data items. Subsequent chapters discuss the optional clauses in this form of the data-description entry.

7.2   Records, Groups and Elementary Data Items

Frequently, a program will deal with a set of items that form a hierarchy, i.e. the data items will have some ordered relationship to each other. A collection of data-description-entries is called a *record*.

Consider the items that a college Admissions Officer may wish to store for each applicant. The list might include:

Name of student,   Address,   Birth date,   Date of application,   etc.

Some of these items may be divided into sub-items. The student's name will have at least two parts: surname and given names. We shall need to code these items in a way that shows their relationships. We do this by putting their identifiers in a *record* using *level numbers* to establish the hierarchy.

Let consider two possible ways to code this record.

```
       Example A                        Example B

01 ADMISSION-REC.                   01 ADMISSION-REC.
   02  NAME       PIC X(40).           02 STUDENT-NAME.
   02  STREET     PIC X(30).              03 SURNAME      PIC X(20).
   02  CITY       PIC X(20).              03 GIVEN-NAMES  PIC X(20).
   02  PROVINCE   PIC X(4).            02 ADDRESS.
   02  POST-CODE  PIC X(6).              03 STREET       PIC X(30).
   02  BIRTHDAY   PIC 9(6).              03 CITY         PIC X(20).
   02  APPLY-DATE PIC 9(6).              03 PROVINCE     PIC X(4).
                                         03 POST-CODE    PIC X(6).
                                      02 BIRTHDAY.
                                         03 BYEAR        PIC 99.
                                         03 BMON         PIC 99.
                                         03 BDAY         PIC 99.
                                      02 APPLY-DATE      PIC 9(6).
```

The indentations as level numbers increase and the alignment of PIC clauses are not required but are strongly recommended since they make the code more readable. Each line in the code consists of a *level number* followed by a *data-name* with, occasionally, a PICTURE clause. The PICTURE clause is discussed in the next chapter. It may help the reader to know at this stage that the clause specifies the type (alphanumeric or numeric) of the item and its size.

We now introduce the concepts of record, group and elementary items. It is essential that the reader becomes familiar with these concepts before proceeding to subsequent chapters.

Record   The 01 level indicates the beginning of a record. A record ends when the next 01 or 77 level data-description-entry occurs. The 01 level is considered the highest level.

How do the two examples differ? Example A is shorter but is not as useful. We have no way of referencing the student's surname in A. In B, we have identifiers for both parts of the name. Conversely, in A we have no way of referencing the full address as a single item, only the component parts. In code B we have grouped similar items together under headings. Not surprisingly, the four identifiers used for these headings are called *group items.*

Group Item   A *group item* names the group of items appearing below it. A group at a particular level ends when another item at the same level begins. The identifier ADDRESS is a group item containing four *elementary items.* The record in Example A contains no group items, only elementary items. Note that a group item may not have a PICTURE clause.

Elementary Item The items that are not further sub-divided are *elementary items.* An elementary item has a level number between 02 and 49; see also *independent items* below. Note that only elementary items have PICTURE (abbreviated to PIC) clauses. Elementary items are said to be at the lowest level in the record. It will be seen that, within a group, the elementary items have the numerically highest *level numbers.* We must exercise care to distinguish *level* from *level number.* Recall that a record, like an organizational chart, defines a hierarchy. The person at the top of the chart (level 1) has a higher level than the person at level 5. So it is with items in a record.

In summary: A *record* may be divided into *groups.* A group consists of a collection of *elementary items.* An elementary item is said to be *subordinate* to its group item.

It is not required that a record be divided into further items. Thus, we may code:

```
01 PRINT-REC  PIC X(132).
```

One may think of the identifier PRINT-REC as being both a record (it has a 01 level number), and an elementary item (it is not further subdivided.)

It is not required that level-numbers be incremented by one. For example, the record above could be coded as:

```
01 ADMISSION-REC.
    03 STUDENT-NAME.
       05 SURNAME          PIC X(20).
       05 GIVEN-NAMES      PIC X(20).
    03 ADDRESS.
       05 STREET           PIC X(30).
       05 CITY             PIC X(20).
       05 PROVINCE         PIC X(4).
       05 POST-CODE        PIC X(6).
    03 BIRTHDAY.
       05 BYEAR            PIC 99.
       05 BMON             PIC 99.
       05 BDAY             PIC 99.
    03 APPLY-DATE          PIC 9(6).
```

All items at the *same level* of subdivision of the record have the *same level numbers.* As the record is further divided, the level numbers increase. Thus, if we wished to divide STREET into STREET-NUMBER and STREET-NAME, these two new items would have a level number of 06 or higher. Using an increment greater than 1 enables the programmer to later introduce a new group item without the need to renumber everything. For example, using the example above, we could insert after the 01 entry a new group 02 NAME-AND-ADDRESS, and, just before the BIRTHDAY group, insert 02 OTHER-DATA. We could then reference the two groups NAME and ADDRESS by the single item called NAME-AND-ADDRESS.

In the procedure division we can reference record, group and elementary items, as needed.

```
MOVE SPACES TO ADMISSION-REC.
MOVE "N.S." TO PROVINCE.
IF BYEAR > 69 DISPLAY "This student is too young" END-IF.
```

7.3 Level Numbers in a Record

The following rules apply to the values of level numbers in a record:

1) To set out the hierarchy of the items, the level numbers must be in the range 01 to 49.

2) A record item begins with 01.

3) It is not required that the level numbers be incremented by 1. Indeed, it is advantageous to increment by more than 1 since one can then insert a new group level item without the need to renumber the items below the new one. The level numbers of groups at the same level of subdivision of the record must be the same.

4) All items that are immediately subordinate to a group item must have an identical level number which is greater than that used for the group item.

5) Elementary items are those with the highest numerical level number *within that group*.

6) Each elementary item must have PICTURE clause. So must a record with no subordinate items. A group item may not have a PICTURE clause. See Chapter 8 for details of the picture clause and some exceptions to this rule.

7) Within a group, *either* the group item *or* its elementary items, may have optional VALUE clauses.

8) Level 77 is reserved for independent items — see below. An independent item must have a PICTURE clause and may optionally have a VALUE clause.

9) Levels 66 and 88 have special meanings as mentioned in Chapter 6. Level 88 items are covered in detail later.

10) The ANSI standard requires items at the 01 or 77 level to begin in Area A. All other items must begin in Area B. Most compilers relax this rule and allow all levels to begin in either area.

7.4 Data-names and Identifiers

In the previous chapter, we discussed rules for data-names. Some additional comments may be helpful.

a) An elementary item must have a unique name within its group; a group item must have a unique name within its record.

    When one wishes to use either a MOVE CORRESPONDING statement or an ADD CORRESPONDING statement, it is necessary to use the same name for different items in two or more records or groups. Let BDATE occur in two records; A-REC and B-REC. To reference either one of the BDATE identifiers we must use a *name qualifier*:

    ```
    either        MOVE  BDATE  IN  A-REC  TO …
    or            MOVE  BDATE  OF  A-REC  TO …
    ```

    Whereas BDATE is a *data-name,* BDATE IN A-REC is an *identifier.* Similarly, if the identifier name, BDATE, occurs within two groups (say A-GROUP and B-GROUP) which are members of the same or of different records, we may use the group name to qualify BDATE as in BDATE IN A-GROUP.

b) Some programmers like to preface the names of all items in a way that indicates the records to which the items belong. Thus the items in our ADMISSION-REC record might be coded as ADM-FULL-NAME, ADM-SURNAME, etc. The ADM part of the names would remind the programmer that the items were part of the admission record.

c) The word FILLER is optional in COBOL 85. For example, these two lines of code are functionally identical:

    ```
    05 FILLER     PIC XXX.
    05            PIC XXX.
    ```

7.5 Independent Items; level 77

Most programs also contain data items that are not related to each other. For example, we may have an identifier that counts the number of records read from a file. Independent data items may be handled in two ways. The first is to use the 77 level. The second is to collect all such items into one or more "dummy" records.

Using 77 level		Using a dummy record	
		01 STUDENT-COUNTERS.	
77 FRESHMAN-COUNT	PIC 99.	03 FRESHMEN-COUNT	PIC 99.
77 SOPHOMORE-COUNT	PIC 99.	03 SOPHOMORE-COUNT	PIC 99.
77 JUNIOR-COUNT	PIC 99.	03 JUNIOR-COUNT	PIC 99.
77 SENIOR-COUNT	PIC 99.	03 SENIOR-COUNT	PIC 99.

7.6 Micro Focus COBOL Level 78

Micro Focus COBOL uses level 78 to specify a constant-name. This level may not be used as part of a record. Example: 78 TAX-RATE VALUE 12.25. We may use the constant-name in any statement where a numeric literal of 12.25 is valid.

7.7 Review Questions

1. A record description begins at level _____ *01* .

2. Data-names within a record use level numbers in the range ____ *1 - 49* .

3. What is wrong with this code?
```
01  X-REC.
    02  X-ONE     PIC XX.
    02  X-TWO     PIC XX.
    03  X-THREE   PIC XX.
    02  X-FOUR    PIC XX.
```
all level numbers within a group must be the same. ie X-THREE

4* What is an elementary item? *lowest level in a record*

5* What is the purpose of indentation in data-description-entries? *readability*

6* A program contains these data-description-entries:
```
01  Z-REC       PIC X(10).
01  J-REC.
    02  J-ALPHA.
        03  J-ONE  PIC XX.
        03  J-TWO  PIC XX.
    02  J-BETA    PIC X(5).
```
Is Z-REC a record item or an elementary item? What type of item is J-ALPHA?
Both   *Group*

7* If X-REC and Z-REC both contain a data-item called TAX-RATE, how do we reference the one in X-REC? *TAX-RATE OF/IN X-REC*

8* A file contains data like this:
```
JOHN        80
MARGARET    90
WILLIAM     75
```
There are 2 spaces between the T of Margaret and the 9. Write a record description that will give us access to the names and the numbers separately.

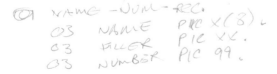
01 NAME-NUM-REC.
03 NAME   PIC X(8).
03 FILLER PIC XX.
03 NUMBER PIC 99.

8
The PICTURE Clause

Objectives

- Know the purpose of the PICTURE clause.
- Be able to use the X and 9 picture string characters.
- Understand the functioning of editing characters.
- Understand the classes: alphanumeric, alphanumeric edited, numeric and numeric edited.

8.1 Purpose and Syntax

The purpose of the PICTURE clause is to describe the *class* of data (alphabetic, alphanumeric, or numeric) that an elementary item may contain, the *size* of the item, and any *editing* to be done. A PICTURE clause is required for most *elementary items*. Data items qualified by certain USAGE clauses do not have PICTURE clauses.

```
             Format for the PICTURE clause

            ⎧ PICTURE ⎫
            ⎨         ⎬  IS picture-string
            ⎩ PIC     ⎭
```

Examples of PICTURE clauses: `PICTURE IS XXXX.`
        `PIC X(4)`
        `PIC Z,ZZZ.ZZ`

The reserved word PICTURE may be abbreviated to PIC. The optional reserved word IS is generally omitted. The picture-string (which is frequently called simply the picture) defines the size of the elementary item, and the type or value of the character allowed in each position of the item.

The picture-string is composed of a sequence of symbols taken from Table 8-1. There are six types of picture string symbols. Three of these are character symbols: data, replacement, and insertion characters. Two are specific to numeric data-items: operational and numeric sign symbols. The sixth, repetition symbol, defines how many times the previous picture string symbol is to be repeated. A picture clause must contain at least either

      (i) one A, X, Z, or 9 symbol, or

or (ii) two characters chosen from: +, –, $(£).

Table 8-1 Picture clause characters

Data Characters
    A alphabetic character   (alphabetic letter or space)
    X alphanumeric character (any COBOL character)
    9 digit   (digit only)

Operational Symbols
    S sign
    V assumed (implied) decimal point location
    P assumed (implied) decimal point scaling position

Replacement Characters
    Z Suppression of leading zeros (leading 0s replaced by spaces)
    * Cheque protection (leading 0s replaced by *s)
    $ Floating dollar sign
    + Floating plus sign; see + in numeric sign symbols below
    − Floating minus sign; see − in numeric sign symbols below

Insertion Characters
    B Blank space inserted
    0 Zero symbol inserted
    / Slash insertion
    , Comma insertion
    . Period insertion

Numeric sign symbols
    + A plus sign will be displayed when the value of the data item is positive. The position of the + symbol in the picture is replaced by a minus symbol when the value is negative.
    − A minus sign will be displayed when the value of the data item is negative. The position of the − symbol in the picture is replaced by a space when the value is positive.
  CR The credit symbol (CR) is displayed when the data item is negative, two blanks are displayed if it is positive.
  DB The debit symbol (DB) is displayed when the data item is negative, two blanks are displayed if it is positive.

Repetition Symbol
    (n) Where n is an integer. For example, X(4) and XXXX are equivalent.

It is most important to remember that editing may occur only when *one elementary item is moved to another elementary item*. No editing occurs when one of the identifiers in a MOVE statement is a group item.

8.2 Data Characters

The type of data (alphabetic, alphanumeric, or numeric) allowed in a position within an item is set by the data character (A, X or 9) used in the item's picture. Pictures containing only the data characters A, X and 9 are said to be unedited.

ALPHABETIC CHARACTER	
The A Data Character	Example: `ITEM-A PIC AAAA or PIC A(4).`
	The A data character permits only alphabetic characters, i.e. the letters A to Z and a to z, and the space character. An item with a picture containing only A characters is called an *alphabetic item*.
Repetition	ITEM-A in the above example may contain 4 letters and/or spaces. Note the use of the repetition symbol, (4), to indicate the A is repeated 4 times. This picture could also have been A(04).
	A literal passed to an item with an A-picture in either a VALUE clause or a MOVE statement, must be enclosed in quotation marks because it has to be a nonnumeric literal.
	An alphabetic picture might be appropriate for fields containing names, for example. It would not be correct for a street-address field since the street number will be in digits. Generally, it is more useful to use an X-picture for all nonnumeric items.
ALPHANUMERIC CHARACTER	
The X Data Character	Example: `ITEM-X   PIC X(10).`
	The X data character permits any COBOL character: letter, digit, or special character. An item with a picture containing only Xs is called an *alphanumeric item*.
	ITEM-X in the above example may contain up to 10 characters, including any of the "printable" characters: letters in both cases, digits and special characters. Clearly, `PIC X(9)` (or `PIC (09)`) is preferable to `PIC XXXXXXXXX`.
	A literal passed to an item with an X-picture in either a VALUE clause or a MOVE statement, must be enclosed in quotation marks because it has to be a nonnumeric literal. An X-pictured item may also receive the figurative constants SPACES, QUOTE and ZERO. A field that is to hold LOW-VALUE or HIGH-VALUE must have an X-picture.

NUMERIC
CHARACTER

The 9 Data Character

Example: `ITEM-N    PIC 9(5).`

The 9 data character allows only one of the digits 0 through 9. An item with a picture containing only 9s is a numeric item.

ITEM-N in the above example may contain a positive integer in the range 0 to 99999.

A literal passed to an item with a 9-picture in either a VALUE clause or a MOVE statement, must not be enclosed in quotation marks because it has to be a numeric literal. An item with a 9-picture may receive the figurative constant ZERO.

An item with a picture composed of only 9s is considered to be a display type item, i.e. an item that may be stored as part of a record, printed on paper or displayed on the terminal. However, it is possible to use such an item in simple, unsigned, integer arithmetic operations. An example would be the page number on a report.

Mixed Data Characters

Example: `ITEM-M    PIC AA99XX.`

For this item, the allowed characters vary. The first two must be letters, the second two must be digits, and the last two may be any of the COBOL character set. An item with such a picture is considered to be an alphanumeric item.

Note

Group items, and records without pictures, behave as if they had alphanumeric pictures.

Example: `05 ITEM-G.`
               `07 ITEM-X    PIC XX.`
               `07 ITEM-N    PIC 99.`

The group item (ITEM-G) has no picture. It occupies four bytes and may be used as it if it had a picture of X(4).

8.3 Operational Symbols (S, V and P)

A data item defined with only 9s in its picture is not suitable for real arithmetic. We need to be able to specify both a sign and a decimal point position. This is done using an S and a V operational symbol, respectively. An item with a picture containing 9s and one or more operational symbols is a *numeric item*. Operational symbols cannot be mixed with As or Xs.

Sign **S** Character	Example: `ITEM-S  PIC S99` The S operation symbol is used to denote a signed field. ITEM-S may have values in the range -99 to +99, and may be used in integer arithmetic.
Implied decimal **V** Character	Example: `ITEM-V PIC 99V9.` The V operational symbol is used to denote the position of the decimal point. The decimal is said to be implied because the value is not stored with a decimal in the V position. ITEM-V may have positive values in the range 0 to 99.9.
Sign with implied decimal **S** and **V** Characters	Example: `ITEM-SV  PIC S99V9.` This item may have values in the range -99.9 to +99.9

Scaling
P Character
	Example: `ITEM-P  PIC PPP99 or PIC P(3)9(2)`
	The P character is a scaling character. It was introduced when memory was expensive and therefore scarce. We shall give two examples to complete the Operation Symbols but we shall not use the P character.
	
	  PIC PPP99 A value of 0.00025 is stored as 25
	  PIC 99PPP A value of 25000 is stored as 25

USAGE Clause	The operational symbols V and S are sufficient for the type of arithmetic operation usually performed in business programs. However, by themselves they are somewhat inefficient. In a subsequent chapter, we discuss the USAGE clauses that improves the efficiency of arithmetic operations.
Printing Numbers	Items containing an operational sign (S,V,P) are normally moved to an edited numeric field (see below) before being printed or displayed. One exception to this is when one wishes to send control characters to the console (e.g. ring the bell) or to the printer (e.g. turn on compressed print).

8.4   Replacement and Insertion Characters

Items with picture-strings containing replacement or insertion characters are called *edited items*. Editing will occur only when *an elementary item is moved to another elementary item*. No editing occurs when one of the identifiers in a MOVE statement is a group item.

We frequently need to do some simple editing on the values in items before we print them. We may, for example, have a file in which Canadian postal codes are in an X(6) field but wish print them as two sets of three characters separated by a blank. We can do this simply by using an edited alphanumeric field. If we wish to print a numeric item having operational symbols in its picture, we must move the value to a numeric edited field and print that field.

8.5 Alphanumeric Editing

Picture-strings for alphanumeric-edited items are formed by combining the A and X data characters with the insertion characters / (slash or stroke), 0 (zero), and B (blank). Table 8-2 shows the use of insertion characters. In these examples we see the result of the following code:

```
MOVE MEMORY-ITEM TO DISPLAY-ITEM.
DISPLAY DISPLAY-ITEM.
```

Table 8-2 Examples of alphanumeric moves

Memory Item		Display Item	
Picture	Value	Picture	Resulting Display
X(6)	abcde	XXXBXXX	abc de
	B2G1C0	XXXBXXX	B2G 1C0
	ABCDE	XX/XX/XX	AB/CD/E
	ABC	XB0BXX	A 0 BC

Note that the results are left-justified since we are dealing with alphanumeric items. When the sending item is smaller than the receiving item, blanks (spaces) are used to right fill.

8.6 Numeric Editing

Picture-strings for numeric-edited fields are formed by combining the insertion and replacement characters, with or without the '9' character. Table 8-3 shows the use of insertion and replacement characters. In these examples we see the result of the following code:

```
MOVE MEMORY-ITEM TO DISPLAY-ITEM.
DISPLAY DISPLAY-ITEM.
```

Note that the + symbol (either fixed or floating) always results in the sign of the value being displayed, whereas the – symbol displays a sign only when the value is negative. The CR and DB characters show when the value is negative, otherwise two spaces are displayed. This may be confusing to the reader unfamiliar with business practices but what is a credit to one party is a debit to another. If your bank balance has a negative value, you owe money to the bank (a debit balance for you) but the bank is owed (has a credit) money. The program will be coded with either DB or CR depending on the intended recipient of the report.

Table 8-3 Numeric Editing

	Memory Item		Display Item	
	Picture	Value	Picture	Display
Insertion	9(6)	123456	99B99B99	12 34 56
		123456	99/99/99	12/34/56
Zero Suppression	9(6)	012345	9(6)	012345
		012345	Z(6)	12345
		01230	Z(6)	1230
Comma Insertion	9(6)	123456	ZZZ,ZZZ	123,456
		012345	ZZZ,ZZZ	12,345
Fixed	$9(6)	123456	$999,999	$123,456
Floating $	9(6)	123456	$,$$$,$$$	$123,456
		000123	$,$$$,$$$	$123
Cheque Protection	9(6)	123456	******9	*123456
		001234	*,***,***	*,**1,234
		123456	$*,***,**9	$*,123,456
Decimal Insertion	9(4)V99	1234.56	9(4).99	1234.56
			9,999.99	1,234.56
			$$$,$$$,$$$.99	$1,234.56
	9(4)	0123	$ZZZZ.99	$ 123.00
Fixed Sign	S999	+123	+9999	+0123
			9999+	0123+
		−123	+9999	−0123
			9999+	0123−
	S999	+123	−9999	0123
			9999−	0123
		−123	−9999	−0123
			9999−	0123−
Floating Sign	S9(6)	+001234	+++++++	+1234
		−001234	+(7)	−1234
		+001234	−(7)	1234
		−001234	−(7)	−1234
Debit and Credit	S999	+123	999CR	123
		−123	999CR	123CR
	S999	+123	999DB	123
		−123	999DB	123DB

8.7 Categories and Classes of Data Items

There are five categories of data items. The category of an item is determined by the symbols used in its picture; see Table 8-4. These categories are grouped into classes; see Table 8-5.

Table 8-4 Data item categories

Category	Data Characters	Editing Characters
Alphabetic[a]	A	None
Numeric[b]	9	None, but may contain operational symbols S, V, P
Alphanumeric[c]	X	None
Alphanumeric-edited	X	Insertion symbols: (0), (,), (B), (/)
Numeric-edited	9	Insertion and/or numeric edit-symbols

a) Prior to COBOL 85, an alphabetic item could also have the B editing character in its picture. Micro Focus COBOL continues to permit this for alphabetic items.
b) A data item lacking a picture clause because it is declared USAGE INDEXED, COMP, BINARY, etc. is numeric.
c) A data item with a mixed picture (two or more of: A, X and 9 data-characters) is alphanumeric. If there are also editing characters, it is alphanumeric-edited.

Table 8-5 Data item classes

Level	Class	Category
Elementary	Alphabetic	Alphabetic
	Numeric	Numeric
	Alphanumeric	Numeric-edited
		Alphanumeric-edited
		Alphanumeric
Group	Alphanumeric	Alphabetic
		Alphanumeric
		Numeric
		Numeric-edited
		Alphanumeric-edited

8.8 Rules for the Picture String

1) The picture-string may contain up to 255 symbols. It is doubtful if many serious programs have ever approached this limit.

2) The picture string must contain at least:
     either   one A, X, Z, 9 or * symbol
     or   two +, –, or $(£) symbols.

3) Some pairs of symbols are mutually exclusive. A picture may contain:

+	(plus)	or	–		(minus)
CR	(credit)	or	DB		(debit)
+ or –		or	CR or DB		
•	(decimal)	or	V		(implied decimal)
•	(decimal)	or	P		(scaling factor)
V	(implied decimal)	or	P		
*	(asterisk)	or	Z		(zero suppression)

4) If CR (or DB) is used, it must be the last symbol.

5) If the SPECIAL NAMES paragraph in the CONFIGURATION DIVISION contains the DECIMAL-POINT IS COMMA entry, then the meaning of the . (period) and , (comma) are reversed; e.g.,1,234.56 becomes 1.234,56.

6) If the SPECIAL NAMES paragraph in the CONFIGURATION DIVISION contains the CURRENCY SIGN IS *literal* entry, then the $ sign in the picture string must be replaced by *literal*. Thus if we code CURRENCY SIGN IS "F", then for a floating currency picture we would code F,FFF rather than $,$$$. Clearly, the use of A, X, P, V, or Z as the literal for the currency symbol is precluded since these are picture string characters.

8.9 Size of Picture

The size of an item's picture (not the count of the number of characters in the picture-string) may be thought of as the number of print positions the item would occupy if it were printed. It is helpful to know each item's size when designing a print line. If we wish to avoid truncation when using the MOVE verb, we will need to know the size of the sending and receiving items. The size of items is important when using a REDEFINES clause.

In computing the size of an item's picture:

1) The data characters A, X and 9 each count as one.
    Each of the following has a size of 4: XXXX, X(4), AAXX, 9999 and 9(4).

2) The insertion characters $; *; /; 0; Z; . (decimal); , (comma); + (plus) and – (minus) count as one. Each of the following has a size of 6: Z(6); 9(4).9; 9(5)+, $Z,ZZZ; **,***.

3)   The credit and debit signs (CR and DB) each count as two.

4)   The implied decimal character (V) does not count.

5)   The operational sign (S) does not count unless the data entry description contains the SIGN IS SEPARATE clause, in which case it counts as one.

6)   See Chapter 12 to determine the size of a data item qualified by a USAGE clause.

8.10   Review Questions

1.   Name the category of each item:
```
     02  ITEM-A        PIC X(4).
     02  ITEM-B        PIC XXBXX.
     02  ITEM-C        PIC 99V99.
     02  ITEM-D        PIC 99.99.
```
Alphanumeric
Alphanumeric edited
Numeric
Numeric edited

2.   Would PIC A(30) be appropriate for an item which is to contain a street address?
No need alphanumeric 'cos of house numbers

3.   If ITEM-N is defined with PIC 99.99, are these statements valid?
```
     ADD  1.25 TO ITEM-N
     MOVE 1.25 TO ITEM-N
```
No Yes ← can only do integer addition/subtraction
Yes

4.   How many 9 characters may appear in the picture of a numeric item?   *≤ 55*

5.   What is the lowest possible value for an item with PIC S9(5)V99?   *= 99999.99*

6*   If ITEM-N is defined with PIC 99V99 VALUE 6.25 what will be displayed by this code?   `SUBTRACT 10.25 FROM ITEM-N`   *4.00*
          `DISPLAY ITEM-N`

7*   If we define two records by
```
     01  X-REC.
         02  X-ONE     PIC 99V99     VALUE 10.50.
         02  X-TWO     PIC XX        VALUE "SF".
     01  Z-REC.
         02  Z-ONE     PIC 99.99.
         02            PIC XX        VALUE SPACES.
         02  Z-TWO     PIC XX.
```
12.50 SF??

what would be displayed by: `MOVE X-REC TO Z-REC`
                              `DISPLAY Z-REC`

8.   If we had these data-description-entries
```
     02  ITEM-1     PIC S99V99    VALUE -10.55
     02  EDIT-1     PIC +Z(4)9.99.
     02  EDIT-2     PIC -Z(4)9.99.
```

what would be displayed by: `MOVE ITEM-1 TO EDIT-1 EDIT-2`
                              `DISPLAY "*" EDIT-1 "* *" EDIT-2 "*"`

*   -10.55 * *   -10.55 *

9
The VALUE Clause

Objectives

▸ Know the purpose of the clause and how to use it with data-names having only simple X or 9 characters in their pictures.

▸ Understand the concept of initailizing a data-name.

9.1 Introduction

The VALUE clause is used, optionally, to set the initial values of data items in the WORKING-STORAGE SECTION, and to define the values associated with condition-names.

Data-definition-entries in the FILE-SECTION and the LINKAGE SECTION may not have VALUE clauses. Such items may have condition-names (88-level items) which, necessarily, have VALUE clauses in their definitions. These clauses are covered in Chapter 21.

In standard ANSI COBOL, a data item declared in WORKING-STORAGE without a VALUE clause has an undefined value when the program is in its initial state. With some compilers data items with "undefined" values may be filled with garbage. RM/COBOL-85 effectively fill alphanumeric items with spaces and numeric items with a null value. Micro Focus COBOL fills both types with spaces. In all cases, it is prudent to initialize data items before using them. The phrase *to initialize a data item* means to give the data item an explicit value.

The VALUE clause permits one to initialize data items to values compatible with the picture clauses of the items. Thus a numeric item could be given the value of 123, while an alphanumeric item may be given the value such as: "Daily report".

Initialization, within the Procedure Division, may also be achieved using the INITIALIZE verb — see Chapter 17.

The syntax of the VALUE clause for items with format-1 data-description-entries is:

<u>VALUE</u> IS literal

9.2 VALUE Clause Rules

Note that these rules do not apply to definitions of condition-names (88 items)

1) A VALUE clause may be used with a record, group or an elementary item. It may not be used in either the FILE SECTION or the LINKAGE SECTION.

2) If the item has an alphabetic, alphanumeric, or alphanumeric edited picture, the literal must be nonnumeric; that is, it must be delimited by a pair of quotation marks. The ANSI standard required double quotation marks (e.g. "ABC"), but most compilers accept single quotations (e.g. 'ABC').

3) If the item's picture is not edited, a literal or an appropriate figurative constant may be used. If the picture is edited, then the literal must be edited.

4) The number of characters in a nonnumeric literal may not exceed the size of the item as defined by its picture. If the literal has fewer characters, alignment is to the left with space fill to the right.

5) If the item is numeric, the numeric value literal must be within the range set by the item's picture. The literal must not cause truncation of nonzero digits.

6) If the item has a signed numeric picture clause or is associated with a USAGE COMP-1 or COMP-2 clause, the numeric literal must be signed.

7) A data description entry may not contain both a VALUE and a REDEFINES clause.

8) When the VALUE clause is used with a group item, additional rules apply:
   a) A nonnumeric literal or a figurative constant must be used.
   b) Items in the group are initialized without regard to the characteristics of the elementary items.
   c) No subordinate item (group or elementary) may contain a VALUE clause.
   d) No subordinate item may contain the clauses: JUSTIFIED, SYNCHRONIZED, or USAGE.

9) When used with an item which contains an OCCURS clause, or an item subordinate to such an item, then the value will be assigned to every occurrence of the item.

10) A data item declared be to EXTERNAL, and identifiers subordinate to such an item, may not have a VALUE clause.

9.3 Examples

The VALUE clause is one of the simpler clauses in the data description entry. We shall look at some examples in terms of the rules given above. The data-names used in these examples were chosen to show the group-elementary item relationship; they would be very poor names in a real program.

a) Rules 1 and 2: The VALUE clause may be at the group or elementary level and must be
    compatible with the PICTURE clause. Note that a group item is always considered to
    be of the alphanumeric type and requires a nonnumeric value literal.

```
05 ITEM-A.                              05 ITEM-B  VALUE "AB12".
    07 ITEM-A1  PIC XX  VALUE "AB".         07 ITEM-B1  PIC XX.
    07 ITEM-A2  PIC 99  VALUE 12.           07 ITEM-B2  PIC 99.
```

The two data descriptions are identical. Note the nonnumeric literal for ITEM-A1 which
is an alphanumeric item. ITEM-A2, being numeric, has a numeric literal. The group item
ITEM-B has a nonnumeric literal, since group items are considered to be in the
alphanumeric category.

b) Rule 3: edited pictures need edited literals.

```
05 ITEM-G PIC 99.99     VALUE 12.34.
05 ITEM-H PIC $99.99    VALUE "$12.34".
05 ITEM-I PIC XX/XX     VALUE "AB/CD".
```

Rule 3: unedited pictures may be assigned Figurative Constants.

```
05 ITEM-C      PIC XXXX      VALUE SPACES.
05 ITEM-D.
    07 FILLER   PIC X         VALUE QUOTE.
    07 ITEM-D2  PIC X(12)     VALUE "A Quotation".
    07 FILLER   PIC X         VALUE QUOTE.
05 ITEM-E      PIC XXX       VALUE ZERO.
05 ITEM-F      PIC XXX       VALUE "000".
05 ITEM-G      PIC X(80)     VALUE ALL "-".
05 ITEM-N      PIC 99V99     VALUE ZERO.
```

ITEM-D has the value "A Quotation"; the quotation marks are part of the value. The
VALUE clauses for ITEM-E and ITEM-F are equivalent; both give their data items the
value of three zero digits. Note that ZERO may be assigned to both alphanumeric and
numeric items. ITEM-G will contain a string of 80 dashes; the figurative constant ALL
relieves us of the need to enter this repetitive string.

c) Rule 5: Numeric identifiers.

```
05 NUMBER-1  PIC 99    VALUE 12.
05 NUMBER-2  PIC 99    VALUE ZERO
05 NUMBER-3  PIC 99V99 VALUE 12.34.
05 NUMBER-4  PIC 99V99 VALUE 1.23.
05 NUMBER-5  PIC 99V99 VALUE ZERO.
05 NUMBER-6  PIC 99V99 VALUE 12.345. <invalid>
```

The decimal in the literal is aligned with the implied decimal (V) in the picture. Data
item NUMBER-4, will have the value 01.23; the leading zero is supplied by the
compiler. The value for NUMBER-6 is incorrect and would cause a compiler error;

three decimal places have been used but the picture has room for only two.

d) Rule 6: Signed numeric data items need signs in the literal.

```
05 NUMBER-7  PIC S99      VALUE +12.
05 NUMBER-8  PIC S99      VALUE -45.
05 NUMBER-9  PIC S99V99   VALUE +12.23.
```

e) Rule 8: VALUE clause with group items.

```
03 GROUP-A     VALUE "ABCDEFGH".
   05 GROUP-AA.
      07 ITEM-AA1    PIC XX.
      07 ITEM-AA2    PIC XX.
   05 GROUP-AB.
      07 ITEM-AB1    PIC 99.
      07 ITEM-AB2    PIC XX.
```

The groups (GROUP-AA and GROUP-AB) and the elementary items may not have VALUE clauses because they are subordinate to GROUP-A which has a VALUE clause.

The value of the numeric item ITEM-AB1 is "EF"; rule 8(b) states that initialization occurs without regard to the characteristics of elementary items. Provided we do not attempt to use ITEM-AB1 while it has this value, all will be well. Numeric items with nonnumeric values are discussed again in the next chapter under the REDEFINES topic.

In the next example ITEM-N has a value of SPACES

```
05 GROUP-X.
   07 ITEM-N     PIC 99.
   07 ITEM-A     PIC XX.
```

In RM/COBOL-85, ITEM-N will behave as if it had a value of zero. In Micro Focus COBOL, a runtime error ("Illegal character in numeric item") will result if we attempt to use ITEM-N in an arithmetic statement while it has this value.

f) Rule 9: VALUE used with OCCURS.

```
02 ITEM-G OCCURS 3 TIMES PIC 99 VALUE ZERO.
02 ITEM-H OCCURS 3 TIMES.
   03 ITEM-H1 PIC X(3) VALUE "ABC".
   03 ITEM-H2 PIC 99   VALUE 1.
```

Every occurrence of ITEM-G (i.e. ITEM-G (1), ITEM-G (2), ITEM-G (3)) will have the value 0. Every occurrence of ITEM-H1 will have the value "ABC" and all occurrences of ITEM-H2 will have the value 1.

9.4 Review Questions

None of these questions refer to level 88 items.

1. The VALUE clause may be used in which sections?   *WORKING STORAGE*

2* Which of these are invalid?

```
a)  02  ITEM-A     PIC XXX    VALUE ABC.         needs  "ABC"
b)  02  ITEM-B     PIC X(5)   VALUE "AB".
c)  02  ITEM-C     PIC 99V99  VALUE 10.25.
d)  02  ITEM-D                VALUE 1234.
        03  ITEM-D1    PIC 99.
        03  ITEM-D2    PIC 99.                    Elementary can't have
        03  ITEM-D3    PIC 99     VALUE 25.        value when group has one.
e)  02  ITEM-E     PIC X(4)   VALUE "ABCDE".       literal too long
```

10
The REDEFINES Clause

Objectives

▸ Know the uses of the clause.
▸ Know how to code the clause.

10.1 Purpose and Syntax

This clause allows the programmer to have two or more data-names for the same memory storage area. The clause has two major uses: (i) to permit different descriptions of the same data and (ii) to initialize tables. A less frequent use is to conserve memory.

```
                    Format for REDEFINES

                       ⎧ data-name-1 ⎫
    level-number       ⎨             ⎬   REDEFINES  data-name-2
                       ⎩ FILLER      ⎭
```

Data-name-1 (or FILLER) occupies the same storage area as data-name-2.

A simple example:
```
                        05  ITEM-X    PIC X(6).
                        05  ITEM-N    REDEFINES ITEM-X  PIC 9(6).
```

The two data items (ITEM-X and ITEM-N) use the same memory space to store their data. In the Procedure Division we may refer to ITEM-A when we wish to use an alphanumeric data item or to ITEM-N when a numeric data item is required.

10.2 Rules for REDEFINES

The rules governing the REDEFINES clause may seem formidable. Novice programmers should not let this deter them from learning to use this powerful tool effectively.

1) The level numbers of data-name-1 and data-name-2 must be the same. The REDEFINES clause may not be used with level 66 or 88 items.

2) In the FILE SECTION, the REDEFINES clause may not be used at the 01 level — see Rule 9(a) below.

3) The REDEFINES clause must immediately follow data-name-1. Other clauses, such as PICTURE, may not be placed between the data-name and the REDEFINES clause.

4) No data item with a level-number numerically lower than that of data-name-1 and data-name-2 may appear between these two items. Thus, the redefinition must follow the definition of data-name-2 as soon as possible. Clearly, any data-names which are subordinate to data-name-2 must be between the two.

```
        A <valid>                        B <invalid>
05 ITEM-A.                         05 ITEM-C PIC X(4).
    07 ITEM-A1 PIC XX.             05 ITEM-D PIC 99.
    07 ITEM-A2 PIC XX.             05 ITEM-E REDEFINES ITEM-C.
05 ITEM-B REDEFINES ITEM-A            07 ITEM-E1  PIC 99.
    07 ITEM-B1 PIC 999.               07 ITEM-E2  PIC XX.
    07 ITEM-B2 PIC X.
```

Example B is invalid because the redefinition of ITEM-C is not the next 05 level entry. It would be necessary to move the data description entry of ITEM-D to the line before ITEM-C or to the line following ITEM-E2.

5) The size of the two data items should be the same. This is a simplification of the actual rules but is the safest course to follow; see Rule 9(b) below. The programmer can always include a FILLER to make the sizes equal. Remember that neither the implied decimal symbol (V), nor the operational sign (S) without the SIGN SEPARATE clause, count towards the size of an item.

6) There cannot be a VALUE clause attached to either data-name-1 nor to any items subordinate to it. Within the program, we may reference data-name-1, data-name-2 and their subordinate item, to place data into the common storage area. This rule does not prevent the use of condition-names (level 88 items) with any of the items in either data description entries.

7) The data-name-2 should not contain an OCCURS clause; see Rule 9(c) below. However, data-name-1 and items subordinate to it may contain an OCCURS clause without the DEPENDING option. Indeed, this is how we initialize tables.

8) To redefine the same area more than once, a series of REDEFINES clauses may be used. The data-name-2 will be the same in all the redefinitions. Note in the example below that in the second REDEFINES it is ITEM-A that is redefined, not ITEM-B.

```
05 ITEM-A    PIC XXXX.
05 ITEM-B    REDEFINES ITEM-A  PIC 9999.
05 ITEM-C    REDEFINES ITEM-A  PIC ZZZZ.
```

9) Rules for the advanced programmer:

a) When a level indicator such as FD is followed by two or more record items, there is an implicit redefinition.

b) Size of the two data-names. When data-name-2 has a level number other than 01, or is an external item, the size of the picture of data-name-2 must be at least equal to that of data-name-1. When data-name-2 is a level 01 item the size of data-name-1 is independent of the size of data-name-2.

c) When data-name-2 is subordinate to an OCCURS clause, a reference to data-name-2 may not be subscripted. Neither data items (data-name-1 and data-name-2) may include a OCCURS DEPENDING clause.

d) If data-name-1 is SYNCHRONIZED, complications may occur; see your compiler manual.

10.3 REDEFINES Used for Different Data-description

Let us return to the first example of the REDEFINES clause:

```
05  ITEM-X     PIC X(6)
05  ITEM-N     REDEFINES ITEM-X PIC 9(6).
```

Perhaps, at some point in the program, we have the statement: MOVE 'ABCD' TO ITEM-X. We know from Chapter 8 that when a data item has a picture-string containing only the '9' data character, only numeric values are permitted for the data-item. Since ITEM-N shares the same storage space as ITEM-X, one might argue that ITEM-N has a nonnumeric value. While this is true, it will not cause a program error to occur unless we attempt to use the item in a statement which requires a numeric value. In Chapter 21 we shall see how to test for nonnumeric values. The program code can be written such that one course of action will be followed if ITEM-X (or ITEM-N) proves to be nonnumeric, another if it is numeric.

The following code is designed to allow the user to type in a series of numbers. We do not know beforehand how many numbers are to be entered. When the last number has been entered the user is to type "EXIT". To show this example we must use COBOL verbs which have not yet been discussed. The English-like characteristic of COBOL should allow you to understand the example even if you could not have written it — something akin to the author's ability with French!

```
MOVE SPACES TO ITEM-X
PERFORM UNTIL ITEM-X = "EXIT"
    DISPLAY "Enter number or type EXIT to quit"
    ACCEPT ITEM-X
    IF ITEM-N IS NUMERIC
        ADD ITEM-N TO TOTAL-COUNT
    END-IF
END-PERFORM
DISPLAY "The sum of the numbers is " TOTAL-COUNT
```

10.4 Using FILLER

We may use FILLER in place of data-name-1 when we use a group of items and do not wish to refer to the entire group. Compare Examples (a) and (b) below. In both we may access TODAY, TODAY-YY, TODAY-MM and TODAY-DD as numeric items. In (a) TODAY-ALPHA is an alphanumeric because it is a group item. Since we are unlikely to need to refer, we can replace it by FILLER as in (b).

```
           (a)                                  (b)

02 TODAY              PIC 9(6).    02 TODAY               PIC
02 TODAY-ALPHA REDEFINES TODAY.                9(6).
   03 TODAY-YY        PIC 99.      02 FILLER REDEFINES TODAY.
   03 TODAY-MM        PIC 99.         03 TODAY-YY        PIC 99.
   03 TODAY-DD        PIC 99.         03 TODAY-MM        PIC 99.
                                      03 TODAY-DD        PIC 99.
```

10.5 REDEFINES Used to Initialize Tables

The topic of Tables is covered in Chapter 18. We will give a simple example here of how REDEFINES is used to initialize (give starting values to) table elements. Consider this code:

```
02 TAX-VALUES
   03 PIC 99V9   VALUE 10.5.
   03 PIC 99V9   VALUE 12.5.
   03 PIC 99V9   VALUE 17.5.
02 TAX-TABLE REDEFINES TAX-VALUES.
   03 TAX-RATE OCCURS 5 TIMES PIC 99V9.
```

Recall that the clause `data-name-1 REDEFINES data-name-2` causes the two data-items to share the same memory space. The VALUE clauses in the example above place data in the memory space used by TAX-VALUES. However, this memory is also used by TAX-TABLE, so it will share this data. In the diagram below the three boxes represent a block of memory. The names at the top of the diagram are assigned to that memory by the data-description-entry for TAX-VALUES while the names on the bottom come from the data-description-entry of TAX-TABLE.

TAX-VALUES	filler-1	filler-1	filler-3
	105	125	175
TAX-TABLE	TAX-RATE(1)	TAX-RATE(2)	TAX-RATE(3)

From this we see that TAX-RATE(1) gets a value of 10.5 (note that the V in the PICTURE denotes an implicit decimal), TAX-RATE(2) has the value 12.5, and TAX-RATE(3) has the value 17.5. Thus we have initialized the table.

10.6 REDEFINES Used to Conserve Memory

We may also use the REDEFINES clause to reduce the memory requirements of a program. Suppose in a program we start by writing a report with a certain heading and that later in the program a second heading is needed with a different grouping of items. The coding may look like this:

```
01 FIRST-HEADING.
    03 FIRST-HEAD-LEFT        PIC X(40).
    03 FIRST-HEAD-CENTRE      PIC X(20).
    03 FIRST-HEAD-RIGHT       PIC X(20).
01 SECOND-HEADING REDEFINES FIRST-HEAD.
    03 SECOND-HEAD-LEFT       PIC X(10).
    03 SECOND-HEAD-CENTRE     PIC X(40).
    03 SECOND-HEAD-RIGHT      PIC X(30).
```

Since SECOND-HEAD shares storage space with FIRST-HEAD we have saved 80 bytes of memory. This is hardly anything to get excited about but illustrates the principle. Memory requirements will generally not be of concern to the average programmer. A program with a number of large tables, however, may require one to use memory saving techniques. With the REDEFINES clause two or more tables could share the same storage area. Clearly, the REDEFINES clause will not be appropriate when we need to keep data in both tables simultaneously.

10.7 Review Questions

1*   Which of the following are invalid?

```
a)  02 A-ONE     PIC X(4).
    02 A-TWO     REDEFINES A-ONE  PIC 9(4).

b)  02 B-ONE     PIC X(4).
    02 B-TWO     PIC X(4).
    02 B-THREE   PIC 9(4)  REDEFINES B-ONE.

c)  02 C-ONE     PIC X(5).
    02 C-TWO     PIC X(4)  REDEFINES C-ONE.

d)  02 D-ONE     PIC 99V99.
    02 D-TWO     PIC 9999  REDEFINES D-ONE.

e)  02 E-ONE     PIC 9(4).
    02 E-TWO     PIC X(4)  REDEFINES E-ONE VALUE SPACES.
```

11
The OCCURS Clause

Objectives

- Know the purpose of the clause.
- Be able to define a simple table.

11.1 Purpose and Syntax

The OCCURS clause is used to define a table or an array; i.e. a group of related data items.
There are two formats for the OCCURS clause:

```
                              Format 1

        OCCURS integer-1 TIMES

               [ { { ASCENDING  }  KEY IS {identifier-3}... }... ]
               [ { { DESCENDING }                              ]

               [ INDEXED  BY { index-name-a }... ]
```

```
                              Format 2

    OCCURS integer-1 TO integer-2 TIMES DEPENDING ON identifier-2

           [ { { ASCENDING  }  KEY IS {identifier-3}... }... ]
           [ { { DESCENDING }                              ]

           [ INDEXED  BY { index-name-a }... ]
```

11.2 OCCURS Clause Rules

1) The OCCURS clause may not be used with identifiers at the 01, 66, 77 or 88 level. This

does *not* preclude identifiers declared with OCCURS from having 88 condition-names associated with them.

2) When Format-1 is used at a group level, subordinate items may also use a Format-1 OCCURS clause. ANSI COBOL permits this to be done to 7 levels; many compilers extend this limit.

3) When Format-1 is used at a group level, subordinate items may not use a Format-2 OCCURS clause.

4) When Format-2 is used at a group level, the group must be the last group in the record. When it is used at an elementary level, this must be the last item (elementary or group) in the record.

5) An index-name, such as index-name-a in the syntax above, must not be declared elsewhere in the program and must have a name that is unique within the program.

11.3 Examples Using OCCURS

Some simple examples follow. Chapter 18 explains more fully how tables are defined and used. The processing of tables is examined again in Chapter 22. The SEARCH verb, in Chapter 24 shows how to find a specific value in a table. Some of the functions described in Chapter 31 are useful for arithmetic operations on tables.

Example 1: Format 1 used at an elementary level.

```
01 A-TABLE.
   02 A-ITEM OCCURS 10 TIMES PIC 99.
```

This defines ten items each with a picture of 99. The items are called A-ITEM(1), A-ITEM(2), etc. We may think of this table as either a column or a row of ten items.

A-ITEM(1)
A-ITEM(2)
A-ITEM(3)
etc....

A-ITEM(1)	A-ITEM(2)	A-ITEM(3)	etc

Example 2: Format 1 used at group level.

```
01 B-TABLE.
   02 B-ITEM OCCURS 5 TIMES.
      03 B-NUM    PIC 99.
      03 B-ALPHA  PIC X(4).
```

This defines 5 group items. Within each there is a numeric and an alphanumeric item. These are B-NUM(1) through B-NUM(5) and B-ALPHA(1) through B-ALPHA(5). The most useful way to conceptualize this table is as shown below.

B-ITEM(1)	B-NUM(1)	B-ALPHA(1)
B-ITEM(2)	B-NUM(2)	B-ALPHA(2)
etc	etc	etc

Example 3: Format 1 used at group level showing the use of an index-name.

```
01 B-TABLE.
    02 B-ITEM OCCURS 5 TIMES INDEXED BY BX.
        03 B-NUM      PIC 99.
        03 B-ALPHA    PIC X(4).
```

We may now refer to individual items in the table using the index BX. For example:

```
SET BX TO 1
DISPLAY B-ITEM (BX)
DISPLAY B-NUM (BX) SPACES B-ALPHA (BX)
IF B-NUM (BX) = 3 .....
```

Chapter 18 examines index-names in detail. The ANSI standard requires a space before a left parenthesis but most compliers relax this rule allowing us to code B-NUM (3) or BNUM(3). A space is always required after a right parenthesis.

Example 4: Format 1 used to define a two-dimensional table.

```
01 C-TABLE.
    02 C-ROW OCCURS 3 TIMES.
        03 C-ITEM  OCCURS 4 TIMES  PIC 99.
```

C-ROW(1)	C-ITEM(1,1)	C-ITEM(1,2)	C-ITEM(1,3)	C-ITEM(1,4)
C-ROW(2)	C-ITEM(2,1)	C-ITEM(2,2)	C-ITEM(2,3)	C-ITEM(2,4)
C-ROW(3)	C-ITEM(3,1)	C-ITEM(3,2)	C-ITEM(3,3)	C-ITEM(3,4)

Note that we need two subscripts (on index-names) to refer to a particular C-ITEM; the first denotes the row number while the second denotes the column number.

11.4 Review Questions

1* Define and initialize a table such that SEASON (1) = "Winter", SEASON (2) = "Spring", etc.

2* Define a table to hold 100 sets of data similar to that shown below; assume you need "miles" and "fare" as numeric items.

Destination	Miles	Fare
SHEFFIELD	150	20.55
LEEDS	175	22.75
YORK	200	25.00

```
01  TRAIN-TABLE.
    03  ROW OCCURS 100 TIMES.
        05  DESTINATION    PIC X(9).
        05  MILES          PIC 9(3).
        05  FARE           PIC 99V99.
```

12
The USAGE Clause

Objectives

▸ Know the effect of this clause on the storage of numbers.
▸ Know the advantages and disadvantages of the use of the clause.

12.1 Purpose and Syntax

The USAGE clause determines how data is stored internally. It is not essential to use any of
the USAGE settings. They may, however, provide a means of improving the performance of
a program or of conserving storage requirements.

```
           Format of the USAGE Clause (ANSI Standard)

                                    ⎧ BINARY          ⎫
                                    ⎪ DISPLAY         ⎪
                  [ USAGE  IS ]     ⎨ COMPUTATIONAL   ⎬
                                    ⎪ INDEXED         ⎪
                                    ⎩ PACKED-DECIMAL  ⎭


           The word COMPUTATIONAL may be abbreviated to COMP
```

The default is USAGE DISPLAY and is applicable to identifiers of all classes. Being the
default, the phrase USAGE DISPLAY is redundant. This format corresponds to the format
used by an editor program running on the computer. Each character is stored in one byte. All
the other types are restricted to numeric data items but may be declared at the group or
elementary level.

12.2 Rules for the USAGE Clause

1) Certain verbs in the PROCEDURE DIVISION impose conditions on the USAGE clause
    which may be associated with their operands.

2) If no USAGE clause is associated with an identifier, the identifier will be stored as a DISPLAY type item; i.e. DISPLAY is the default setting for this clause and the clause USAGE DISPLAY is optional.

3) The USAGE clause may be applied to an elementary or a group item. When a USAGE clause is used with a group item, it applies to all elementary items in the group. The group item may not be used as a numeric item.

4) The types BINARY and COMPUTATIONAL are generally identical but not in RM/COBOL-85.

5) An identifier with USAGE COMPUTATIONAL or BINARY may not also have a SIGN IS SEPARATE clause.

6) When the USAGE INDEX is applied to an elementary item, either directly or through use at the group level, the identifier is called an *index data item*. See also Chapter 18. A group item may not be used as an index data item. The declaration of an index data item may not contain BLANK WHEN ZERO, JUSTIFIED, PICTURE, REDEFINES, VALUE, or SYNCHRONIZED clauses. An index data item may be referenced only in (i) a SEARCH or SET statement, (ii) a relation condition, or (iii) the USING phrase of a Procedure header or of a CALL statement. An index data item may not be a conditional identifier, i.e. no 88 level items may be associated with it.

7) A program in which identifiers are defined with USAGE clauses may not be portable from one system to another because the ANSI standard does not define how each type is to be implemented.

12.3 USAGE BINARY

When a program makes extensive use of arithmetic verbs (ADD, SUBTRACT, MULTIPLY, DIVIDE, and COMPUTE), it may be more efficient if the items used in the arithmetic statements are BINARY or COMPUTATIONAL type items. This is because the data is stored in the same format that the system uses to perform the computation. When the identifiers are of type DISPLAY, the system must convert them first to binary form, which requires a machine operation. However, for there to be any appreciable reduction in the time a program takes to run, it would have to perform a very large number of calculations. Indeed, some experts believe that with modern computers the marginal improvement in computational speed does not warrant the use of this clause. See item 7 above. In Chapter 19 we discuss a program which compares the time to perform arithmetic operations on users of type DISPLAY and BINARY.

```
02 CASH-IN-HAND  PIC S9(4)V99 USAGE BINARY.
02 CASH-IN-BANK  PIC S9(9)V99 USAGE BINARY.
```

The picture of a BINARY/COMPUTATIONAL item may contain the symbols 9, V and S. The first data item may have values in the range −9,999.99 to +9,999.99, while the second allows –999,999,999.99 to +999,999,999.99. The "S" operational symbol permits negative values. While a negative amount of cash-in-hand sounds contradictory, all programs should allow for the unexpected! Furthermore, signed items generally improve program performance.

In standard ANSI COBOL and in Micro Focus COBOL, BINARY and COMPUTATIONAL are synonymous but they are not in RM/COBOL-85.

We will learn in Chapter 20 that there are two types of sequential files. One is called LINE SEQUENTIAL and the other is RECORD SEQUENTIAL in Micro Focus COBOL, and BINARY SEQUENTIAL in RM/COBOL-85. A record description for a LINE SEQUENTIAL file should not contain an identifier with USAGE BINARY/COMP since certain numeric values could be stored in a way that conflicts with the record terminators of these files. Such USAGE is permitted in the second type of file, hence the name BINARY SEQUENTIAL.

12.4 USAGE PACKED-DECIMAL

When the value of an identifier such as ITEM-N PIC 99 is stored in DISPLAY format, each digit is stored as one byte. When USAGE PACKED-DECIMAL is specified, each byte contains two digits — which explains the term "packed-decimal". This clause may be used to decrease the storage space required for numeric items.

The picture of a PACKED-DECIMAL item may contain the symbols 9, V and S.

12.5 Size of Identifier

If a program specifies one of these usages in the data-description-entry for an identifier which is the subject or object of a REDEFINED clause, it is necessary to know the size of the identifer.

DISPLAY   The size of DISPLAY items is discussed in Chapter 8.

PACKED-DECIMAL   If N is the number of 9s in the picture of a PACKED-DECIMAL item (signed or unsigned), its size is ½(N+1) rounded up to the next integer. If we define ITEM-X PIC S99V999 USAGE PACKED-DECIMAL, there are five 9s so the size is three bytes.

BINARY and   The sizes of identifiers with these types depend on the
COMPUTATIONAL   implementation as shown in Tables 12-1 and 12-2. See also the function LENGTH in Chapter 31.

Table 12-1 Size of BINARY and COMPUTATIONAL items in Micro Focus COBOL

Number of digits (9s in picture)		Size in Bytes
Signed	Unsigned	
1 – 2	1 – 2	1
3 – 4	3 – 4	2
5 – 6	5 – 7	3
7 – 9	8 – 9	4
10 – 11	10 – 12	5
12 – 14	13 – 14	6
15 – 16	15 – 16	7
17 – 18	17 – 18	8

Table 12-2 Size of BINARY and COMPUTATIONAL Items in RM/COBOL-85

USAGE BINARY Signed or Unsigned Number of digits (9s in picture)	Size in Bytes
1 – 4	2
5 – 9	4
10 – 18	8
USAGE COMPUTATIONAL Number of digits (9s in picture)	Size in Bytes
N Unsigned	N
N Signed	N + 1

12.6 Non-ANSI USAGE Clauses

Many implementations of COBOL include non-ANSI USAGE clauses. These generally have the form COMP-1, COMP-2, etc. They are used by advanced programmers for such tasks as passing arguments to non-COBOL programs and operations which require the manipulation of bits in a numeric value.

Users of Micro Focus COBOL will come across USAGE COMP-X in many of the sample program supplied with the system. It can be confusing. The picture of an identifier with this usage may contain either Xs or 9s even when the item is numeric. The picture cannot contain an operations sign (S) character. When the picture contains all Xs the number of Xs determines the length (size) of the item. There may be up to eight Xs in the picture with each X representing two characters. When 9s are used for the picture the length is as if the item had usage BINARY — see Table 12-1.

12.7 Review Questions

[handwritten: Adv - efficiency with arithmetic ops.]

1. What are the advantages and disadvantages of defining a data item with USAGE BINARY?

2. What is the advantage of defining a data item with USAGE PACKED-DECIMAL?

[handwritten: Save on storage space]

3. What symbols may be used in the picture clause for an item with a) USAGE BINARY and b) USAGE PACKED-DECIMAL?

[handwritten: 9, S & ✓]

13
The BLANK, JUSTIFIED and SIGN Clauses

Objectives

▸ Know the editing functions performed by these clauses.

13.1 Introduction

This chapter deals with three clauses in the data-description-entry which perform special editing functions. Most programs can be written without the need to use any of these clauses. They can, however, be very useful in certain cases. The reader may wish to review this chapter to become familiar with the purpose of each, and return to it if the need arises to use one of the clauses.

13.2 BLANK WHEN ZERO

When this clause is used in a data-description-entry, the identifier will have its value replaced by spaces when the value is zero.

```
              Format:       BLANK   WHEN   ZERO
```

1) The identifier containing the clause must be numeric or numeric edited.

2) The identifier may have no USAGE clause, other than USAGE DISPLAY.

3) An identifier with this clause is type edited-numeric, even if no edit characters appear in its picture. This means that an identifier with the BLANK ZERO clause may not be used in arithmetic statements, other than as the object of a GIVING option or a COMPUTE verb.

4) The cheque protection symbol (*) overrides the BLANK clause.

EXAMPLES: The following demonstrate the effect on displayed values for identifiers with various pictures with and without the BLANK clause.

PICTURE	VALUE 25	VALUE 0	VALUE 0 BLANK WHEN ZERO
999	25	0	blank
ZZZ	25	blank	blank
ZZ9	25	0	blank
ZZZ+	25	0	blank
+++	+25	+++	blank
***	*25	***	***

Note that the cheque protection symbol (*) overrides the clause making the clause redundant. It is also redundant when the data item has a picture composed only of Z characters or Z characters with commas.

13.3 JUSTIFIED RIGHT

The JUSTIFIED clause is used in a data-description-entry to specify nonstandard positioning of alphabetic or alphanumeric data within a receiving data item.

```
Format:      { JUSTIFIED }
             { JUST      }
```

1) A data-name with a JUSTIFIED clause must have an alphabetic or edited alphanumeric picture.

2) The clause may be used only with an elementary data-name.

3) Data is transferred to an identifier having the JUSTIFIED clause in a nonstandard manner. The standard alignment for alphanumeric data is left justified; the first character in the data is placed in the left-most position of the receiving field. If the data contains more characters than there are positions in the receiving item, the excess characters to the right are lost; this is right-truncation. The JUSTIFIED clause, reverses this procedure. The right-most character of the data is placed in the last (right-most) position of the receiving item. If the data is larger than the receiver, left truncation occurs. It is important to note that when data is assigned to an identifier having the JUSTIFIED clause, trailing blanks are not truncated but are treated as valid characters.

EXAMPLES: *The caret symbol (^) in the examples is used to denote a blank character.*

a) Used in the value clause:
```
PIC X(5)    VALUE    "AB"      JUSTIFIED    gives ^^^AB
PIC X(5)    VALUE    "^AB^"    JUSTIFIED    gives ^^AB^
```

b) Used with the MOVE verb: `MOVE ITEM-A TO ITEM-B ITEM-C`

	ITEM-A	value	ITEM-B PIC X(6).	ITEM-C PIC X(6) JUST.
i	X(4)	ABCD	ABCD^^	^^ABCD
ii	X(4)	AB^^	AB^^^^	^^AB^^
iii	X(8)	ABCDEFGHI	ABCDEFG	DEFGHI

In (i) there are no trailing blanks in the value of the sending item; note that the D is aligned with the last position in ITEM-C. In (ii) there are two blank characters in the value of ITEM-A, note the effect on alignment. Example (iii) demonstrates left truncation. Remember that the JUSTIFIED clause will be effective only when it is used as an elementary item in a MOVE statement.

13.4 SIGN IS SEPARATE

The SIGN clause in a data-description-entry specifies the position and representation type of the operational sign.

```
Format:   [ SIGN IS ] { LEADING  }  [ SEPARATE CHARACTER ]
                      { TRAILING }
```

1) The SIGN clause may be applied only to a signed numeric identifier; the picture must contain the S operational sign symbol. The clause may also be used with a group item containing elementary items of this type.

2) The identifier must have DISPLAY usage.

3) If a group item and one of its elementary items both contain a SIGN clause, the clause attached to the elementary item overrides that for the group.

4) The SIGN clause does not impose any limitations on the use of the identifier.

5) The SEPARATE CHARACTER phrase causes the operational sign symbol (S) in the picture to count as one character in computing the size of the item, otherwise the S does not count towards the size.

To understand the purpose of this clause it is necessary to understand how signed numeric items are stored in the absence of the clause. First, consider an unsigned numeric item with PICTURE 99 and display usage. Let it be given the value of 10. The two digits are stored as the ASCII representation of the characters "1" and "0", respectively. An identifier with a signed picture is stored differently. If the item had PICTURE S99 and was given the value of -10, the 1 is stored as before but the 0 is combined with the sign. Each combination of digit and sign symbol has its own representation which is not defined by the ANSI standard but by the implementor. Table 13-1 shows the representations used by Micro Focus COBOL and RM/COBOL-85. Program CHAP13-A (on disk) may be used to explore this topic.

Table 13-1 Representation of digits and negative sign

```
Digit:               0  1  2  3  4  5  6  7  8  9
Micro Focus encoding p  q  r  s  t  u  v  w  x  y
RM\COBOL-85 encoding }  J  K  L  M  N  O  P  Q  R
```

Consider these declarations:

```
(a) 02 ITEM-A PIC S99  VALUE -25.
(b) 02 ITEM-B PIC S99  VALUE -25  SIGN TRAILING.
(c) 02 ITEM-C PIC S99  VALUE -25  SIGN LEADING.
(d) 02 ITEM-D PIC S99  VALUE -25  SIGN TRAILING SEPARATE.
(e) 02 ITEM-E PIC S99  VALUE -25  SIGN LEADING SEPARATE.
```

Codes (a) and (b) are equivalent since TRAILING is the default; the sign and the 5 are combined when the value is stored. In case (c), the sign and the 2 are combined. In cases (d), and (e), the sign is kept on a separate field either to the right (TRAILING) or to the left (LEADING) of the numeric value. We will discuss, in Chapter 16, a program which demonstrates the effect of this clause.

13.5 Review Questions

1* A program has these definitions,

```
02 X-GROUP.
   03 X-ONE  PIC X(6)  VALUE "ABC".
   03 X-TWO  PIC 999   VALUE ZERO.
02 Z-GROUP.
   03 Z-ONE  PIC X(6)  JUSTIFIED.
   03 Z-TWO  PIX ZZ9   BLANK WHEN ZERO.
```

Why would the following code not give the desired editing?

```
MOVE X-GROUP TO Z-GROUP
DISPLAY Z-GROUP
```

How could you get the desired editing?

-2. If ITEM-N is defined with PIC 99 BLANK WHEN ZERO, what limitations are there in using it in an arithmetic statement?

3. What is the size of each of these identifiers?

```
02 A-ONE  PIC S99.
02 A-TWO  PIC S99    SIGN IS LEADING SEPARATE.
```

14
The SYNCHRONIZED Clause

Objectives

▶   This chapter is for advanced programmers using mainframes.

14.1 Purpose and Syntax

The SYNCHRONIZED clause is used to align elementary items on natural boundaries of the computer memory. On a personal computer the natural boundary is a byte so the SYNC clause has no effect since data is always byte-aligned. On larger machines the natural alignment is a word, which may be 2, 4 or 8 bytes long. Aligning elementary items on a word may improve program efficiency.

```
Format:    {SYNCHRONIZED}  [LEFT ]
           {SYNC         }  [RIGHT]
```

On most computers, the LEFT/RIGHT options have identical effects and are therefore redundant.

Examples:
```
05 CASH-SUM      PIC 9999V99   COMP SYNC.
05 TABLE-INDEX   USAGE INDEX SYNC.
```

1)   The clause affects the alignment only of BINARY, COMPUTATIONAL and INDEX data items. It may be used only with elementary data items.

2)   When the clause is used with an identifier which also has an OCCURS clause, all the occurrences of the data item, and all occurrences of data items subordinate to the identifier, are SYNCHRONIZED.

3)   The SYNCHRONIZED clause, like the SIGN clause, is concerned with the internal storage of data. In the absence of a SYNCHRONIZED clause, each record (01 level) and each 77 level item begins on a word boundary. Elementary items are stored on contiguous bytes.

   The SYNCHRONIZED clause causes elementary items to be aligned on word boundaries rather than on byte boundaries. The item is aligned on a 2, 4 or 8-byte word depending on its USAGE type and/or size. The interested reader should refer to the system manual for more details.

4) **Program efficiency:** When a numeric (or index-name) item is used without the SYNCHRONIZED clause, each operation involving the item must first move it to a **word boundary.** The SYNCHRONIZED clause saves this a machine step and can result in a more efficient program.

5) It is sometimes necessary for parameters used to CALL non-COBOL subprograms to be on word boundaries. The SYNCHRONIZED clause achieves this.

15
The Procedure Division

Objectives

- ▶ Know what is meant by a procedure and a paragraph.
- ▶ Know the four types of statement.
- ▶ Understand what is meant by the scope of a statement.

15.1 Purpose and Syntax

It is in the Procedure Division that we code the instructions for processing the files and the data described in the Environment and Data divisions.

```
PROCEDURE DIVISION     [USING identifier-1…]●
{ [ section-name SECTION●]
    { paragraph-name●
        { sentence● }…  }…  }…
```

The USING clause is required in a subprogram (a program that is called by another program) which receives and/or passes data to the calling program. Chapter 28 explains the use of this clause.

From the remainder of the diagram we see that sections are composed of paragraphs which, in turn, are composed of sentences. We noted earlier that a sentence contains one or more statements and ends with a period. A statement always begins with a COBOL verb.

15.2 Sections

The procedure division may be divided into sections. Each section starts with a section heading consisting of a user-defined section-name and the word SECTION. The heading is terminated by a period and followed by one or more paragraphs. When no sections are explicitly defined, the procedure division is considered to consist of one, unnamed section.

We omit any discussion of segmentation since this feature is scheduled for deletion in the next COBOL standard.

One or more DECLARATIVE sections may optionally be placed immediately following the division header. These sections are used to instruct the program what actions to take in the event of I/O errors; see Chapter 32 .

15.3 Paragraphs and Procedure-names

Paragraphs are used in the Procedure Division to modularize the program. A paragraph consists of a user-defined paragraph-name terminating with a period and followed by one or more sentences. The paragraph-name must begin in Area A while statements must begin in Area B. When the compiler finds a paragraph name it knows that the previous paragraph has ended. Paragraph names must be unique within each section. A paragraph name that appears in more than one section must be referenced by a qualified name: e.g. PERFORM PARA-A IN AAA-SECTION. It is frequently convenient in large programs to begin the paragraph names with a number (e.g. 100-OPEN-ALL-FILES.); this enables the programmer to show the relationships (hierarchy) between the paragraphs.

A paragraph must have at least one sentence. The minimal sentence reads: EXIT. A program with this sentence would do nothing. When EXIT is used, it must be the only statement in the paragraph — see Chapter 22 for the use of EXIT.

A procedure-name may refer to: a single paragraph-name, a series of consecutive paragraph-names, a single section, or a series of consecutive sections. For example, the syntax for one of the PERFORM verb formats begins:

        PERFORM procedure-name ...

In coding this verb we could use lines such as:

```
        PERFORM PARA-TWENTY
        PERFORM PARA-TWENTY THRU PARA-THIRTY
        PERFORM ABC-SECTION
        PERFORM ABC-SECTION THRU XYZ-SECTION
```

15.4 Sentences and Statements

A *sentence* consists of one or more statements and is terminated by a period. A *statement* is a syntactically correct series of words beginning with a COBOL verb. As in English, a verb is a word expressing an action. Examples of verbs include: MOVE, ADD, PERFORM. However, for the sake of consistency, the definition of verb is expanded to include the word IF. What dictionary will contain the verb "to if", one may ask. In this context, it helps to think of IF as an instruction: "DO the following IF ...".

Here are three sample sentences, with periods emphasised.

```
    (a)    ADD 1 TO ITEM-M●                        <1 statement>
    (b)    MOVE ITEM-A TO ITEM-C    ADD 1 TO ITEM-C●  <2 statements>
    (c)    MOVE ITEM-1 TO ITEM-2                    <3 statements>
           ADD  ITEM-2 ITEM-5 GIVING ITEM-3
           DISPLAY "VALUE OF ITEM-3 IS " ITEM-3●
```

15.5 Statement Types

Statements are grouped into four types: compiler directed, conditional, imperative and delimited-scope. Table 15-1 lists the COBOL verbs and the type of statement each defines.

Table 15-1: Statement types and verbs

Type	Category	Verb
Imperative	Arithmetic	ADD, COMPUTE, DIVIDE, MULTIPLY, SUBTRACT, without the optional `SIZE  ERROR` phrase. INSPECT (TALLYING)
	Data Movement	ACCEPT (DATE, DAY, DAY-OF-WEEK, TIME) INITIALIZE INSPECT (REPLACING or CONVERTING) MOVE SET (TO TRUE) STRING, UNSTRING without OVERFLOW phrase
	Ending	STOP
	Input-Output	ACCEPT identifier CLOSE DELETE without INVALID KEY DISPLAY OPEN READ without INVALID KEY REWRITE without INVALID KEY START without INVALID KEY UNLOCK WRITE without INVALID KEY or END-OF-PAGE
	Inter-program	CALL without EXCEPTION, OVERFLOW or END-CALL
	Procedure Branching	ALTER CONTINUE EXIT GO TO PERFORM without END-PERFORM
	Table Handling	SET (TO, UP BY, or DOWN BY)
	Ordering	MERGE RELEASE RETURN SORT

Table 15-1: Statement types and verbs *continued*

Type	Verb
Conditional	EVALUATE
	IF
	RETURN
	SEARCH
	Arithmetic verbs with SIZE ERROR phrase
	ADD, COMPUTE, DIVIDE, MULTIPLY, SUBTRACT
	Input verbs with ON END phrase
	ACCEPT (with ANSI extension), READ
	IO verbs with INVALID KEY phrase
	DELETE, READ, REWRITE, START, WRITE
	Output verb with END-OF-PAGE (EOP) phrase
	WRITE
	Data movement verbs with OVERFLOW phrase
	STRING, UNSTRING
	Inter-program communication verb
	CALL (EXCEPTION or OVERFLOW)
Delimited-scope	EVALUATE (END-EVALUATE)
	IF (END-IF)
	RETURN (END-RETURN)
	Arithmetic verbs with END-verb phrase
	ADD, COMPUTE, DIVIDE, MULTIPLY, SUBTRACT
	IO verbs with END-verb phrase
	ACCEPT (with ANSI extension), DELETE
	READ, REWRITE, START, WRITE
	Data movement verbs with END-verb phrase
	STRING, UNSTRING
	Inter-program communication verb
	CALL (END-CALL)
	Procedure branching verb
	PERFORM (END-PERFORM)
Compiler-directing	COPY
	REPLACE
	USE

Note that some verbs may define more that one type of statement depending upon the use of optional phrases. For example, the ADD verb may define an imperative statement. When the phrase ON SIZE ERROR is used with the verb, it defines a conditional statement.

Imperative	A statement that directs the program to unconditionally perform the action defined by its verb. As shown in Table 15-1, statements of this type are further divided into categories.
Conditional	A statement that requires the program to take an action that depends on the truth value of an expression. The most obvious verb defining a conditional statement is IF. Another is EVALUATE. As mentioned above, other verbs define conditional statements when certain optional phrases are used.
Delimited-scope	These are statements that end with a scope terminator having the form *END-verb*. Thus, we may code IF... END-IF. Delimited-scope statements enhance the programmer's ability to write structured programs. A delimited-scope statement may be used wherever a COBOL syntax requires an imperative statement.
Compiler-directed	These are statements that instruct the COBOL compiler to perform an action at compilation time. All other statements are executed at run time. The most commonly used compiler-directed statement uses the COPY verb that is examined in Chapter 30.

NOTE: When the format of a verb calls for an *imperative-statement* (as in IF condition-1 THEN imperative-statement-1 ...), a *delimited-scope statement* may be used as imperative-statement-1. The next section of this chapter discusses the scope of statements.

15.6 Scope of Statements

Consider these two fragments of code:

```
    (a)                              (b)
DISPLAY "Item = " ITEM-N         IF ITEM-N > 20
PERFORM PARA-ZODIAC                  DISPLAY "Item = " ITEM-N
                                     PERFORM PARA-ZODIAC
```

In (a) the action of the verb in each statement is terminated by the occurrence of the next verb. The compiler recognizes PERFORM as a verb and terminates the action of the DISPLAY statement.

Now look what happens in (b). When does the IF action stop? How many statements following the IF are to be executed when the condition (ITEM-N > 20) is true? How do we delimit the scope of a conditional statement? One way is to use a period, i.e. to make a separate sentence. We show this in (c) below where the indented statement is to be executed when the condition is true.

```
(c) IF ITEM-N > 20
        DISPLAY "Item = " ITEM-N●
    PERFORM PARA-ZODIAC
```

The DISPLAY (and any other statements we place before the period) will execute only when the condition in true. The PERFORM will execute whatever the truth value of the condition.

The period, however, is often too powerful. There is a neater and much more flexible way of delimiting the scope of conditional verbs; use the scope-terminator that has the form: END-verb.

```
(d) PERFORM 5 TIMES
        DISPLAY "Enter a number less than 50 " NO ADVANCING
        ACCEPT ITEM-N
        IF ITEM-N < 50
            ADD ITEM-N TO SUM-OF-N
        END-IF
    END-PERFORM
    DISPLAY "Sum is " SUM-OF-N
```

Here we could not have terminated the IF statement with a period at the end of the ADD statement. A period here would terminate both the IF and the PERFORM statements. The END-IF solves the problem of delimiting only the IF statement. Note that END-PERFORM is legal only with in-line PERFORM statements.

15.7 Notes on Coding Style

a) *Scope-terminators.* The reader is advised always to use a scope-terminator rather than the period as a means of delimiting the scope of a statement. There are two advantages to using this style of coding. Firstly, if this style is always used and the programmer avoids the use of NEXT SENTENCE, then only two periods are required in a paragraph: one to terminate the paragraph name and one at the end of the final statement in the paragraph. Secondly, it makes the program very easy to follow since the reader sees clearly when a structure is ended.

b) *Using indentation.* In the last example there are two levels of indentation. Everything between PERFORM and END-PERFORM is indented to one level. The statement between IF and END-IF is indented to a second level. This again improves the readability of the code.

c) *Paragraphs.* The novice programmer often asks when he/she should use a paragraph. There are two rules-of-thumb. The first states that a paragraph should perform one and only one function. Now this has to be tempered with good sense. Opening a file is a function but does not need a paragraph all to itself. The code for opening a file and reading all its records would be a good candidate for a single paragraph.

```
READ-FILE-PARA.
    OPEN INPUT X-FILE
    READ X-FILE AT END SET MOVE "Y" TO FOUND-END   END READ
    PERFORM UNTIL FOUND-END = "Y"
       DISPLAY X-RECORD
       READ X-FILE AT END SET MOVE "Y" TO FOUND-END   END READ
    END-PERFORM
    CLOSE X-FILE
    •                          < a structured period - see (e) below >
```

If we wish to do more with the record than just display it then we have two options. We could replace the DISPLAY statement by all the statements needed for our task, or we could replace it by a PERFORM statement and code all the task in its own paragraph. Only when the task can be coded in a few lines is the first option recommended.

The second rule-of-thumb is that a paragraph should contain no more that three levels of indentation if there is more than a line or so of code at each level. Again the programmer should use common sense when considering this rule.

Providing you do not go to ridiculous extremes, nobody will fault you for having too many paragraphs. You may well be faulted for having too few.

d) *Paragraph names.* In a long program, it may help with readability if a system is used to name the paragraphs. The major paragraphs may be called 100-READ-FILE, 200-PRINT-REPORT, etc. Any paragraph called from within 100-READ-FILE would be given a name beginning with 110, 120, etc. The naming system then reflects the hierarchy of the paragraphs.

e) *Structured periods.* We noted above that the last statement in a paragraph must end with a period and that we may wish to have only one period in the paragraph other than the period that ends its name. What then should we do if we need to add an additional line to a paragraph? Do we go to the bother of removing the period above the new line? Some programmers use what are called "structured periods". The paragraph-terminating period is placed in column 12 of the line following the last statement.

15.8 Review Questions

1.   What differentiates a sentence from a statement?

2.   Write a program to display "Hello, world" using the minimum number of lines of code.

3*   The syntax of arithmetic statements contain the phrase ON SIZE ERROR *imperative-statement.* Is there any way we could use an IF statement for *imperative-statement?*

4*   What is wrong with this code?
```
     PARA-ONE
         MOVE ZERO TO ITEM-N
         MOVE SPACES TO ITEM-A
     PARA-TWO
         DISPLAY "Value of Item-A is   " ITEM-A
         STOP RUN.
```

16
The ACCEPT and DISPLAY Verbs

Objectives

- ▸ Know how to use format-1 of the two verbs.
- ▸ Know how to access the system date and time.

16.1 Introduction

The ACCEPT and DISPLAY verbs allow for low volume input and output. Data may be obtained from, or displayed upon, the user's terminal or other system devices. A simple example:

```
DISPLAY   "Please type in your name"
ACCEPT    USER-NAME
DISPLAY   "Your name is " USER-NAME
```

An important feature of COBOL is that it is standardized so that programs are portable (can be moved from one type of computer to another). Many implementations include enhancements to the ACCEPT and DISPLAY verbs. We shall examine first the ANSI forms of the ACCEPT and DISPLAY verbs. Later sections explore the enhancements offered by Micro Focus COBOL and RM/COBOL-85.

16.2 Simplest Forms (Format-1)

```
                        ACCEPT Format-1

        ACCEPT identifier-1 [ FROM mnemonic-name ]
```

```
                        DISPLAY Format-1

DISPLAY {identifier-1 / literal-1}... [UPON mnemonic-name] [WITH NO ADVANCING]
```

Some typical uses of statements using these verbs are:

a) To prompt the user for data and accept it from the terminal. The NO ADVANCING may be used to retain the cursor at the end of the data that has been displayed; in the absence of this phrase the cursor is positioned at the beginning of the next line.

```
DISPLAY "Enter account number " NO ADVANCING.
ACCEPT ACCOUNT-KEY.
```

b) To give the user information on the progress of the program; this can be comforting to the user especially if there will be a long wait before he/she is next asked for input. The DISPLAY statement is also helpful when debugging a program.

```
DISPLAY "Please wait while file is sorted ....."
DISPLAY "In PARA-ABC; COMPUTE-TOTAL = " COMPUTE-TOTAL.
```

c) To report error conditions to the user.

```
ADD ITEM-A TO ITEM-B
    ON SIZE ERROR  DISPLAY "Size error in ITEM-B"
END-ADD
```

d) In a mainframe environment your program may use a DISPLAY UPON mnemonic-name statement to request the operator in the computer room to mount a tape on the tape drive unit. If a corresponding ACCEPT FROM mnemonic-name statement was used, the program could wait until operator sent a suitable reply.

16.2.1 Notes on the DISPLAY and ACCEPT verbs (Format-1)

You may wish to print and run the program CHAP16-1 (on disk) to observe how your implementation of COBOL behaves with these verbs. The identifiers used in the program are defined by:

```
01 GROUP-AN.
   02 ITEM-A PIC X(5)  VALUE "ABCDE".
   02 FILLER PIC XX    VALUE SPACES.
   02 ITEM-N PIC S99   VALUE -25.
```

1) The sending item size is the sum of the sizes of each identifier or literal in the statement. There must be one space (or a comma and a space) between each item when two or more are displayed.

```
05  ITEM-A  PIC X(5) VALUE "ABCD".
DISPLAY  "*" ITEM-A  "*"
```

The output will be *ABCD * , with ITEM-A using five character positions — the last one being blank.

2) The NO ADVANCING may be used to retain the cursor at the end of the data displayed.

Without this phrase the cursor is positioned at the beginning of the next line.

3) Displaying numeric data: In the ANSI standard, Format-1 of the DISPLAY verb does not convert numeric data. Thus, for example, if ITEM-N PIC S99 has a value of -25, DISPLAY ITEM-N will result in "2N" being displayed in RM/COBOL-85 or "2u" in Micro Focus COBOL when the item is part of a group; see SIGN SEPARATE in Chapter 13 for an explanation. This is not very meaningful to most of us. The SIGN IS {LEADING/TRAILING} SEPARATE clause may be used to overcome this problem. Alternatively, MOVE the numeric item to a numeric-edited item and display that item.

When an elementary item is displayed using Format-1 with Micro Focus COBOL, the system performs the conversion to human-readable form. RM/COBOL-85 does not. Carefully note that this conversion applies only to Format-1. With either application, you may wish to add a SIGN clause to the item to observe the effect with group and elementary displays.

4) Suppose that, in reply to ACCEPT ITEM-A, the user types five characters such as JKLMN. At this point, because the item is full, some compilers (e.g. RM/COBOL-85) complete the statement without requiring the user to press the Enter key. Other compilers (e.g. Micro Focus COBOL) require the Entry key to be pressed. While this automatic completion is often very useful in saving keystrokes, it has the drawback of not allowing the user to check for typo errors. If this is needed, you should use one of the other formats shown below.

5) Generally, if in reply to ACCEPT, you press Enter without typing any characters, a numeric item will be given the value of zero and an alphanumeric item would be filled with spaces. Some ill-behaved compilers leave the identifier with the value it had before the ACCEPT statement was executed.

6) Some compilers (fortunately not Micro Focus COBOL or RM/COBOL-85) have a very nasty habit. Suppose ITEM-A currently has a value of "abcde", and in reply to ACCEPT ITEM-A the user types "ABC". The poorly-behaved compiler gives ITEM-A a value of "ABCde"; the last two characters are left over from the previous value. The programmer must move spaces to the item before the ACCEPT statement.

7) In the ANSI standard, the ACCEPT verb does not convert numeric data. For example, if you wish to enter a value with less than 2 digits into ITEM-N, it is necessary to type the leading zero. Most compilers are somewhat more friendly and do not require leading zeros to be typed.

In the program, ITEM-N has a picture of S99. That is to say, it is a signed numeric item. Both Micro Focus COBOL and RM/COBOL-85 allow the user to type data in various formats for signed items. For a positive value we may type: 25, +25, 25+; likewise a negative value may be typed as 25- or -25. The system converts the number to the correct storage format. Carefully note that this conversion applies only to Format-1. Experiment with CHAP16-1 to see what happens if you type nonnumeric data in response to ACCEPT ITEM-N.

16.3 ACCEPT Format-2: System Date and Time

```
                      ACCEPT Format-2

                                    ┌ DATE        ┐
                                    │ DAY         │
     ACCEPT identifier-2 FROM  ⟨ DAY-OF-WEEK ⟩
                                    │ TIME        │
                                    └             ┘
```

This form of the ACCEPT verb gives the programmer access to the current date and time as stored by the computer's operating system. The sending items (DAY, DAY-OF-WEEK, DATE and TIME) are not true identifiers and do not appear in the Data Division. They function as if they were numeric items with the pictures as shown below. In addition to this verb, one may use the more extensive date functions as described in Chapter 31, if your compiler supports them.

Item	Picture	Format	Explanation
DATE	9(6)	YYMMDD	YY = year; MM = month; DD = day of month
DAY	9(5)	YYJJJ	YY = year; JJJ = Julian date Julian date: Jan 1st = 001, etc
DAY-OF-WEEK	9(1)	N	Monday = 1 ... Sunday = 7
TIME	9(8)	HHMMSShh	HH = hours on 24-hr clock MM = minutes; SS = seconds; hh = hundredths of seconds

The program CHAP16-2 on the disk demonstrates the use of this verb to accept and display each of the options. Part of the code in this program is:

```
02 TODAY-DATE              PIC 9(6).
02 REDEFINES TODAY-DATE.
   03 TODAY-YY             PIC 99.
   03 TODAY-MM             PIC 99.
   03 TODAY-DD             PIC 99.
...
02 SHOW-DATE               PIC 99/99/99.
```

The identifier TODAY-DATE gets a value such as 950613 from ACCEPT TODAY-DATE FROM DATE. This value is displayed with insertion editing by moving it to SHOW-DATE. We may also access the components (year, month and day) from the redefining item.

16.4 Enhanced Forms of the Verbs

At the time the standard was originally developed for COBOL, the vast majority of output was to files and printers, and input was from files — or punched cards! Only the computer operator had a terminal so there was minimal use for ACCEPT and DISPLAY. Unfortunately, the standard has not kept up with computer hardware developments. The standard forms of the console input and output verbs are too limited. This will be addressed in the next standard. Meanwhile complier vendors have added enhanced versions of the verbs. There are two forms. One which accepts and displays identifiers defined in the FILE SECTION, WORKING-STORAGE or LINKAGE SECTION of the program in a manner similar to Format-1 but with additional control of features such as the position on the screen and the colours used. We will call this the *Field-Oriented* mode. The other form allows the program to display on the screen an object which is similar to a form that one would use a typewriter to complete. This is the *Screen* mode.

While the enhancements provided by Micro Focus COBOL and RM/COBOL-85 are similar, there are sufficient differences to make it necessary to treat them in separate sections. We do not have the space to give a comprehensive discussion on the use of all the various options. The interested reader should consult the appropriate language reference manual. In the discussion two options are omitted: UNDERLINE since it functions only with monochrome monitors, and TIMEOUT since it is unlikely to be of use to the intermediate-level programmer.

16.5 Micro Focus Field-Oriented ACCEPT and DISPLAY

```
ACCEPT identifier-1
        [[ [ AT [ LINE NUMBER { identifier-2 }  ]          ] ]
         [ [        { integer-1    }  ]          ] ]
         [ {   COLUMN NUMBER { identifier-3 } ]  } ]
         [ {                 { integer-2    } ]  } ]
         [ [ AT { identifier-4 }              ]  ] ]
         [ [    { integer-3    }              ]  ] ]
        [ FROM CRT ]    [ MODE IS BLOCK ]
        [ WITH { control-option-1 }... ]
        [ON EXCEPTION imperative-statement-1 ] ]
        [NOT ON EXCEPTION imperative-statement-2 ]
        [ END-ACCEPT ]
```

The data item *identifier-1* may be an elementary or a group item. If it is elementary it may not be defined with a USAGE other than DISPLAY. See section 16.5.1 for information on accepting a group item and the purpose of the MODE phrase.

The optional phrase to control the screen position of *identifier-1* may be paraphrased as:
```
{ AT [LINE line-number] [COLUMN column-number] }
{ AT combined-number                           }
```

where the items *line-number, column-number,* and *combined-number* may be integer valued identifiers or literals. The phrase AT LINE 3 COLUMN 5 will cause the item to be displayed or accepted starting on line 3 at column position 5 of the screen. The phrase AT 0305 will the same effect. Similarly AT PUT-HERE would start the item on line 10 at column 12 if the ACCEPT/DISPLAY statement was preceded by MOVE 1012 TO PUT-HERE.

Users of Personal COBOL need not be concerned with the optional FROM CRT phrase other than to note that an ACCEPT statement with one of the phrases AT, FROM CRT, WITH *control-option,* or EXCEPTION is needed for the system to recognise this format. The system treats the statement as Format-1 if none of these is used. Users of the full version of Micro Focus COBOL may wish to read the manual to learn how to the ACCEPT statement may take data from the command line when a linked program is run.

When an elementary item is accepted, the user presses the ENTER key to complete the statement. When a group is displayed the TAB key is used to move from field to field. These two keys are called normal termination keys. The user may also press the ESCAPE key or a function key. The optional ON EXCEPTION clause in the ACCEPT statement allows field termination characteristics and conversion errors to be reported. We shall not explore this topic since Micro Focus provides a demonstration program called FUNKEY to show a better way of trapping function keys.

In the WITH phrase of an ACCEPT statement, a *control-option* may be:

a) Any of the following which are described in Table 16-1: AUTO, BELL, ERASE, FULL, GRID, HIGHLIGHT/LOWLIGHT, LEFTLINE, OVERLINE, PROMPT (with a literal only), REQUIRED, REVERSE-VIDEO, SECURE, SIZE, FOREGROUND-COLOUR and BACKGROUND-COLOUR with numeric literals only, CONTROL.

b) When *identifier-1* is an elementary item and the compiler is configured for free-format for the input of numeric data, the following may be used.

SPACE-FILL	Causes zero-suppression of all positions including the least significant.
ZERO-FILL	Suspends the normal zero suppression; all zeros are shown.
RIGHT-JUSTIFY	The item is displayed right-justified.
TRAILING-SIGN	The operational sign is displayed to the right of the value.

c) UPDATE — Specifies that the current value of the identifier is displayed by the ACCEPT statement. Your compiler may be configured to do this automatically.

d) The following options are available only in the full version of Micro Focus COBOL, not in Personal COBOL.

UPPER	Specifies that keyed in data be converted to uppercase.
LOWER	Specifies that keyed in data be converted to lowercase.

Table 16-1 Micro Focus COBOL screen attribute options

AUTO	Positions the cursor to the next screen item when the last character is keyed into a screen item without the user pressing TAB. If this is the last screen item, the ACCEPT statement is completed. The keyword AUTO-SKIP may be used in place of AUTO.
BACKGROUND COLOUR	$\left\{ \begin{array}{l} \underline{\text{BACKGROUND-COLOR}} \\ \underline{\text{BACKGROUND-COLOUR}} \end{array} \right\}$ IS $\left\{ \begin{array}{l} integer\text{-}1 \\ identifier\text{-}1 \end{array} \right\}$ The value of identifier-1 or integer-1 determines the colour of the background. The same values are used with FOREGROUND-COLOUR.
	0 black 1 blue 2 green 3 cyan
	4 red 5 magenta 6 brown 7 white
	The colour 6 is yellow if HIGHLIGHT is also specified, otherwise it is brown. If a screen description contains a BLANK SCREEN clause, and contains this phrase or is subordinate to one that does, then the default background colour is set by a DISPLAY statement.
BELL	BELL (or BEEP) causes a bell sound each time the item containing it is displayed or accepted. The data item must be elementary.
BLANK	BLANK SCREEN causes a DISPLAY statement to move the cursor to line 1 column 1, blank the screen and set colours to their default values. May be used only with colour options; other options for the same screen are ignored. BLANK LINE causes a DISPLAY statement to blank the line on which an elementary item is displayed.
BLANK WHEN ZERO	Causes a numeric item with zero value to be displayed as spaces.
BLINK	The screen field is displayed in characters that flash on and off.
COLUMN	Specifies the starting column (in absolute value or a position relative to the current position) in which an elementary item is displayed or accepted.
	$\underline{\text{COLUMN}} \left[\text{NUMBER IS} \left[\left\{ \begin{array}{l} \underline{\text{PLUS}} \\ + \\ - \end{array} \right\} \right] \left\{ \begin{array}{l} identifier\text{-}1 \\ integer\text{-}1 \end{array} \right\} \right]$
CONTROL	With field-oriented verbs the syntax of the CONTROL phrase is CONTROL {identifier-1/ literal-1}, with screens the CONTROL operand must be an identifier. The keywords shown below are allowed in the CONTROL phrase: BELL, BLINK, HIGHLIGHT, LOWLIGHT, GRID, LEFTLINE, OVERLINE, REVERSE-VIDEO, UNDERLINE, FOREGROUND-COLOUR integer-1, BACKGROUND-COLOUR integer-1, JUSTIFY, TRAILING-SIGN, AUTO, SECURE, FULL, REQUIRED, PROMPT, PROTECT, ZERO-FILL, BLANK LINE or SCREEN.
ERASE	ERASE LINE causes a DISPLAY statement to erase the rest of the line. ERASE SCREEN causes a DISPLAY statement to erase the remainder of the screen.
FOREGROUND-COLOUR	Specifies the foreground screen colour. For syntax and colours see BACKGROUND-COLOUR.
FULL	Specifies that the user must either leave the field empty or fill it completely with data. This clause may be used with group and elementary items. It is valid only with input and update items. See also REQUIRED.

Table 16-1 Micro Focus COBOL screen attribute options *continued*

GRID	Used with group or elementary items, GRID specifies that each item is to be displayed with a vertical line to the left of each character.
HIGHLIGHT	Causes the item or group of items to be displayed in high intensity.
JUSTIFIED RIGHT	Specifies right justification when data is moved or keyed in to a elementary item. The keyword RIGHT is optional; JUST is acceptable for JUSTIFIED.
LEFTLINE	Causes a vertical line to be displayed to the left of the item.
LINE	Specifies the line on which the item is to start. The syntax and usage parallels that of COLUMN.
LOWLIGHT	Causes the item or group of items to be displayed in low intensity.
OCCURS	OCCURS integer-1 TIMES. The clause, which may appear at an 01 level, may be used in place of separate entries for a table. A receiving item must have the same number of occurrences; a sending item must have either the same number of occurrences or none at all.
OVERLINE	Used with group or elementary items, OVERLINE specifies that each item is to be displayed with a horizontal line below each character.
PICTURE	The PICTURE clause is used to define the size, characteristics and edition of a screen item. See text for details.
PROMPT	PROMPT CHARACTER IS *prompt* is used with ACCEPT to display a fill character on the screen in each position where data is to be accepted. The operand *prompt* must be a single-character alphabetic or alphanumeric identifier, or a single-character literal or figurative constant.
PROTECT	Specifies that input to an ACCEPT item is to be prevented.
REQUIRED	Used with an elementary or group item, REQUIRED specifies that the user may not leave the item(s) empty.
REVERSE-VIDEO	Causes the background and foreground colours to be reversed. If a monochrome screen is used, data appears in reverse video: dark characters on a bright background.
SECURE	Used with an elementary or group item, SECURE specifies that the data keyed in by the user does not appear on the screen. NO-ECHO and SECURE are equivalent.
SIGN	SIGN IS {LEADING / TRAILING } SEPARATE CHARACTER is very useful when displaying an identifier with a operational sign (S in its picture).
SIZE	SIZE IS {identifier-1 / integer-1} is used to specify the size of an elementary item on the screen.
VALUE	Specifies the literal data to be displayed on the screen.
ZERO-FILL	Causes trailing prompt characters to be replaced by zeros rather than spaces when an alphabetic or alphanumeric data item is moved to the receiving item in an ACCEPT statement. When JUSTIFY is also in effect, the leading spaces are replaced by zeros.
UPPER	Causes any data typed in lower case characters to be converted to upper case when the ACCEPT statement is executed. This phrase cannot be used as static phrase, it must be used within a CONTROL phrase.

```
     DISPLAY  {{identifier-1}
               {literal-1   }}
          [[ [AT [LINE NUMBER {identifier-2}]         ]  ]
          [  [         {integer-1   }]                ]  ]
          [  [    COLUMN NUMBER {identifier-3}]     ] ]
          [  {          {integer-2   }]          } ]
          [  [AT {identifier-4}                   ]  ]
          [  [   {integer-3   }                   ]  ]
          [ UPON { CRT       }     [ MODE IS BLOCK ]
          [      { CRT-UNDER }
          [ WITH { control-option-1 }... ]}...
```

The operand *identifier-1* may be an elementary or a group item. Note that more than one operand may be used:

```
        DISPLAY  ITEM-A AT 0101 WITH BLANK SCREEN
                 ITEM-B AT 0140 WITH REVERSE-VIDEO.
```

If *identifier-1* is the figurative constant SPACES, the screen is cleared from the specified cursor position to the end of the screen:

```
        DISPLAY SPACES AT 0101 WITH FOREGROUND-COLOUR 3.
```

The AT phrase is as described above for the ACCEPT verb.

A simple DISPLAY SPACES UPON CRT statement at the start of a program will clear the screen and place the cursor in column 1 of line 1. The option UPON CRT-UNDER may be used to highlight an item on some monitors.

In the WITH phrase of a DISPLAY statement, a *control-option* may be any of the following which are described in Table 16-1: BELL, GRID, HIGHLIGHT/LOWLIGHT, LEFTLINE, OVERLINE, PROMPT (with a literal only), REQUIRED, REVERSE-VIDEO, SIZE, FOREGROUND-COLOUR and BACKGROUND-COLOUR with numeric literals only, CONTROL, BLANK SCREEN/LINE and ERASE. The program CHAP16-C (on disk) shows the use of a control option and may be used to view various colour combinations.

The program CHAP16-F demonstrates many of the options. Run the program and note the effect of typing numbers such as 10, 12.25, 1275, 13. You will find that, in general, you must type four digits to get the required value but the decimal may be omitted.

```
 1     IDENTIFICATION DIVISION.
 2     PROGRAM-ID.    CHAP16-F.
 3     * Demonstrates 'field' ACCEPT and DISPLAY statements
 4     DATA DIVISION.
 5     WORKING-STORAGE SECTION.
 6     01 WORK-ITEMS.
 7        02 J          PIC 99.
 8        02 LYNE       PIC 99      VALUE 5.
 9        02 IN-VALUE   PIC 99V99   VALUE ZERO.
10        02 OUT-VALUE  PIC $ZZ,ZZ9.99.
```

```
11          02 TOTAL-VALUE  PIC 999V99   VALUE ZERO.
12          02 LAST-CHAR    PIC X        VALUE SPACES.
13      PROCEDURE DIVISION.
14      MAIN-PARA.
15          DISPLAY SPACES AT 0101
16              WITH FOREGROUND-COLOUR 1 BACKGROUND-COLOUR 7
17          DISPLAY "Example of using fields"
18              AT LINE 3 COLUMN 20 WITH HIGHLIGHT, BLINK
19          PERFORM VARYING J FROM 1 BY 1 UNTIL J > 5
20              DISPLAY J  LINE LYNE COLUMN 3
21                   "Enter a number (real or integer): "
22                      LINE LYNE POSITION 6
23              ACCEPT IN-VALUE AT LINE LYNE COLUMN 45
24                  WITH FOREGROUND-COLOUR 6
25              ADD IN-VALUE TO TOTAL-VALUE
26              MOVE IN-VALUE TO OUT-VALUE
27              DISPLAY OUT-VALUE AT LINE LYNE COLUMN  60
28                  WITH FOREGROUND-COLOUR 4 REVERSE-VIDEO
29              ADD 1 TO LYNE
30          END-PERFORM
31          DISPLAY "Total value is" AT 1810
32          MOVE TOTAL-VALUE TO OUT-VALUE
33          DISPLAY OUT-VALUE  AT 1825
34                  WITH FOREGROUND-COLOUR 6 HIGHLIGHT
35          DISPLAY "Press any key to continue" AT 2010
36          ACCEPT LAST-CHAR AT 2036 WITH SECURE
37          STOP RUN.
```

16.5.1 Accepting and displaying group items

When the MODE IS BLOCK phrase is omitted and *identifier-1* is a group item, the ACCEPT statement behaves as if you had coded a series of ACCEPT statements, one for each non-FILLER item in the group. Use the TAB key to move from one item to another. Press the ENTER key to terminate the statement. When MODE IS BLOCK is used and *identifier-1* is a group item, the group is treated as if it were one elementary item including any FILLER items. The DISPLAY statement operates in a similar fashion.

16.5.2 Accepting and displaying numeric data

There can be problems accepting/displaying a numeric item with an operational sign and/or an implied decimal unless you configure Micro Focus COBOL to accept/display numeric data in free-format— a topic beyond the scope of this book. To overcome this, the identifier in the ACCEPT statement should be a numeric-edited item which is then moved to the numeric item after the ACCEPT statement. With a DISPLAY, the reverse is used — move the numeric item to a numeric-edit item and display the edited item.

16.5.3 Dynamic options using CONTROL

The CONTROL option gives dynamic control of the various options used in the ACCEPT and DISPLAY statement. As a simple example consider the case where you wish sometimes to display an item in blue and another time in red with blinking.

Without using CONTROL we might code:

```
01 WARNING-ITEM.
    02        PIC X(18) VALUE "The value of X is "
    02 X      PIC 99.

IF X = 0
    DISPLAY WARNING-ITEM WITH FOREGROUND-COLOUR 4 BLINK
ELSE
    DISPLAY WARNING-ITEM WITH FOREGROUND-COLOUR 1
END-IF
```

Using CONTROL we may use:

```
IF X = 0
    MOVE 4 TO CONTROL-FORE
    MOVE "BLINK" TO CONTROL-BLINK
    DISPLAY WARNING-ITEM WITH CONTROL CONTROL-ITEM
ELSE
    MOVE 3 TO CONTROL-FORE
    MOVE SPACES TO CONTROL-BLINK
    DISPLAY WARNING-ITEM WITH CONTROL CONTROL-ITEM
END-IF
```

We would need to define CONTROL-ITEM as:

```
01 CONTROL-ITEM.
    02                  PIC X(20) VALUE "FOREGROUND-COLOUR".
    02 CONTROL-FORE     PIC 99.
    02                  PIC X     VALUE SPACES.
    02 CONTROL-BLINK    PIC X(5).
```

Unfortunately, because a simple example was used for clarity, it makes the use of CONTROL seem less desirable as it takes more code. This will be reversed in more complex situations. The control-identifier may use the following options which are described in Table 16-1: AUTO, BELL, BLINK, FULL, GRID, HIGHLIGHT/LOWLIGHT, LEFTLINE, OVERLINE, PROMPT, PROTECT, REQUIRED, REVERSE-VIDEO, SECURE, SIZE, UNDERLINE, FOREGROUND-COLOUR and BACKGROUND-COLOUR. To override static options, each option here may be preceded with the keyword NO. When used as an optional phrase in an ACCEPT or DISPLAY statement, the control-identifier may be replaced by a literal: ACCEPT ...CONTROL "BLINK, REVERSE-VIDEO". The use of a literal is not permitted when CONTROL is used in a screen data-description-entry.

16.6 Screens in Micro Focus

A *screen-name* item is defined in the SCREEN SECTION in a manner which is similar to, but has some major departures from, the way identifiers are defined in WORKING-STORAGE. The screen-name item is displayed and accepted using these forms of the verbs.

$$
\text{ACCEPT } screen\text{-}name \left[\left\{\begin{array}{l} \text{AT}\left[\begin{array}{l} \underline{\text{LINE}}\text{ NUMBER } \left\{\begin{array}{l} identifier\text{-}2 \\ integer\text{-}1 \end{array}\right\} \\ \underline{\text{COL}}\text{UMN NUMBER } \left\{\begin{array}{l} identifier\text{-}3 \\ integer\text{-}2 \end{array}\right\} \end{array}\right] \\ \underline{\text{AT}}\left\{\begin{array}{l} identifier\text{-}4 \\ integer\text{-}3 \end{array}\right\} \end{array}\right\}\right]
$$

$$
\text{DISPLAY } screen\text{-}name \left[\left\{\begin{array}{l} \text{AT}\left[\begin{array}{l} \underline{\text{LINE}}\text{ NUMBER } \left\{\begin{array}{l} identifier\text{-}2 \\ integer\text{-}1 \end{array}\right\} \\ \underline{\text{COL}}\text{UMN NUMBER } \left\{\begin{array}{l} identifier\text{-}3 \\ integer\text{-}2 \end{array}\right\} \end{array}\right] \\ \underline{\text{AT}}\left\{\begin{array}{l} identifier\text{-}4 \\ integer\text{-}3 \end{array}\right\} \end{array}\right\}\right]
$$

We will look at a simple example of a screen definition and its use before going into the details of how to define a screen.

```
WORKING-STORAGE SECTION.
01 ITEM-A      PIC X(10) VALUE "ABCD".
01 ITEM-B      PIC 9(4)  VALUE 1234.
01 ITEM-C      PIC 9(4)  VALUE 1234.

SCREEN SECTION.
01 X-SCREEN.
   03 VALUE "Demonstration screen" BLANK SCREEN.
   03 LINE 2 COLUMN 5  PIC X(10) FROM   ITEM-A REVERSE-VIDEO.
   03 LINE 4 COLUMN 5  PIC 9(4)  TO     ITEM-B.
   03 LINE 6 COLUMN 5  PIC ZZZ9  USING ITEM-C.

DISPLAY X-SCREEN
ACCEPT X-SCREEN
```

The DISPLAY statement will show the items on the screen. The ACCEPT statement will wait for the user to key-in data for ITEM-B and ITEM-C but not ITEM-A which has a FROM clause — see below. *When a screen accepts more than one item, press TAB to move from field to field and press ENTER to terminate the ACCEPT statement.*

The data-description-entry for each screen begins with an 01-level just as a record does. The data-description-entries in the SCREEN SECTION have the form:

$$
\text{level-number} \left[\begin{array}{l} screen\text{-}name \\ \text{FILLER} \end{array}\right] \{\ screen\text{-}option\text{-}1\ \}...
$$

We may think of there being three types of screen-data items:
      group items including the 01 level item which names the entire screen,
      literal items which are used to display text on the screen, and
      field items which are items associated with an input, output or update item.

A screen data item requires a name only if it is to be referenced in a DISPLAY or ACCEPT statement. Clearly, the 01 item which names the screen must be named. You may name other items if you wish to display or accept just part of a screen. The screen-options, with the exception of PICTURE, are described in Table 16-1.

The PICTURE clause has the form:

$$\left\{ \begin{array}{l} \underline{\text{PICTURE}} \\ \underline{\text{PIC}} \end{array} \right\} \text{ IS } picture\text{-}string$$

$$\left\{ \begin{array}{l} \left[\underline{\text{FROM}} \left\{ \begin{array}{l} identifier\text{-}1 \\ literal\text{-}1 \end{array} \right\} \right] \; [\; \underline{\text{TO}} \; identifier\text{-}2 \;] \\ \underline{\text{USING}} \; identifier\text{-}3 \end{array} \right\}$$

The *picture-string* defines the type and size of the identifer. The rules we studied in Chapter 8 apply with some caveats.

a)   The main exception is that when a PIC clause is used, a VALUE clause may not be used.

b)   The size of the picture should be at least large enough to make the implied move statement that occurs with ACCEPT and DISPLAY legal.

c)   It is recommended that every numeric screen item be either an edited item or contain only 9s in its picture. The DISPLAY and ACCEPT verbs will perform the required editing and de-editing.

The FROM, TO and USING clauses determine how operands will be treated by ACCEPT and DISPLAY statements.

a)   When FROM is used, a DISPLAY statement will display *identifier-1* or *literal-1*. If the operand is an identifier it is classed as an *output identifier*. An ACCEPT statement will not affect the identifier.

b)   When TO is used, an ACCEPT statement accepts the value of the identifier which is classed as an *input identifier*.

c)   When USING is specified, the identifier is classified as an *update identifier* and is both displayed and accepted.

The CONTROL option permits the programmer to specify dynamic screen options, i.e. screen options that can be changed as the program progresses. A static option is one that is coded in the screen definition and may not be used in a CONTROL identifier. The use of the CONTROL option with screens is clearly illustrated by the program SSCNTRL which is supplied by Micro Focus with its COBOL development systems.

The program CHAP16-S displays a number of screens: a header, an input, a result and a terminating screen. The input screen is displayed and accepted five times. Run the program and compare its actions to the code. Experiment by typing some alphanumeric data when the program expects numeric data.

```
1     IDENTIFICATION DIVISION.
2     PROGRAM-ID.    CHAP16-S.
3     *       Screen demonstration program
4     DATA DIVISION.
5     WORKING-STORAGE SECTION.
6     01 WORK-ITEMS.
7         02 THE-NUMBER    PIC 999.
8         02 THE-COUNT     PIC 99     VALUE 0.
9         02 THE-TOTAL     PIC 9999   VALUE 0.
10        02 THE-AVERAGE   PIC 99.99.
11        02 J             PIC 99.
12        02 LYNE          PIC 99     VALUE 14.
13        02 EXIT-CHAR     PIC X      VALUE SPACES.
14    SCREEN SECTION.
15    01 SCREEN-A.
16        02 VALUE "Sample screen program - averages 5 integers"
17                    LINE 5 COLUMN 20 BLANK SCREEN
18                    FOREGROUND-COLOUR 6 BACKGROUND-COLOUR 3 HIGHLIGHT.
19    01 SCREEN-B.
20        02 VALUE "Enter an integer less than 1000"
21                    LINE 8 COLUMN 5 FOREGROUND-COLOUR 1.
22        02 PIC ZZZ TO THE-NUMBER   COLUMN 40.
23    01 SCREEN-C.
24        02 VALUE "Count Number Total" LINE LYNE COLUMN 5
25            FOREGROUND-COLOUR 4.
26    01 SCREEN-D FOREGROUND-COLOUR 2 HIGHLIGHT.
27        02 PIC ZZ    FROM THE-COUNT LINE LYNE COLUMN 5.
28        02 PIC ZZ9   FROM THE-NUMBER COLUMN 12.
29        02 PIC Z(3)9 FROM THE-TOTAL   COLUMN 18.
30    01 SCREEN-E.
31        02 VALUE "Average is" LINE 12 COLUMN 5 FOREGROUND-COLOUR 4.
32        02 PIC ZZ.ZZ FROM THE-AVERAGE REQUIRED COLUMN 20 BLINK.
33    01 EXIT-SCREEN.
34        02 VALUE "Press any key to continue " LINE 22 COLUMN 20.
35        02 PIC X TO EXIT-CHAR SECURE.
36
37    PROCEDURE DIVISION.
38    MAIN-PARA.
39        DISPLAY SCREEN-A
40        DISPLAY SCREEN-C
41        PERFORM 5 TIMES
42           DISPLAY SCREEN-B
43           ACCEPT  SCREEN-B
44           ADD THE-NUMBER TO THE-TOTAL
45           ADD 1 TO THE-COUNT
46           COMPUTE THE-AVERAGE ROUNDED = THE-TOTAL / THE-COUNT
47           ADD 1 TO LYNE
48           DISPLAY SCREEN-D  SCREEN-E
49        END-PERFORM
50        DISPLAY EXIT-SCREEN
51        ACCEPT EXIT-SCREEN
52        STOP RUN.
```

16.7 RM/COBOL-85 Field Oriented DISPLAY and ACCEPT

```
ACCEPT { identifier-1 [ control-item ]... }...
    [                         ⎧ imperative-statement-1 ⎫ ]
    [ ON EXCEPTION [ identifier-2 ] ⎨ NEXT SENTENCE         ⎬ ]
    [                         ⎩                        ⎭ ]
    [ [NOT ON EXCEPTION imperative-statement-2 ]            ]
    [ END-ACCEPT ]
```

```
DISPLAY ⎧ ⎧ identifier-1 ⎫                    ⎫
        ⎨ ⎨ literal-1    ⎬ [ control-item ]... ⎬ ...
        ⎩ ⎩             ⎭                    ⎭
```

Note that both verbs permit more than one operand to be processed in a single statement.

The optional ON EXCEPTION clause in the ACCEPT statement allows field termination characteristics and conversion errors to be reported. Note there can be only one ON EXCEPTION clause and it is associated with the last (or only) *identifier-1*. When *identifier-2* (a numeric integer item) is used, the value of the termination code is stored in it.

Table 16-2 lists the optional control phrases. All are permitted in an ACCEPT statement. DISPLAY statements may use: BEEP, BLINK, CONTROL, CONVERT, ERASE, HIGH/LOW, LINE, POSITION, REVERSE, and SIZE. Where alternate keywords are shown they are available with version 5 .

Table 16-2 Optional control phrases for RM/COBOL-85

[NO] BEEP	BEEP (or BELL) causes the bell to sound in a DISPLAY statement; NO BEEP suppresses the bell which normally accompanies the ACCEPT statement.
BLINK	The screen field is displayed in characters that flash on and off.
CONTROL	The use of the CONTROL phrase is demonstrated below. The keywords shown below are allowed in the CONTROL phrase; where two or more are bracketed, only one may be used: [ERASE, ERASE EOL, ERASE EOS, NO ERASE], [BEEP, NO BEEP], [HIGH, LOW, OFF], [BLINK, NO BLINK], [REVERSE, NO REVERSE], [TAB, NO TAB], [PROMPT, NO PROMPT], [CONVERT, NO CONVERT], [UPDATE, NO UPDATE], [ECHO, NO ECHO]. Note that negation is allowed in the CONTROL phrase for certain keywords. Additional keywords are valid in a CONTROL phrase:

BCOLOR   Sets the background colour; BCOLOR=colour, where *colour* has one of the following values: black, blue, green, cyan, red, magenta, brown, white.

BORDER   Sets the colour of the screen border; BORDER=colour. See BCOLOR above for a list of colours.

Table 16-2 Optional control phrases for RM/COBOL-85 *continued*

FCOLOR	Sets the colour of the foreground; FCOLOR=colour. See BCOLOR above for a list of colours.
UPPER	Causes any data typed in lower case characters to be converted to upper case when the ACCEPT statement is executed.
GRAPHICS	See section 16.8.2

Literals in the control expression must be separated by commas:
CONTROL "HIGH, REVERSE"

CONVERT	Causes conversion of signed numeric data. Conversion is implied if the identifier is numeric and UPDATE is specified. The ON EXCEPTION phrase is triggered if a conversion error occurs.
CURSOR *cursor-item*	An identifier or a literal may be used for *cursor-item*. The value of the operand sets the initial position of the cursor within screen field. Operative only with ACCEPT.
ERASE ERASE EOL ERASE EOS	After moving to the position set by LINE and POSITION but before displaying the screen field: (i) the screen is completely cleared by ERASE,(ii) the current line is cleared by ERASE EOL (end-of-line), or (iii) the remainder of the screen is cleared by ERASE EOS (end-of screen).
HIGH LOW OFF	Only one of these may be specified. HIGH gives bright intensity to the characters, LOW gives normal intensity. The defaults are HIGH for ACCEPT statements and LOW for DISPLAY statements. When OFF is specified, the data typed in response to an ACCEPT statement is not visible on the screen. Alternate keywords are: HIGHLIGHT, LOWLIGHT, and SECURE.
LINE *line*	The cursor is positioned on line *line* before the item is accepted/displayed. An identifier or a literal may be used for *line*.
POSITION *column*	The cursor is positioned on column *column* before the item is accepted/displayed. An identifier or a literal may be used for *column* POSITION 0 keeps the cursor at its current position. If POSITION is omitted, POSITION 1 is implied. The alternate keywords are COLUMN and COL.
PROMPT *prompt*	Used with ACCEPT to display a fill character on the screen in the positions where data is to be accepted. The operand *prompt* must be a single-character literal or a figurative constant such as SPACE. When *literal* is included, the literal is used as the fill character; otherwise, the underscore character is used.
REVERSE	Causes the background and foreground colours to be reversed. If a monochrome screen is used, data appears in reverse video: dark characters on a bright background. Alternate keywords are: REVERSED and REVERSE-VIDEO.
SIZE *size*	An identifier or a literal may be used for *size* to set the size of the item as it appears on the screen.
TAB	When TAB is specified, the user must press Enter to complete the input of *identifier-1* in an ACCEPT statement. If it is not specified, filling the field automatically completes the statement.
UPDATE	Causes the current value of *identifier-1* to be displayed on the screen with output conversion when the ACCEPT statement begins.

16.7.1 Using a CONTROL option

These two lines of code will have the same effect:
a) DISPLAY ITEM-X HIGH BLINK   b) DISPLAY ITEM-X CONTROL "HIGH, BLINK"
If we use an identifier for the CONTROL phrase rather than a literal, we may change the
control item as the program executes. In this way we achieve *dynamic* control. For example:

```
02 CONTROL-ITEM.
   03 CONTROL-INTENSE  PIC X(4).
   03                  PIC X   VALUE ",".
   03 CONTROL-BLINK    PIC X(10).

EVALUATE MY-ITEM
   WHEN    0
    MOVE "LOW"  TO CONTROL-INTENSE MOVE "NO BLINK" TO CONTROL-BLINK
   WHEN    1
    MOVE "LOW"  TO CONTROL-INTENSE MOVE "BLINK" TO CONTROL-BLINK
   WHEN OTHER
    MOVE "HIGH" TO CONTROL-INTENSE MOVE "NO BLINK" TO CONTROL-BLINK
END-EVALUATE
DISPLAY MY-ITEM CONTROL CONTROL-ITEM.
```

The sample program (CHAP16-C), which illustrates the use of CONTROL, may be used to
experiment with the colours of the foreground (the FCOLOR=colour part of the control
item), the background (BCOLOR=), and the border (BORDER=) on the runtime screen. The
reader is encouraged to experiment with this program.

```
1     IDENTIFICATION DIVISION.
2     PROGRAM-ID. CHAP16-C.
3    * Purpose: Illustrates the use of CONTROL
4     DATA DIVISION.
5     WORKING-STORAGE SECTION.
6     01 ITEM-D1 PIC X(45) VALUE "PERMITTED COLOURS ARE:".
7    -01 ITEM-D2 PIC X(45) VALUE
8        "BLACK BLUE GREEN CYAN RED MAGENTA BROWN WHITE".
9     01 ITEM-D3 PIC X(45) VALUE
10       "Experiment with valid and invalid colours".
11    01 ITEM-D4.
12       02 PIC X(24) VALUE "This is a line of text. ".
13       02 PIC X(18) VALUE "The Foreground is ".
14       02 ITEM-FORE  PIC X(08).
15       02 PIC X(20) VALUE ", the Background is ".
16       02 ITEM-BACK PIC X(08).
17    01 CONTROL-COLOUR.
18          03               PIC X(10) VALUE "FCOLOR=".
19          03 FORE-COLOUR  PIC X(10) VALUE "BLUE".
20          03               PIC XX     VALUE ", ".
21          03               PIC X(10) VALUE "BCOLOR=".
22          03 BACK-COLOUR  PIC X(10) VALUE "CYAN".
23          03               PIC XX     VALUE ", ".
24          03               PIC X(10) VALUE "BORDER=".
```

```
25              03 BORD-COLOUR  PIC X(10) VALUE "GREEN".
26    01 WORK-ITEMS.
27       02 QUESTION          PIC X VALUE "Y".
28          88 NO-MORE        VALUE "N" "n".
29          88 VALID-REPLY    VALUE "Y" "y" "N" "n".
30       02 LYNE              PIC 99 VALUE 12.
31    PROCEDURE DIVISION.
32    MAIN-PARA.
33       DISPLAY SPACES LINE 1 POSITION 1 ERASE EOS
34                         CONTROL CONTROL-COLOUR
35       DISPLAY ITEM-D1  LINE 4 POSITION 24
36       DISPLAY ITEM-D2  LINE 5 POSITION 12
37       DISPLAY ITEM-D3  LINE 6 POSITION 14
38       PERFORM UNTIL NO-MORE
39          MOVE SPACES TO FORE-COLOUR BACK-COLOUR
40          DISPLAY "Enter Foreground colour           "
41            LINE 8 POSITION 10  CONTROL "FCOLOR=BLUE,BCOLOR=CYAN"
42          ACCEPT FORE-COLOUR LINE 8 POSITION 36
43          DISPLAY "Enter Background colour           "
44                LINE 9 POSITION 10
45          ACCEPT BACK-COLOUR LINE 9 POSITION 36
46          MOVE FORE-COLOUR TO ITEM-FORE
47          MOVE BACK-COLOUR TO ITEM-BACK
48          DISPLAY ITEM-D4 LINE LYNE POSITION 2
49                  CONTROL CONTROL-COLOUR
50          ADD 1 TO LYNE
51          IF LYNE > 20 MOVE 8 TO LYNE END-IF
52          PERFORM TEST AFTER UNTIL VALID-REPLY
53            DISPLAY "Do you want to try again? "
54              LINE 22 POSITION 22 CONTROL "FCOLOR=BLUE,BCOLOR=CYAN"
55            ACCEPT QUESTION
56              LINE 22 POSITION 50 CONTROL "FCOLOR=BLUE,BCOLOR=CYAN"
57          END-PERFORM
58       END-PERFORM
59       STOP RUN.
```

The next program (CHAP16-F) is a very simple program to accept and re-display five numbers. It is recommended that the reader runs this program and observes the effects it produces. The program may then be used to experiment with other control phrases. The reader may wish to observe the program's behaviour when an alphanumeric literal is typed into a numeric field and to contrast this program's behaviour with that of the program CHAP16-S discussed in this chapter.

```
1     IDENTIFICATION DIVISION.
2     PROGRAM-ID.   CHAP16-F.
3     * Purpose: to demonstrate fields
4     DATA DIVISION.
5     WORKING-STORAGE SECTION.
6     01 WORK-ITEMS.
7        02 J        PIC 9.
8        02 LYNE     PIC 99      VALUE 5.
```

```
 9        02 IN-VALUE       PIC 9999V99.
10        02 TOTAL-VALUE    PIC 9999V99 VALUE 0.
11        02 OUT-VALUE      PIC $ZZ,ZZ9.99.
12        02 C-ITEM         PIC X(25)   VALUE "FCOLOR=BLUE,BCOLOR=WHITE".
13        02 EXIT-CHAR      PIC X       VALUE SPACES.
14     PROCEDURE DIVISION.
15     MAIN-PARA.
16        DISPLAY " " LINE 1 ERASE EOS CONTROL C-ITEM
17        DISPLAY "Example of using fields"
18                           LINE 3 POSITION 20 HIGH
19        PERFORM VARYING J FROM 1 BY 1 UNTIL J > 5
20           DISPLAY J  LINE LYNE POSITION 3
21                 "Enter a number (real or integer): "
22                           LINE LYNE POSITION 6
23           ACCEPT IN-VALUE LINE LYNE POSITION 45
24                           CONTROL "FCOLOR=GREEN"
25           ADD IN-VALUE TO TOTAL-VALUE
26           MOVE IN-VALUE TO OUT-VALUE
27           DISPLAY OUT-VALUE LINE LYNE POSITION 60
28                           CONTROL C-ITEM REVERSE
29           ADD 1 TO LYNE
30        END-PERFORM
31        MOVE TOTAL-VALUE TO OUT-VALUE
32        DISPLAY "Total = "   LINE 18 POSITION 10
33                           CONTROL "FCOLOR=CYAN"
34              OUT-VALUE
35        DISPLAY "Press any key to continue"
36              LINE 22 POSITION 10
37              CONTROL "BLINK,FCOLOR=RED"
38        ACCEPT EXIT-CHAR  LINE 22 POSITION 36 OFF
39        STOP RUN.
```

16.8 Screens in RM/COBOL-85

A *screen-name* item is defined in the SCREEN SECTION in a manner which is similar to, but has some major departures from, the way identifiers are defined in WORKING-STORAGE. The screen-name item is displayed and accepted using these forms of the verbs.

```
ACCEPT screen-name │ AT ⎧⎧ LINE NUMBER ⎰identifier-2⎱ ⎫⎫ │ ⎤
                   │    ⎨⎨              ⎱integer-1 ⎰ ⎬⎬ │ │
                   │    ⎨⎨ COLUMN NUMBER⎰identifier-3⎱⎬⎬ │ │
                   │    ⎩⎩              ⎱integer-2 ⎰⎭⎭ │ │

     [ON EXCEPTION imperative-statement-1 ] ]
     [NOT ON EXCEPTION imperative-statement-2 ]
     [ END-ACCEPT ]
```

```
              ┌    ┌┌                ┌ identifier-2┐ ┐ ┐
              │    ││ LINE NUMBER    │ integer-1   │ │ │
DISPLAY screen-name │ AT │           └             ┘ │ │
              │    ││ COLUMN NUMBER  ┌ identifier-3┐ │ │
              └    └└                │ integer-2   │ ┘ ┘
                                     └             ┘
```

The vertical bar in the syntax diagrams indicate that the LINE and COLUMN phrases may appear in any order. The keyword COLUMN may be abbreviated to COL.

We will look at a simple example of a screen definition and its use before going into the details of how to define a screen.

```
WORKING-STORAGE SECTION.
01 ITEM-A       PIC X(10) VALUE "ABCD".
01 ITEM-B       PIC 9(4)  VALUE 1234.
01 ITEM-C       PIC 9(4)  VALUE 1234.

SCREEN SECTION.
01 X-SCREEN.
   03 VALUE "Demonstration screen" BLANK SCREEN.
   03 LINE 2 COLUMN 5  PIC X(10) FROM  ITEM-A     REVERSE-VIDEO.
   03 LINE 4 COLUMN 5  PIC 9(4)  TO    ITEM-B.
   03 LINE 6 COLUMN 5  PIC ZZZ9  USING ITEM-C.

DISPLAY X-SCREEN
ACCEPT X-SCREEN
```

The DISPLAY statement will show the items on the screen. The ACCEPT statement will wait for the user to key-in data for ITEM-B and ITEM-C but not ITEM-A which has a FROM clause — see below.

When a screen accepts more than one item, press TAB to move from field to field and press ENTER to terminate the ACCEPT statement.

The data-description-entry for each screen begins with an 01-level just as a record does. The data-description-entries in the SCREEN SECTION have the form:

```
level-number ┌ screen-name ┐ { screen-option-1 }...
             └ FILLER      ┘
```

We may think of there being three types of screen data items:

       group items including the 01 level item which names the entire screen,
       literal items which are used to display text on the screen, and
       field items which are items associated with an input, output or update item.

A screen data item requires a name only if it is to be referenced in a DISPLAY or ACCEPT statement. Clearly, the 01 item which names the screen must be named. You may name other items if you wish to display or accept just part of a screen.

Group items may use the options BACKGROUND IS, FOREGROUND IS, SIGN IS, AUTO, SECURE, REQUIRED and FULL as described in Table 16-3.

Literal items may use BELL, BLANK, BLINK, ERASE, [NO] HIGHLIGHT/LOWLIGHT, REVERSE, BACKGROUND, FOREGROUND, LINE, COLUMN, and VALUE clauses as described in Table 16-3.

Field items may use BELL, BLANK, BLINK, ERASE, [NO] HIGHLIGHT/LOWLIGHT, REVERSE, BACKGROUND, FOREGROUND, LINE, COLUMN, PIC, BLANK WHEN ZERO, JUSTIFY, SIGN, AUTO, SECURE, REQUIRED, and FULL clauses as described in Table 16-3.

The PICTURE clause has the form:

$$\left\{ \begin{array}{l} \underline{\text{PICTURE}} \\ \underline{\text{PIC}} \end{array} \right\} \text{ IS } \textit{picture-string}$$

$$\left\{ \begin{array}{l} \left[\underline{\text{FROM}} \left\{ \begin{array}{l} \textit{identifier-1} \\ \textit{literal-1} \end{array} \right\} \right] \ [\ \underline{\text{TO}} \ \textit{identifier-2} \ ] \\ \underline{\text{USING}} \ \textit{identifier-3} \end{array} \right\}$$

The *picture-string* defines the type and size of the identifer. The rules we explore in Chapter 8 apply with some caveats.

a)   The main exception is that when a PIC clause is used, a VALUE clause may not be used.

b)   The size of the picture should be at least large enough to make the implied move statement that occurs with ACCEPT and DISPLAY legal.

c)   It is recommended that every numeric screen item be edited or contain only 9s in its picture. The DISPLAY and ACCEPT verbs will perform the required editing and de-editing.

The FROM, TO and USING clauses determine how operands will be treated by ACCEPT and DISPLAY statements.

a)   When FROM is used, a DISPLAY statement will display *identifier-1* or *literal-1*. If the operand is an identifier it is classed as an *output identifier*. An ACCEPT statement will not affect the identifier.

b)   When TO is used, an ACCEPT statement accepts the value of the identifier which is classed as an *input identifier*.

c)   When USING is specified, the identifier is classified as an *update identifier* and is both displayed and accepted.

Table 16-3 Optional screen clauses in RM/COBOL-85

AUTO	Positions the cursor to the next screen item when the last character is keyed into a screen item without the user pressing TAB. If this is the last screen item, the ACCEPT statement is completed.
BACKGROUND	BACKGROUND IS *colour-name*, where *colour-name* may have one of the values BLACK, BLUE, GREEN, CYAN, RED, MAGENTA, BROWN, WHITE. Starting with version 5.2 a format similar to that used by Micro Focus may be used: BACKGROUND-COLOR *colour-integer,* where *colour-integer* may have one of the values:

0	black	1	blue	2	green	3	cyan
4	red	5	magenta	6	yellow	7	white

BELL	BELL (or BEEP) causes a bell sound each time the item containing it is displayed or accepted. The data item must be elementary.
BLANK	BLANK may be used only with an elementary item and is operative with a DISPLAY statement. BLANK SCREEN moves the cursor to line 1 column 1 and blanks the screen. BLANK REMAINDER blanks from the right of the cursor to the end of the screen. BLANK LINE causes the line to be blanked from the right of the cursor.
BLANK WHEN ZERO	Causes a blanking of the screen when an item with zero value is displayed. May be used only with elementary numeric or numeric-edited item.
BLINK	The screen field is displayed in characters that flash on and off.
COLUMN	Specifies the starting column (in absolute value or relative the current position) in which an elementary item is displayed or accepted.

$$\underline{\text{COLUMN}} \left[\text{NUMBER IS} \left\{ \begin{array}{l} [\ \underline{\text{PLUS}}\ ]\ \textit{integer-1} \\ \textit{identifier-1} \end{array} \right\} \right]$$

	The keyword COLUMN may be abbreviated to COL. In version 5.2, the keyword PLUS may be replaced by the + symbol. When COLUMN is used without an operand, it is equivalent to COLUMN PLUS 1.
ERASE	ERASE EOL causes a DISPLAY statement to erase the rest of the line. ERASE EOS erases from the cursor to the end of the screen. ERASE SCREEN or ERASE causes a DISPLAY statement to erase the remainder of the screen.
FOREGROUND	Specifies the foreground screen colour — see BACKGROUND.
FULL	Specifies that the users must either leave the field empty or fill it completely with data. See also REQUIRED. This clause may be used with group and elementary items. It is valid only with input and update items.
[NO] HIGHLIGHT	Causes the item or group of items to be displayed in high intensity.
JUSTIFIED RIGHT	Specifies right justification when data is moved in to or keyed into the elementary screen item. The keyword RIGHT is optional; JUST is acceptable for JUSTIFIED.
LINE	Specifies the line on which the item is to start. The syntax and usage parallels that of COLUMN.
LOWLIGHT	Causes the item or group of items to be displayed in low intensity.

Table 16-3 Optional screen clauses in RM/COBOL-85 *continued*

PICTURE	The PICTURE clause is used to define the size, characteristics and edition of a screen item. See text for details.
PROMPT	PROMPT <u>CHARACTER</u> IS *prompt* is used with ACCEPT to display a fill character on the screen in the positions where data is to be accepted. The operand *prompt* must be a single-character alphabetic or alphanumeric identifier, or a single-character literal or figurative constant.
REQUIRED	Used with an elementary or group item, REQUIRED specifies that the user may not leave the item(s) empty.
REVERSE	Causes the background and foreground colours to be reversed. Alternate keywords are REVERSED and REVERSE-VIDEO.
SECURE	Prevents user input from being displayed on the screen.
SIGN	<u>SIGN</u> IS {<u>LEADING</u> / <u>TRAILING</u> } <u>SEPARATE</u> CHARACTER is very useful when displaying an identifier with a operational sign (S in its picture). This option is equivalent to the same clause used in other sections — see Chapter 13.
SIZE	<u>SIZE</u> IS {identifier-1 / integer-1} is used to specify the size of an elementary item on the screen.
UPPER	Causes any data typed in lower case characters to be converted to upper case when the ACCEPT statement is executed. This phrase cannot be used as a static phrase — it must be used within a CONTROL phrase.

When the optional ON ESCAPE clause is used in an ACCEPT statement, the *imperative-statement-1* is executed if the user presses the Escape key or a function key (F1, F2, etc.). These keys are called "field termination keys". Pressing one of them is said to "raise the escape condition". This terminates the input operations. If Escape is used, the current screen field and all subsequent fields retain the values they had before the ACCEPT statement. If a function key (or any other field termination key, other than Enter) and the current field is complete, then the current field is given its new value. The program can test which key is pressed with a statement such as ACCEPT *termination-key* FROM ESCAPE, where *termination-key* is used to represent a user-defined numeric identifier.

If no escape condition is raised (the user does not press Escape or a function key) and the statement includes the NOT ON ESCAPE clause, then *imperative-statement-2* is executed after all the fields have been processed.

The RM/COBOL-85 version of the program CHAP16-S on the disk is essentially the same as that shown in section 16.6. It differs only in the syntax used for the foreground and background colour options. RM/COBOL-85 allows us to specify words where Micro Focus requires numbers. The reader may wish to run this program and observe the output. The program may then be modified to experiment with the screen control phrases. The reader should also observe what happens when an alphanumeric literal is typed into a numeric field and compare this program's behaviour to that of the CHAP16-F program shown earlier.

The final two examples are for the more adventurous programmers. The first deals with "capturing" functions keys and the second with with graphics characters.

16.8.1 Capturing termination keys

The program CHAP16-T demonstrates how to capture "termination keys". These are the function keys (including CTRL-Fn and ALT-Fn), ESCAPE, TAB, combinations of CTRL and a character, combinations of ALT and a character, and the cursor control keys HOME, PgUp, PgDn, right arrow, etc. The program shows how the capture can occur with an ACCEPT screen statement in which only the keys F1 through F10 are captured, and with field ACCEPT statements where a wider range of keys is captured. Note that the F11 and F12 keys are captured by neither with RM/COBOL-85.

```
1     identification division.
2     program-id.     chap16-t.
3     ************************************************
4     *   Shows how to capture "termination codes"
5     *     e.g. F keys, ESC, CTRL-letter, ALT-letter
6     ************************************************
7     data division.
8     working-storage section.
9     01 work-item.
10        02 fkey     pic 99.
11        02 item-a   pic x(10).
12        02 lyne     pic 99 value 5.
13    screen section.
14    01 screen-a.
15        02   value "Try pressing an F key or ESC key"
16             line 2 col 8 blank screen
17             background blue foreground white.
18    01 screen-b.
19        02 value "Type here >" line lyne col 10.
20        02 pic x(10) to item-a col 30 reverse.
21    01 screen-c.
22        02 value "Function key " line lyne col 50.
23        02 pic 99 from  fkey.
24    01 screen-d.
25        02 value "No function key pressed" line lyne col 50.
26    procedure division.
27    main.
28        perform screen-para
29        perform field-para
30        stop run.
31
32    screen-para.
33    * With screen only ESC and F1-F10 captured
34        display screen-a
35        perform 15 times
36          display screen-b
37          accept  screen-b
38              on escape perform screen-capture
```

```
39                   not on escape display screen-d
40            end-accept
41            add 1 to lyne
42         end-perform
43         display "Press any key to continue " line 22 position 10
44         accept item-a line 22 position 36 size 1.
45     screen-capture.
46         accept fkey from escape key end-accept
47         display screen-c.
48
49     field-para.
50   * With field ACCEPT Fkeys, CTRL-key and ALT-key capture
51         move 5 to lyne
52         display
53             "Try pressing F keys; ALT-letter; CTRL-letter"
54               line 2 position 8    erase eos
55         display
56             "or cursor control keys HOME, END, PgDown, arrows"
57               line 3 position 8
58         perform 15 times
59            display  "Type here"  line lyne position 8
60                    control "bcolor=blue,fcolor=white"
61                    "          " line lyne position 20
62                    control "bcolor=white,fcolor=blue"
63            accept item-a line lyne position 20
64                 on exception fkey perform field-capture
65            end-accept
66            add 1 to lyne
67         end-perform
68         display "Press any key to continue " line 22 position 10
69         accept item-a line 22 position 36 size 1.
70     field-capture.
71         display "Key pressed was " line lyne position 40
72         display fkey               line lyne position 58.
```

16.8.2 Drawing boxes

The RM/COBOL-85 editor does not give the user access to the extended ASCII characters (i.e. by holding the ALT-key and typing a number on the numeric keyboard). There are two methods of overcoming this limitation. The first, which may be used with screens, normal displays, or in printer records uses hexadecimal notation. The second which works only with with the CONTROL phrase uses the GRAPHICS option. We shall be interested here in the line-drawing characters.

In this table the middle row of each cell shows the graphic line-drawing character. The value above is the ASCII value in hexadecimal, and the letter below is used with the GRAPHICS option. For example, the character ╬ has an ASCII value of 206, or a hexadecimal value of CE. The character "N" is used in the GRAPHICS option. Note that the GRAPHICS option is limited in what can be displayed.

B3	B4	B5	B6	B7	B8	B9	BA	BB	BC	BD	BE	BF	C0
│	┤	┥	┨	┐	┑	┩	║	┒	┛	┛	┘	┐	└
x	u						U	X	K	J			k	m

C1	C2	C3	C4	C5	C6	C7	C8	C9	CA	CB	CC	CD	CE
┴	┬	├	─	┼	┝	╂	╙	╒	╨	╤	╟	=	╪
v	w	t	q	n			M	L	V	W	T	Q	N

CF	D0	D1	D2	D3	D4	D5	D6	D7	D8	D9	DA		
╧	╨	╤	╥	╙	╘	╒	╓	╂	╆	┘	┌		
										j	l		

The defintion 02 ITEM-G PIC X VALUE H"CE" with the statement DISPLAY ITEM-G will display the "╪" character. The statement DISPLAY "N" CONTROL "HIGH, GRAPHICS" will do the same. The program CHAP16-B demonstrates how to draw a simple box on the screen. CHAP16-G (on disk) demonstrates the GRAPHICS option method to draw a box.

```
 1     identification division.
 2     program-id.    chap16-b.
 3
 4     ****************************************************
 5     *        Program to draw a box                    *
 6     ****************************************************
 7
 8     data division.
 9     working-storage section.
10
11     01 box-items.
12         02 k          pic 99      value 6.
13         02 akey       pic x.
14         02 top-line.
15             03                pic x      value H"c9".
16             03                pic x(40) value ALL H"cd".
17             03                pic x      value H"bb".
18         02 vert-line.
19             03                pic x      value H"ba".
20             03                pic x(40) value spaces.
21             03                pic x      value H"ba".
22         02 bottom-line.
23             03                pic x      value H"c8".
24             03                pic x(40) value ALL H"cd".
25             03                pic x      value H"bc".
26     screen section.
27     01 screen-a.
28         02  pic x(42)  from top-line line k col 10
29                        foreground magenta.
30     01 screen-b.
31         02  pic x(42) from vert-line   line k col 10.
```

```
32    01 screen-c.
33        02  pic x(42) from bottom-line line k col 10.
34    procedure division.
35    main-para.
36        display " " line 1 position 1
37                control "bcolor=green,fcolor=yellow"
38                erase eos
39        display "Sample box program" line 3 position 20
40        display screen-a
41        perform 4 times
42           add 1 to k
43           display screen-b
44        end-perform
45        add 1 to k
46        display screen-c
47        display "Press any key to continue " line 18 position 20
48        accept akey line 18 position 48
49        stop run.
```

16.9 Review Questions

1. In the ANSI standard, format-1 of the ACCEPT and DISPLAY verbs do not convert signed numbers. How does your compiler behave?

2. A typical monitor can display _____ lines of _____ columns of text.

3* A single format-1 DISPLAY statement may be used to display ____
    a) only one identifier, or   b) one identifier or one literal, or
    c) a number of identifiers and/or literals.

4* The enhanced "field oriented" DISPLAY verb in your implementation, may be used to display ___. Select an answer from question 3.

5* Explain why the results of this code are probably not what was intended by the programmer.
```
        DISPLAY "Please enter your password " LINE 3 COLUMN 5
        ACCEPT USER-PASSWORD   LINE 3 COLUMN 10.
```

6* A. Micro Focus COBOL: What is wrong with this statement?
```
        DISPLAY ITEM-A FOREGROUND 3
```
    B. RM/COBOL-85:   What is wrong with this statement?
```
        DISPLAY ITEM-A CONTROL "FCOLOR = GREEN    REVERSE"
```

7. The Screen Section must come _____ {before/after} the Working-Storage Section.

8* Only screen-data-name items declared at the 01 level may be displayed or accepted. True or false?

17
The MOVE and INITIALIZE Verbs

Objectives

▸ Know the syntax and use of format-1 of the MOVE verb.
▸ Know the requirement for editing to occur.
▸ Know the syntax and use of the INITIALIZE verb.

17.1 Purpose and Syntax of the MOVE Verb

The MOVE verb transfers data from a sending identifier to one or more receiving identifiers and performs any necessary editing functions. The sending identifier is unchanged.

```
                        Format-1

        MOVE  { identifier-1 }  TO  { identifier-2 }...
              { literal       }
```

```
                        Format-2

        MOVE  { CORRESPONDING }  identifier-1 TO identifier-2
              { CORR          }
```

1) The MOVE causes the value in the sending area to be copied to the receiving area. Data in the sending area is unchanged.

2) The data moved overlays (replaces) any data previously in the receiving area. The length of each receiving item is assumed to be the maximum length in the data description.

```
        MOVE "ABCD" TO ITEM-X
        DISPLAY ITEM-X              <result is ABCD>
        MOVE "XX" TO ITEM-X
        DISPLAY ITEM-X              <result is XX  >
```

In the second case the rightmost two bytes of ITEM-X will be filled with spaces.

3) The MOVE verb cannot be used with index data types (as sending or receiving items); the SET verb must be used with these data items.

4) When there are two or more receiving items the result is equivalent to a series of MOVES. Thus the code (a) is equivalent to code (b):

```
        (a)                              (b)
MOVE  ITEM-A TO ITEM-X ITEM-Y    MOVE   ITEM-A  TO temp
                                 MOVE   temp    TO ITEM-X
                                 MOVE   temp    TO ITEM-Y
```

Generally, the order of the receiving items (ITEM-X and ITEM-Y) does not affect the result. However, this is not true if (a) ITEM-X is subordinate to ITEM-Y, or (b) ITEM-X is the subscript of ITEM-Y.

5) In Format-2, both identifier-1 and identifier-2 must be group items; there may be only one receiving item.

```
02 GROUP-A.
     03 ITEM-A    PIC 99.
     03 ITEM-B    PIC XX.
     03 ITEM-C    PIC XX.
02 GROUP-B.
     03 ITEM-B    PIC XX.
     03 ITEM-C    PIC XX.
     03 ITEM-A    PIC 99.
     03 ITEM-X    PIC XX.
```

The result of: `MOVE CORRESPONDING GROUP-A TO GROUP-B.`
is equivalent to: `MOVE ITEM-A IN GROUP-A TO ITEM-A IN GROUP-B`
                      `MOVE ITEM-B IN GROUP-A TO ITEM-B IN GROUP-B`
                      `MOVE ITEM-C IN GROUP-A TO ITEM-B IN GROUP-C`

Note that the corresponding items in the two groups need not be in the same order. Furthermore, it is not necessary for the elementary items in the two groups to be the same in number. Indeed, if the two groups were identical, then a simple group move (MOVE GROUP-A TO GROUP-B) would suffice.

17.1.1 Elementary moves

A move is said be an elementary one when the receiving item is an elementary data item and the sending item is either an elementary data item or a literal.

1) The validity of an elementary move depends on the category (alphabetic, alphanumeric, alphabetic edited, numeric, numeric edited) of the sending and receiving items. Table 17-1 shows the legal and illegal elementary moves.

2) When the receiving item is alphabetic, alphanumeric or alphanumeric edited, the moved data is aligned at the left most character position of the receiving item. When the number of characters moved is less than the size of the receiving item, space filling to the right occurs. If there are more characters in the moved data then truncation occurs to the right.

When the receiving item has a JUSTIFIED clause, rule 2 is overridden by the rules of the JUSTIFIED clause.

Table 17-1 Legality of elementary moves

| | Category of Receiving Item | | |
Category of Sending Item	Alphabetic	Alphanumeric or Alphanumeric-edited	Numeric or Numeric-edited
Alphabetic	Y	Y	N
Alphanumeric	Y	Y	N
Alphanumeric-edited	Y	Y	N
Numeric integer	N	Y	Y
Numeric non-integer	N	N	Y
Numeric-edited	N	Y	Y[a]
ZERO	N	Y	Y
SPACES	Y	Y	N
HIGH-VALUE or LOW-VALUE	Y	Y	N
QUOTE	Y	Y	N
Alphanumeric literal	Y	Y	N
Numeric literal			
integer	N	Y	Y
non-integer	N	Y	Y
ALL literal	Y	Y	Y[b]

a) This COBOL 85 feature, is called a *de-editing move*. Symbols such as $, decimal, and comma are removed.

b) If the receiving item is USAGE COMP-1 or COMP-2, only one occurrence of the literal is moved.

3) Data moved to a numeric field is aligned by the decimal point. When there is no explicit decimal point specified, the data item is treated as if there were a decimal point to the right of the rightmost digit. Left and/or right zero fill or truncation will occur as necessary. Certain edit characters (e.g. the cheque-protection symbol, "*") in a numeric edited receiving field will replace leading zeros with another symbol; see Chapter 8.

Examples of numeric moves:
```
03  INTEGER-NUM  PIC  99.
03  FLOAT-NUM    PIC  9999V99.
03  DISPLAY-NUM  PIC  999.99.
```

```
MOVE 10 TO INTEGER-NUM  FLOAT-NUM  DISPLAY-NUM
DISPLAY    INTEGER-NUM                        <result is 10>
DISPLAY    DISPLAY-NUM                     <result is 010.00>
MOVE FLOAT-NUM TO DISPLAY-NUM
DISPLAY DISPLAY-NUM                        <result is 010.00>
MOVE 1234.56 TO DISPLAY-NUM
DISPLAY DISPLAY-NUM.                       <result is 234.56>
```

NOTE: Editing (see Chapter 8) can occur only when both the receiving and the sending items are elementary. In other cases, the result is as if an alphanumeric item had been moved to another alphanumeric item.

17.1.2 Nonelementary moves

When the sending item and/or the receiving item is a group item, the move is a non-elementary one. Groups are treated as belonging to the alphanumeric class of items. No internal conversion of data occurs, and the move is not affected by the categories of the items subservient to the group. Consider the following:

```
02 GROUP-A.
    03 ITEM-A1    PIC XX.
    03 ITEM-A2    PIC XX.
    ....
02 GROUP-B.
    03 ITEM-B1    PIC 99.
    03 ITEM-B2    PIC XX.

MOVE   "ABCD"  TO  GROUP-A.
MOVE GROUP-A TO GROUP-B.
```

The value of GROUP-B will be "ABCD". Thus ITEM-B1, a numeric field, has the nonnumeric value "AB". The MOVE statement is valid and will not give an error. However, any subsequent statement requiring an initial numeric value in ITEM-B1 will result in a run-time error. Thus, ADD 1 TO ITEM-B1 would cause the program to abort with a run-time error if ITEM-B1 has the nonnumeric value "AB".

17.2 Purpose and Syntax of the INITIALIZE Verb

The INITIALIZE verb behaves very much like a series of elementary moves. It has two principal uses. If, at the start of the program, the compiler does not initialize those identifiers that have no value clauses (see Chapter 6), the INITIALIZE verb may be used to do this. Secondly, in a program where a record or group is repetitively used, the verb may be used to re-initialize elementary items at the start of the various stages of the program.

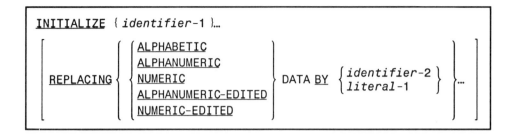

a) When *identifier-1* is an elementary item and the verb is used without the REPLACING phrase (for example: INITIALIZE ITEM-X) the statement will cause ITEM-X to be initialized to spaces if it is an alphabetic, alphanumeric or alphanumeric-edited item, or to zero if it is a numeric or a numeric-edited item. Refer to Chapter 8 for a discussion on categories of identifiers.

b) When a group item or a record is named as identifier-1, then each elementary item in the group (or record) is initialized as explained in (a) above. See also (c) below.

c) The following items do not have their values changed by the INITIALIZE statement:
    FILLER items
    Items with VALUE clauses
    Items declared to be index-data items by USAGE INDEX clauses.

d) Several identifiers (elementary, group, and/or record) may be initialized in one statement: INITIALIZE   ITEM-A ITEM-B GROUP-A RECORD-X

e) The REPLACING phrase makes the verb very flexible:
             INITIALIZE GROUP-A
                 REPLACING   ALPHANUMERIC BY ALL "*"
                              NUMERIC   BY 1

f) Identifier-1 May not have a RENAMES clause in its data-description entry.

    May not have an OCCURS...DEPENDING clause, nor may it have a subordinate item with such a clause.

    May contain a REDEFINES clause or be subordinate to an item with this clause. Note, however, that items subordinate to identifier-1 are not initialized if the subordinate items contain the REDEFINES clause.

    May not be an index-data item; the same rule applies to identifier-2.

17.3 Review Questions

1* A program defines these data items:

```
02 ITEM-A      PIC X(10).
02 ITEM-N      PIC 99.99.
```

What will be displayed by this code?

```
MOVE "Weekly Report" TO ITEM-A
MOVE 100.00 TO ITEM-N
DISPLAY ITEM-A " " ITEM-N
```

2* In a program you have coded `MOVE A-ONE TO RIGHT-ITEM` where RIGHT-ITEM was declared with a justified clause. The output was not right-justified. What is the probable reason?

3* Your program contains this declaration:

```
01 X-REC.
   02 X-A        PIC XXXX.
   02 X-B        PIC XBX.
   02 X-NE       PIC ZZ9.99.
   02 X-C        PIC X(5).
   02 X-COUNT    PIC 999.
```

Code a single initialize statement that will leave the values of X-A, X-B and X-C unchanged, give X-NE a value of zero, and X-COUNT a value of 100.

18
Tables

Objectives

▸ Understand the concept of a table.
▸ Be able to code a one and two dimensional table.
▸ Know the similarities and differences between subscripts and index-names.
▸ Know the use of the SET verb.
▸ Be able to initialize a table using REDEFINES and INITIALIZE.

18.1 The Table Data Structure

A table is a group of similar data items. The data structure which COBOL refers to as a "table" is often called an "array" in other languages. Tables are defined in the DATA DIVISION by attaching the OCCURS clause to an identifier definition. The format of the OCCURS clause and the rules that apply are set out in Chapter 11. The reader is encouraged to review Chapter 11 (OCCURS) and Chapter 7 (REDEFINES) before studying this chapter.

In this chapter we shall see how tables are defined and given initial values. We shall also look at some ways of manipulating the data in tables in the Procedure Division. These examples use the various verbs that we have yet to introduce formally. The reader will be able to judge the truth of the assertion that COBOL's use of English-like constructions makes it easy to interpret COBOL programs.

Consider an identifier with 10 subordinate elementary items each with the same PICTURE:

```
01 A-RECORD.
   03 A-ITEM-1  PIC XX.
   03 A-ITEM-2  PIC XX.
   ...
   03 A-ITEM-10 PIC XX.
```

This could be replaced by a simple table:

```
01 A-TABLE.
   03 A-ITEM  OCCURS 10 TIMES   PIC XX.
```

To reference a specific element in the table, we shall need to use a *subscript* or an *index*. Using the example above, we may write code such as DISPLAY A-ITEM (AX), where the identifier AX is a subscript or an index having a value in the range 1 to 10. The terms *subscript* and *index* are not synonyms in COBOL, as we shall see shortly. We may also use numeric literals and arithmetic expressions: A-ITEM (4), A-ITEM (AX + 3).

Note that in COBOL, the first element in a table has an occurrence number of one, not zero as is the case in some other languages.

18.2 Subscript and Index Items

18.2.1 Subscripts

A subscript may be an integer expression or an elementary item having an integer numeric picture.

```
05 SUB-A  PIC 99.
05 SUB-B  PIC 99   USAGE COMP.
...
MOVE 4 TO SUB-A  SUB-B
DISPLAY A-ITEM (4)           <use of integer literal>
DISPLAY A-ITEM (SUB-A)       <subscript is DISPLAY type>
DISPLAY A-ITEM (SUB-B)       <subscript is COMP type>
```

18.2.2 Index-name data item

An index-name is defined by the INDEXED BY phrase in the OCCURS clause.

```
(a)  01 A-TABLE.
        02 A-ITEM OCCURS 10 TIMES  INDEXED BY INDEX-N  PIC XX.
(b)  01 A-TABLE.
        02 A-ITEM PIC XX OCCURS 10 TIMES  INDEXED BY INDEX-N.
```

Examples (a) and (b) are equivalent. INDEX-N is an index-name. It is not defined elsewhere in the Data Division. The PIC clause refers to A-ITEM not to the index-name.

When we use code such as DISPLAY A-ITEM (INDEX-N), we are using an *index*. An index-name data item may be given a value using the SET verb (see below). Such an item may not be used in a MOVE statement.

18.2.3 Index data item

An index data item is defined by using the USAGE INDEX phrase in the data description of an identifier: 05 INDEX-DI USAGE INDEX. Note that with USAGE INDEX there may not be a PIC clause. Index data items are stored in binary form. An index data item may not be used to reference a table element; it may be used to store the value of an index-name item. Index data items are used in SET statements not in MOVE statements.

18.3 The SET Verb

A subscript may be assigned a value using a VALUE clause, a MOVE statement, or an arithmetic statement such as ADD 1 TO SUB-A. None of these is available for assigning values to an index-name or an index data item. The SET verb must be used to assign a value to an index or to give a subscript the value stored by an index.

$$\text{Format-1:}\quad \underline{\text{SET}}\ \left\{\begin{array}{l} identifier\text{-}1 \\ index\text{-}name\text{-}1 \end{array}\right\}\ \underline{\text{TO}}\ \left\{\begin{array}{l} identifier\text{-}2 \\ index\text{-}name\text{-}2 \\ integer\text{-}1 \end{array}\right\}$$

$$\text{Format-2:}\quad \underline{\text{SET}}\ index\text{-}name\text{-}3\ \left\{\begin{array}{l} \underline{\text{UP}}\ \underline{\text{BY}} \\ \underline{\text{DOWN}}\ \underline{\text{BY}} \end{array}\right\}\ \left\{\begin{array}{l} identifier\text{-}3 \\ integer\text{-}2 \end{array}\right\}$$

identifier-1, etc.	index data item (defined with USAGE INDEX) or elementary numeric identifer.
integer-1,	integer literal; integer-1 must be positive.
index-name-1, etc.	index associated with a table (INDEX BY index-name).

We may write Format-1 in the form: `SET receiving-item TO sending-item` .
Table 18-1 shows the valid combination of identifier types for this format of the SET verb.

Table 18-1 Legal uses of the SET verb

Sending-item	Receiving-item		
	Integer identifier	Index data item	Index-name
Integer literal	N	N	Y
Integer data item	N	N	N
Index data item	N	Y	Y
Index-name	Y	Y	Y

In the examples below, INDEX-N is an index-name, INDEX-DI is an index data item and SUB-A is an elementary integer identifier.

```
SET INDEX-N  TO 5.
SET INDEX-DI TO INDEX-N.
SET INDEX-N  TO INDEX-DI.
SET SUB-A    TO INDEX-N.
```

NOTE: An index-name and an index data item may not be referenced within a MOVE statement. Conversely, the SET verb must reference at least one index-name or index data item.

18.4 Using a Subscript or an Index

As we have seen, a table element may be referenced using either a subscript or an index. The first question the reader will ask is "What is the difference?"

We have seen that to modify the value of an index we must use the SET verb. This is because the internal representation of an index differs from that of a numeric identifier. This difference is also responsible for the fact that indexes are more efficient than subscripts, requiring less work by the operating system and therefore less time. Furthermore, as we shall see in a subsequent chapter, a table must have an index when we need to examine it with the SEARCH verb.

It is the programmer's responsibility to ensure that the index or subscript has a legal value. When a value is assigned to an index name, the result must be a valid occurrence number in its associated table. The value of a subscript or an index must be a valid occurrence number when used to reference a table element. Thus if we have A-ITEM OCCURS 10 TIMES INDEXED BY AX, then, when we code for example, MOVE A-ITEM (AX) or MOVE A-ITEM (SUB-X), AX or SUB-X must have a value in the range 1 to 10. Other values will cause a run-time error called a bounds violation.

The reader should note that an index may be modified (a) with the SET verb, (b) with the VARYING clause in a PERFORM, and (c) in a SEARCH statement, implicitly or explicitly.

When *relative subscripting* or *relative indexing* is used, the subscript or index is followed by a + or a − sign and an integer. Consider the following examples. The code in all four examples produces the same result, except that in (a) and (c) the values of the subscript and the index, respectively, are changed at the completion of the module.

```
   03 SUB-A   PIC 99   COMP.              <USAGE COMP is optional>
                                          <it improves program speed>


   01 A-TABLE.
      AN-ITEM OCCURS 10 TIMES INDEXED BY AIX  PIC X(12).


        (a)                          (b)
      MOVE 3 TO SUB-A              MOVE 3 TO SUB-A
      DISPLAY A-ITEM (SUB-A)       DISPLAY A-ITEM (SUB-A)
      ADD 2 TO SUB-A
      DISPLAY A-ITEM (SUB-A)       DISPLAY (SUB-A + 2)


        (c)                          (d)
      SET AIX TO 3                 SET AIX TO 3
      DISPLAY A-ITEM (AIX)         DISPLAY A-ITEM (AIX)
      SET AIX UP BY 2
      DISPLAY A-ITEM (AIX)         DISPLAY (AIX + 2)
```

It should be noted that in multidimensional tables, one may use either subscripts or indexes to refer to a table element but a specific reference may not use a mixture of both.

You may declare more than one index in a single OCCURS clause.

```
   01 A-TABLE.
      03 AN-ELEMENT OCCURS 10 TIMES INDEXED BY AEX AEZ PIC X(20).
```

18.5 Initializing Values in Table Elements

Tables may be initialized by: 1) a VALUE clause in a data-description-entry, 2) a REDEFINES clause in a data-description-entry, and 3) an INITIALIZE statement.

1) Use of the VALUE clause.

```
02 A-ITEM OCCURS 5 TIMES PIC X(20) VALUE SPACES.

02 B-ITEM OCCURS 10 TIMES.
   03 B-ALPHA  PIC 9(4) VALUE 0.
   03 B-BETA   PIC 9(3) VALUE 1.

01 WEEK     VALUE "SunMonTueWedThuFriSat"
   02 WEEK-DAY OCCURS 7 TIMES INDEXED BY WX PIC X(3).
```

Every A-ITEM item will have the value of SPACES. The B-ALPHA elements will all have values of 0, while the B-BETA items are all set to 1. In the third example, WEEK-DAY(1) = "Sun", WEEK-DAY(2) = "Mon", etc.

2) The use of a REDEFINES clause.

```
01 MONTHS-OF-YEAR.
   03 MONTH-VALUES.
      05 FILLER  PIC X(10) VALUE "January".
      05 FILLER  PIC X(10) VALUE "February".
      05 FILLER  PIC X(10) VALUE "March".
      05 FILLER  PIC X(10) VALUE "April".
      05 FILLER  PIC X(10) VALUE "May".
      05 FILLER  PIC X(10) VALUE "June"
      05 FILLER  PIC X(10) VALUE "July"
      05 FILLER  PIC X(10) VALUE "August"
      05 FILLER  PIC X(10) VALUE "September".
      05 FILLER  PIC X(10) VALUE "October".
      05 FILLER  PIC X(10) VALUE "November".
      05 FILLER  PIC X(10) VALUE "December".
   03 MONTH-TABLE REDEFINES MONTH-VALUES.
      05 MONTH OCCURS 12 TIMES    INDEXED BY MX   PIC X(10).
```

It is important to remember that the size of the redefining item (here, MONTH-TABLE) must be the same size as the redefined item (MONTH-VALUES). In the example, both have a size of 12 × 10.

The first element in MONTH-TABLE (i.e. MONTH(1)) will have the value "January", the second "February", etc. To understand better how this method works, let us initialize the MONTH-TABLE in a different way. Suppose we omit REDEFINES MONTH-VALUES in the description of MONTH-TABLE. Now, in the Procedure Division, we will need to code MOVE MONTH-VALUES TO MONTH-TABLE. The same result is obtained but now we have used twice as much memory. We have the names of the months stored in both MONTH-VALUES and in MONTH-TABLE. The REDEFINES method avoids this waste of memory by giving the same name (MONTH-VALUES and MONTH-TABLE) to the one block of memory. Furthermore, we are saved the chore of having to remember to code the MOVE statement.

3) A table may be initialized at any point in the program with the INITIALIZE verb — see Chapter 17.

```
03 COUNT-ITEM OCCURS 100 TIMES INDEXED BY CIX.
   05 COUNT-ALPHA    PIC X(4).
   05 COUNT-BETA     PIC 9(3).

INITIALIZE COUNT-TABLE
   REPLACING ALPHANUMERIC BY SPACES NUMERIC BY 1.
```

All occurrences of COUNT-ALPHA will have the value of spaces and all COUNT-BETA items will have the value of 1.

18.6 Examples Using Tables

Example 1: In this example we shall use the system date to display the current month in text. The table needed is as shown in 3) above. The code to perform the task is:

```
01 THIS-DATE.
   03 THIS-YEAR     PIC 99.
   03 THIS-MONTH    PIC 99.
   03 THIS-DAY      PIC 99.

ACCEPT THIS-DATE FROM DATE.
SET MX TO THIS-MONTH.
DISPLAY "Date is " THIS-DAY " " MONTH (MX) " " THIS-YEAR.
```

Example 2: Suppose we have a data file giving daily sales data for a company and that we wish to calculate the total sales for each month. Let the data records have this layout:

```
01 SALES-REC.
   02 SALES-DATE.
      03 SALES-YY   PIC 99.
      03 SALES-MM   PIC 99.
      03 SALES-DD   PIC 99.
   02 SALES-AMOUNT  PIC 9(4)V99.
```

We shall need a table with 12 elements — one for each month. Element 1 will hold the total for January, element 2 the total for February, etc. A table with this structure will suffice:

```
01 RESULT-TABLE.
   02 RESULT-AMOUNT OCCURS 12 TIMES INDEXED BY RX
                    PIC 9(7)V99  VALUE 0.00.
```

As we read each record from the file we will add the sales amount to the corresponding table element. Clearly, the value of SALES-MM could be used as a subscript since it will have a value of 01 for January sales, 02 for February sales, etc. The code to add the data would be:

```
ADD SALES-AMOUNT TO RESULT-AMOUNT(SALES-MM)
```

Alternatively, we could use SALES-MM to set the table index:

```
SET RX TO SALES-MM
ADD SALES-AMOUNT TO RESULT-AMOUNT(SALES-MM)
```

In either case the subscript or the index must be in the range 1 to 12. If the file had bad data, such that we tried to add to a table element outside this range, the program would abort with a run-time error. We could guard against this using:

```
IF SALES-MM > 0 AND SALES-MM < 13
    SET RX TO SALES-MM
    ADD SALES-AMOUNT TO RESULT-AMOUNT(SALES-MM)
ELSE
    DISPLAY "Bad data ! - Sales month has value of " SALES-MM
END-IF
```

The COBOL functions, discussed in Chapter 31, are useful for performing calculations on tables.

Example 3: Frequently a program requires a look-up table. The following example allows us to convert Canadian provincial abbreviations to full names.

```
01 PROVINCES-OF-CANADA.
03 PROVINCE-VALUES.
    05    PIC X(30) VALUE "NF Newfoundland".
    05    PIC X(30) VALUE "NS Nova Scotia".
    05    PIC X(30) VALUE "PE Prince Edward Island".
    05    PIC X(30) VALUE "NB New Brunswick".
    05    PIC X(30) VALUE "PQ Quebec".
    05    PIC X(30) VALUE "ON Ontario".
    05    PIC X(30) VALUE "MN Manitoba".
    05    PIC X(30) VALUE "SK Saskatchewan".
    05    PIC X(30) VALUE "AB Alberta".
    05    PIC X(30) VALUE "BC British Columbia".
    05    PIC X(30) VALUE "YK Yukon".
    05    PIC X(30) VALUE "NT North West Territories".
03 PROVINCE-TABLE REDEFINES PROVINCE-VALUES.
    05 PROVINCE OCCURS 12 TIMES INDEXED BY PX.
        07 PROV-ABREV      PIC X(2).
            07 FILLER         PIC X.
            07 PROV-NAME      PIC X(27).
```

Note that the identifier PROVINCE, which has the OCCURS phrase, has three subordinate items. The FILLER item allows for the space between the abbreviation and the name; this serves to make the data easier to read.

A table look-up is usually done with the SEARCH verb that we will study in a later chapter. To demonstrate the use of this table we shall use a looping structure. Assume the program has just read a file record in which one of the items is ADDRESS-PROV, a two-character abbreviation for a customer's province. We wish to use the value of ADDRESS-PROV to find the full name of the province as given in our table.

```
PERFORM  VARYING PX FROM 1 BY 1 UNTIL PX > 12
        IF ADDRESS-PROV = PROV-ABREV (PX)
            MOVE PROV-NAME (PX) TO OUTPUT-PROVINCE
        END-IF
END-PERFORM
```

Even after a match has been found, the PERFORM loop will continue until PX has a value greater than 12. This would be inefficient, especially in a long table. We may improve upon this code with:

```
MOVE "N" TO FOUND-IT
PERFORM  VARYING PX FROM 1 BY 1 UNTIL PX > 12  OR FOUND-IT = "Y"
        IF ADDRESS-PROV = PROV-ABREV (PX)
            MOVE PROV-NAME (PX) TO OUTPUT-PROVINCE
            MOVE "Y" TO FOUND-FLAG
        END-IF
END-PERFORM
```

18.7 Hard-coded and Soft-coded Data

The data in PROVINCE-TABLE in Example 3 is said to be *hard-coded* because its values are contained in the program and cannot be changed without modifying the program. What would happen if, as is expected to happen soon, the North West Territories were to be divided into two new territories or provinces? We would need to modify our program. This may be avoided if we *soft-code* the data by placing the data in a file. Our program would read the data and add it to the table before we need to use the table. If there were to be a change in the data, all we would need to do is edit the data file — a much quicker operation than modifying one or more programs.

18.8 Two Dimensional Tables

The table in the third example of section 18.6 above has 12 items each with the format:
```
        abbreviation     filler     name
```
Ignoring the filler, we have a table in which each element has two dissimilar items. Let us now consider a table with several similar subordinate items. The code below would serve as a table for a teacher to record the grades obtained in 10 tests by members of a class of 50 students.

```
01  STUDENT-TABLE.
    03  STUDENT-DATA OCCURS 50 TIMES INDEXED BY SDX.
        05  STUDENT-ID     PIC 9999.
        05  STUDENT-GRADE  PIC 99    OCCURS 10 TIMES INDEXED BY SGX.
01  OUTPUT-RECORD VALUE SPACES.
    03  OUT-ID    PIC 9999.
    03  OUT-DATA   OCCURS 10 TIMES INDEX BY OGX.
    05  FILLER        PIC X.
    05  OUT-GRADE     PIC ZZ9.
```

The following code will print the table, one line at a time:

```
PERFORM  VARYING SDX FROM 1 BY 1 UNTIL SDX > 50
    MOVE STUDENT-ID (SDX) TO  OUT-ID
    PERFORM  VARYING SGX FROM 1 BY 1 UNTIL SGX > 10
        SET OGX TO SGX
        MOVE STUDENT-GRADE (SDX, SGX) TO OUT-GRADE (OGX)
    END-PERFORM
    WRITE PRINT-RECORD FROM OUTPUT-RECORD
END-PERFORM.
```

18.9 Multi-Dimensional Tables

We have seen examples of one and two dimensional tables. Standard ANSI COBOL permits tables with a maximum of 7 dimensions when Format-1 of the OCCURS clause is used. Some implementations of COBOL allow a larger number of dimensions.

For an example of a three dimensional table, let us design a table to hold the monthly sales data for a company which sells two products from five outlets.

```
01  SALES-TABLE.
    02  SALES-OUTLET           OCCURS 5 TIMES    INDEXED BY SALES-S.
        03  SALES-MONTH        OCCURS 12 TIMES   INDEXED BY SALES-M.
            05  SALES-PRODUCT  OCCURS 2 TIMES    INDEXED BY SALES-P.
                07  SALES-TOTAL  PIC 9(6)V99.
```

Since the last item SALES-PRODUCT is not further subdivided an equivalent table could be coded using:

```
01  SALES-TABLE.
    02  SALES-OUTLET    OCCURS 5   INDEXED BY SALES-S.
        03  SALES-MONTH  OCCURS 12 INDEXED BY SALES-M.
            05  SALES-PROD OCCURS 2  INDEXED BY SALES-P PIC 9(6)V99.
```

There are several ways of picturing this table. We will look at just two. In the first, we may think of a table with 5 rows — one for each outlet. Each row has 12 elements — one for each month. Each month element is divided into 2 — each holding the data for one of the products. In the second, we may think of a stack of 5 two-dimensional tables — one for each outlet. The diagrams below attempt to illustrate these views. The second diagram shows the top table in a stack of five.

outlet(1)	month(1)		month(2)		etc.	
	prod(1)	prod(2)	prod(1)	prod(2)		
outlet(2)	month(1)		month(2)		etc.	
	prod(1)	prod(2)	prod(1)	prod(2)		
etc.						

month(1)	prod(1)	prod(2)
month(2)	prod(1)	prod(2)
month(3)	prod(1)	prod(2)
etc.	prod(1)	prod(2)

18.10 The KEY Phrase in an OCCURS Clause

The KEY phrase may be used with either of the OCCURS formats when the values in one or more of the elements of the table are in order. If we wish to use the binary search format of the SEARCH verb, our table must be sorted and a key must be declared.

```
{  { ASCENDING  }   KEY IS  {identifier -3}…   }…
   { DESCENDING }
```

If the table K-TABLE has an item K-ITEM-ONE, whose values are arranged in ascending order, then we could code:

```
01 K-TABLE.
     03 K-ITEM OCCURS 100 TIMES        ASCENDING KEY K-ITEM-ONE.
       05 K-ITEM-ONE       PIC XX.
       05 K-ITEM-TWO       PIC 99.
```

If, additionally, K-ITEM-TWO values were in descending order we could code:

```
     03 K-ITEM OCCURS 10 TIMES    ASCENDING  KEY K-ITEM-ONE
               DESCENDING KEY K-ITEM-TWO.
```

18.11 Format-2 OCCURS Clause

This format is used primarily to conserve memory, or disk or tape space. A table may be declared with variable size using:

```
OCCURS integer-1 THRU integer-2 TIMES
       DEPENDING ON  identifier-2
```

Both integer-1 and integer-2 must be numeric literals; identifier-2 must be a numeric identifier and may not be part of the table. Example:

```
01 A-TABLE.
      03 A-ITEM OCCURS 1 TO 100 TIMES DEPENDING ON ELEMENT-COUNT.
         05 A-ITEM-ONE    PIC XX.
         05 A-ITEM-TWO    PIC 99.
```

When Format-2 is used at a group level, the group must be the last group in the record. When it is used at an elementary level, this must be the last item (elementary or group) in the record. The value of ELEMENT-COUNT may be varied during the course of the program's execution. Suppose that at some point it has a value of 10, then only table items with an occurrence number (subscript or index) of 1 to 10 are available. We shall not use this format.

18.12 Review Questions

1.   What is the advantage of using an index rather than a subscript with a table? What verb requires a table to be defined with an index-name?

2*   a)   Write a statement that will increase the value of the index-name TAB-X by 2.
      b)   What must you do to display the value of TAB-X?
      c)   The table to which TAB-X belongs is defined with the clause OCCURS 10 TIMES. When is this statement valid? MOVE ITEM-N TO TAB-X.

3*   You have a file containing 50 records, each with data similar to; LAX   LOS ANGELES. The file record description is
```
           01 AIRPORT-REC.
              02 AIRPORT-CODE      PIC X(3).
              02                   PIC XX.
              02 AIRPORT-NAME      PIC X(20).
```
Define a table to hold the data. Write an algorithm to load the file data into the table.

4*   In section 18.9 we defined a table to hold a company's data for one year. Modify the table to hold the data for 10 years. How many bytes of storage will the new table use?

19
The Arithmetic Verbs

Objectives

▸ Know the syntax and use of all formats of these verbs.
▸ Understand the use of the ON SIZE ERROR phrase.
▸ Know why COMPUTE can limit program portability.

19.1 Introduction

There are five arithmetic verbs: ADD, SUBTRACT, DIVIDE, MULTIPLY and COMPUTE. These enable the programmer to achieve most of the arithmetic operations required in a business program. COMPUTE allows exponentiation. Thus we can find the square, the cube, the square root, the cube root, etc., of numbers. In addition to these verbs, the programmer should become familiar with the mathematical and business functions of COBOL as described in Chapter 31.

Each verb, other than COMPUTE, has several formats. All the verbs include an ON SIZE ERROR phrase which we examine at the end of the chapter.

With two exceptions, the identifiers in these formats must.be elementary, unedited, numeric items. The first exception is that identifiers used in the ADD/SUBTRACT formats with the CORRESPONDING clause must be group items. The second is the identifier-3 that follows the keyword GIVING; this may be a numeric edited item. Clearly every literal must be numeric.

A numeric item may contain up to 18 digits. There is also a rule concerning what is called the "composite of operands"; it is unlikely that the reader will be dealing with numbers so large that he/she will be concerned with this rule.

19.2 The ADD Verb

There are three formats for this verb. We may paraphrase them as ADD TO..., ADD GIVING... and ADD CORRESPONDING....

Format-1: ADD $\begin{Bmatrix} identifier\text{-}1 \\ literal\text{-}1 \end{Bmatrix}$... TO { identifier-2 [ROUNDED] }...
[ON SIZE ERROR imperative-statement-1]
[NOT ON SIZE ERROR imperative-statement-2]
[END-ADD]

Format-2: ADD $\begin{Bmatrix} identifier\text{-}1 \\ literal\text{-}1 \end{Bmatrix}$... TO $\begin{Bmatrix} identifier\text{-}2 \\ literal\text{-}2 \end{Bmatrix}$
GIVING { identifier-3 [ROUNDED] }...
[ON SIZE ERROR imperative-statement-1]
[NOT ON SIZE ERROR imperative-statement-2]
[END-ADD]

In Format-1 and Format-2, the *identifier-1, identifier-2* must be numeric items; *literal-1* and *literal-2* must be a numeric literals. In Format-2, *identifier-3* may be either a numeric or a numeric-edit item.

Format-3: ADD CORRESPONDING identifier-1 TO identifier-2 [ROUNDED]
[ON SIZE ERROR imperative-statement-1]
[NOT ON SIZE ERROR imperative-statement-2]
[END-ADD]

In Format-3, the two *identifiers* must be group items — see example below.

In the examples that follow we use the identifiers shown below. Note that the calculations are executed as a sequence. The calculations in (a) use the values set by the VALUE clauses, the new values are used in calculation (b), and so on.

```
03 ITEM-N          PIC 99          VALUE 85.
03 ITEM-N2         PIC 99V99       VALUE 25.75.
03 ITEM-N3         PIC Z,ZZZ.99.
03 GROUP-1.
   05 NUMBER-A     PIC 99          VALUE 10.
   05 ITEM-X       PIC XX          VALUE "ZZ".
   05 NUMBER-B     PIC 99          VALUE 20.
03 GROUP-2.
   05 NUMBER-B     PIC 99          VALUE 12.
   05 NUMBER-C     PIC 99          VALUE 24.
   05 NUMBER-A     PIC 99          VALUE 18.
```

(a) ADD 5.876 TO ITEM-N2 ROUNDED   ITEM-N
New values: ITEM-N2 = 33.63 (25.75 + 5.876 = 33.626; rounded to 2 places = 33.63)
ITEM-N = 90   (85 + 5.876 = 90.876; but ITEM-N has no decimal places) If the ROUNDED clause was included for ITEM-N, it would receive a value of 91.

(b) ADD ITEM-N2 TO ITEM-N

New values: ITEM-N = 23
(the numbers sum to 123.63, but the PIC for ITEM-N is too small; the ON SIZE ERROR could be used to give a warning)
ITEM-N2 unchanged.

(c) `ADD 1234.75 ITEM-N2 TO ITEM-N GIVING ITEM-N3 ROUNDED.`
New values: ITEM-N3 = 1,291.38. The others are unchanged.

(d) `ADD CORRESPONDING GROUP-1 TO GROUP-2.`
New values: Nothing changes in GROUP-1
NUMBER-C is unchanged since GROUP-1 does not contain an item with this name.
In GROUP-2: NUMBER-B = 32 (20 +12) NUMBER-A = 28 (10 + 18)

Since NUMBER-A and NUMBER-B are not unique data names (they appear in GROUP-1 and in GROUP-2), if we wish to reference one of them we need to use a *qualifier*. For example: NUMBER-A IN GROUP-1 or NUMBER-A OF GROUP-1.

19.3 The SUBTRACT Verb

The three formats for SUBTRACT (SUBTRACT FROM..., SUBTRACT GIVING... and SUBTRACT CORRESPONDING...) parallel the ADD verb formats.

```
Format-1:  SUBTRACT  { identifier-1 }... FROM {identifier-2 [ROUNDED]}...
                     { literal-1    }
           [ ON SIZE ERROR imperative-statement-1 ]
           [ NOT ON SIZE ERROR imperative-statement-2 ]
           [ END-SUBTRACT ]
```

```
Format-2:  SUBTRACT  { identifier-1 }... FROM { identifier-2 }
                     { literal-1    }         { literal-2    }
           GIVING  { identifier-3 [ ROUNDED ] }...
           [ ON SIZE ERROR imperative-statement-1 ]
           [ NOT ON SIZE ERROR imperative-statement-2 ]
           [ END-SUBTRACT ]
```

In Format-1 and Format-2, the *identifier-1, identifier-2* must be numeric items; *literal-1* and *literal-2* must be a numeric literals. In Format-2, *identifier-3* may be either a numeric or a numeric-edit item.

```
Format-3:
    SUBTRACT CORRESPONDING identifier-1 FROM identifier-2 [ ROUNDED ]
            [ ON SIZE ERROR imperative-statement-1 ]
            [ NOT ON SIZE ERROR imperative-statement-2 ]
            [ END-SUBTRACT ]
```

In Format-3, the two *identifiers* must be group items — see example below.

19.4 The MULTIPLY Verb

There are two formats for the MULTIPLY verb: MULTIPLY BY... and MULTIPLY GIVING....

```
Format-1:   MULTIPLY  { identifier-1 }  BY { identifier-2 [ ROUNDED ] }...
                      { literal-1     }
                [ ON SIZE ERROR imperative-statement-1 ]
                [ NOT ON SIZE ERROR imperative-statement-2 ]
                [ END-MULTIPLY ]
```

```
Format-2:   MULTIPLY  { identifier-1 }  BY  { identifier-2 }
                      { literal-1     }      { literal-2    }
            GIVING  { identifier-3 [ ROUNDED ] }...
                [ ON SIZE ERROR imperative-statement-1 ]
                [ NOT ON SIZE ERROR imperative-statement-2 ]
                [ END-MULTIPLY ]
```

The items *identifier-1, identifier-2* must be numeric; *literal-1* and *literal-2* must be numeric literals. In the GIVING phrase of Format-2, *identifier-3* may be either a numeric or a numeric-edit item.

Format-1 operates in a manner which differs from the way most people think. Thus to double the value of ITEM-N we might say "Multiply ITEM-N by 2". To code this we must use MULTIPLY 2 BY ITEM-N. When we code MULTIPLY ITEM-A BY ITEM-B, the product is placed in ITEM-B not ITEM-A as we might expect. For example,

```
02 ITEM-A    PIC 99       VALUE 4.
02 ITEM-B    PIC 99       VALUE 2.
....
MULTIPLY ITEM-A BY ITEM-B
DISPLAY "ITEM-A = " ITEM-A SPACES SPACES "ITEM-B = " ITEM-B
```

The product of this calculation ($4 \times 2 = 8$) is placed in ITEM-B not in ITEM-A. The last line of code will give the output: ITEM-A = 4   ITEM-B = 8

NOTE: When used with two identifiers, or a literal and an identifier, the product in MULTIPLY BY is placed in the second identifier.

If you find this too confusing you can always use Format-2 (MULTIPLY GIVING). If we code:

```
MULTIPLY ITEM-A BY ITEM-B GIVING ITEM-A
DISPLAY "ITEM-A = " ITEM-A SPACES SPACES "ITEM-B = " ITEM-B
```

the last line of code will give the output: ITEM-A = 8   ITEM-B = 2

It is important to know that the effects of Format-1 are cumulative. Let ITEM-C have a value of 3. The two coding examples below are equivalent.

(a)   ```
MULTIPLY 2 BY ITEM-C
MULTIPLY 2 BY ITEM-C
```

(b)     ```
MULTIPLY 2 BY ITEM-C ITEM-C
```

Both will yield a value of 12 for ITEM-C (2 ×3 = 6, 2 ×6 = 12).

19.5 The DIVIDE Verb

There are five formats for this verb. They have the form:
(a) DIVIDE divisor INTO dividend …
or (b) DIVIDE dividend BY divisor …
In the first format, which is of form DIVIDE INTO, the quotient is placed into the dividend identifier. Format 2 and 3 place their results in quotient-identifiers - format-2 is a DIVIDE INTO while format-3 is a DIVIDE BY. The last two formats are similar to formats 2 and 3 except that a remainder is also calculated. Note also that while formats 2 and 3 allow for more than one quotient-identifier, only one is permitted in formats 4 and 5.

```
Format-1:  DIVIDE  { identifier-1 }  INTO  { identifier-2 [ ROUNDED ] }…
                   { literal-1    }
               [ ON SIZE ERROR imperative-statement-1 ]
               [ NOT ON SIZE ERROR imperative-statement-2 ]
               [ END-DIVIDE ]
```

```
Format-2:  DIVIDE  { identifier-1 }  INTO  { identifier-2 }
                   { literal-1    }        { literal-2    }
                  GIVING { identifier-3 [ ROUNDED ] }…
               [ ON SIZE ERROR imperative-statement-1 ]
               [ NOT ON SIZE ERROR imperative-statement-2 ]
               [ END-DIVIDE ]
```

```
Format-3:  DIVIDE  { identifier-1 }  BY  { identifier-2 }
                   { literal-1    }      { literal-2    }
                   GIVING { identifier-3 [ ROUNDED ] }...
                   [ ON SIZE ERROR imperative-statement-1 ]
                   [ NOT ON SIZE ERROR imperative-statement-2 ]
                   [ END-DIVIDE ]
```

```
Format-4:  DIVIDE  { identifier-1 }  INTO  { identifier-2 }
                   { literal-1    }        { literal-2    }
                   GIVING identifier-3 [ ROUNDED ]
                   REMAINDER identifier-4
                   [ ON SIZE ERROR imperative-statement-1 ]
                   [ NOT ON SIZE ERROR imperative-statement-2 ]
                   [ END-DIVIDE ]
```

```
Format-5:  DIVIDE  { identifier-1 }  BY  { identifier-2 }
                   { literal-1    }      { literal-2    }
                   GIVING identifier-3 [ ROUNDED ]
                   REMAINDER identifier-4
                   [ ON SIZE ERROR imperative-statement-1 ]
                   [ NOT ON SIZE ERROR imperative-statement-2 ]
                   [ END-DIVIDE ]
```

In each format, *identifier-1, identifier-2* and *identifier-4* must be numeric items; *literal-1* and *literal-2* must be numeric literals. In the GIVING phrases, *identifier-3* may be either a numeric or a numeric-edit item.

For examples (a), (b) and (c) let the identifiers be declared using:

```
02 ITEM-A     PIC 99       VALUE 15.
02 ITEM-B     PIC 99       VALUE 15.
02 ITEM-C     PIC 99       VALUE 15.
02 ITEM-D     PIC 99       VALUE 15.
02 RESULT-A   PIC 99.9.
02 RESULT-B   PIC 99.9.
```

(a) DIVIDE 4 INTO ITEM-A ITEM-B ROUNDED
(b) DIVIDE 4 INTO ITEM-C GIVING RESULT-A ROUNDED
(c) DIVIDE ITEM-D BY 4 GIVING RESULT-B ROUNDED

In all these examples the arithmetic result is 3.75 ($15 \div 4 = 3.75$). The effect of (a) is to give ITEM-A a value of 3. The PICTURE of ITEM-A has no decimal point, so the result is truncated to integer 3. The ROUNDED phrase in (a) applies only to the identifer it immediately follows (here, ITEM-B). This item, therefore, will get a value of integer 4 which is what 3.75 rounds to with no decimal point.

Example (b) uses a GIVING and a ROUNDED phrase. The receiving item (RESULT-A) has place for one digit following the decimal so the value of 3.75 is rounded to 3.8. Example (c) is equivalent to (c) but uses the DIVIDE BY rather than the DIVIDE INTO form. Note that in both examples we elected to use a numeric-edited identifier for the quotients; there is an explicit decimal in their pictures.

The REMAINDER clause needs careful study. We start with examples using integer division. In integer division (*dividend ÷ divisor = quotient*) the dividend, divisor and quotient all have integer values. The remainder for this division is calculated using the expression *remainder = dividend - (divisor × quotient)*. If the integer division expression is $17 ÷ 3$ the quotient is integer 5. The remainder expression is *remainder* = 17 - (5 × 3) = 2.

Consider the following equivalent statements in which lower case words represent identifiers:

    DIVIDE dividend BY divisor GIVING quotient REMAINDER remainder
    DIVIDE divisor INTO dividend GIVING quotient REMAINDER remainder

If the identifiers each had a PICTURE composed only of 9s, our COBOL code would perform integer divisions. This is sometimes called *modulus arithmetic*.

When the identifiers contain decimal points, the picture becomes more complex. For the next examples let RESULT-D and REMAIN-D each have a picture of 99.99. For clarity we will use literals for the divisor and dividend; identifiers would give similar results.

```
(d) DIVIDE 18.75 BY 6 GIVING RESULT-D REMAINDER REMAIN-D
(e) DIVIDE 18.75 BY 6 GIVING RESULT-D ROUNDED REMAINDER REMAIN-D
```

The division $18 ÷ 6$ yields a result of 3.125. Since RESULT-A can hold only two digits after the decimal it gets a value of 3.12 in example (d). We find the remainder using remainder = 18 - (6 × 3.12), giving a value of 0.03. In our example, REMAIN-D can hold two digits after the decimal, so its value is 0.03. Had REMAIN-D been given a picture of 9v9, its value would have been 0.0. When quotient-identifier is qualified by ROUNDED it is the truncated value, not the rounded value, that is used to calculate the remainder. This tells us that example (e) will yield the same REMAIN-D value as example (d) although RESULT-A will have a value of 3.13. The program CHAP19-1 (on disk) uses DIVIDE...REMAINDER to convert seconds to hours, minutes and seconds.

19.6 The COMPUTE Verb

A COMPUTE statement may be used in place of a series of other arithmetic statements. It may also be used to raise the value of an identifier to a noninteger power, something that is not possible with the other statements. The operator of exponentiation (raising to a power) is **; two asterisks with no space between them.

```
COMPUTE { identifier-1 [ ROUNDED ] = arithmetic-expression
    [ ON SIZE ERROR imperative-statement-1 ]
    [NOT ON SIZE ERROR imperative-statement-2 ]
    [ END-COMPUTE ]
```

The arithmetic-expression may be any COBOL valid arithmetic expression composed of identifiers, literals, the mathematical operator symbols +, −, /, * and **; and matching pairs of parentheses ( ) symbols. The order of precedence is ; (1) operations in parentheses are performed first, (2) exponentiation, (3) multiplication/division from left to right, and (4) addition/subtraction from left to right. It is advisable to make use of parentheses to ensure the correct order of calculation. There must be a space on each side of an operator — something that is expected to disappear in COBOL 9x. Some examples using the COMPUTE verb follow.

```
(a)    COMPUTE   SQUARE-OF-A   =   A ** 2
(b)    COMPUTE   SQUARE-ROOT-OF-A =  A ** 0.5
(c)    COMPUTE   B-CUBED = B ** 3
(d)    COMPUTE   A = ( ( B − 3.5 ) + ( C − D ) ) / ( Z * ( 4 − G ) )
(e)    COMPUTE   CELSIUS = ( FAHRENHEIT - 32 ) * ( 5 / 9 )
(f)    COMPUTE   DAILY-INTEREST ROUNDED =
                          ( YEARLY-INTEREST / 360 ) * NUMBER-OF-DAYS
```

The first three examples use exponentiation. When, mathematically, a positive and a negative value can result, as in the second example, the COMPUTE verb always returns the positive value. There are three rules to remembers — see section 19.7.

Examples (d) and (e) shows the use of parentheses to control the order in which items are calculated. In (e), for example, we wish to subtract 32 before multiplying by the second term. The parentheses around 5/9 do not affect the calculation; they serve to make the expression more readable.

In the last example the ROUNDED phrase has been used as it normally should be with monetary calculations. It also show how to use two lines of code for a long formula. The parentheses are not essential in this example but they do make clearer what is being computed.

The author prefers to avoid the COMPUTE statement when the calculation can be performed with a single ADD, SUBTRACT, DIVIDE or MULTIPLY statement. It is more in keeping with the spirit of COBOL to use English-like statements. It is also more efficient since the COMPUTE verb requires more CPU overhead — a matter of concern only when many calculations are being performed. See program CHAP19-1 on disk for an example of the COMPUTE verb.

There is an even more important consideration which suggests that COMPUTE should only be used when essential; i.e. for non-integer exponentiation. In a complex COMPUTE a number of intermediate values are evaluated. Unfortunately, notwithstanding that COBOL is highly standardized, these intermediate values are stored with varying accuracy in different COBOL implementations. COBOL 9x will, hopefully, address this problem.

19.7 SIZE ERROR Phrase

There are three common ways in which a size error condition may occur: (1) when the receiving field is too small, (2) when division by zero is attempted, and (3) when the rules of exponentiation are violated.

a) If, in any of the five arithmetic verbs, the number of digits to the left of the decimal point in the arithmetic result (i.e. the integer part of the result) exceeds the number of digits to the left of the decimal in the picture of the receiving field then a size error occurs. This type of problem results in incorrect data.

Example:
```
02 ITEM-A PIC 99    VALUE 99.
02 ITEM-B PIC 99    VALUE 33.
```

(i)
```
ADD ITEM-B TO ITEM-A
DISPLAY "ITEM-A = " ITEM-A              result is: ITEM-A = 32
```

(ii)
```
ADD ITEM-B TO ITEM-A
    ON SIZE ERROR DISPLAY "ITEM-A is too small"
END-ADD
DISPLAY "ITEM-A = " ITEM-A              result is: ITEM-A = 99
```

Recall that when there is no decimal point in a picture, COBOL behaves as if there were a decimal point after the right-most 9 in picture string. In (i), 99 + 33 = 132, but ITEM-A can hold only two digits before the assumed decimal. Therefore it receives the left truncated value of 32.

In (ii), the SIZE ERROR clause "traps" the size error and lets the user know that an erroneous addition would occur. When the SIZE ERROR clause is used and a size error condition occurs, the value of the receiving field is left at its value before the calculation was attempted.

If there are two (or more) resultants (e.g. ADD A TO B GIVING C D) and a SIZE ERROR occurs for one resultant, then the value in the second resultant is unaffected by the error.

In DIVIDE...GIVING...REMAINDER, a size error in the remainder item will not affect the quotient item result.

b) If a DIVIDE or COMPUTE statement attempts to divide by zero a size error occurs. This type of problem causes the program to terminate in an error state unless the ON SIZE ERROR clause is used.

Example: A program is designed to accept a series of numbers and tally the sum of the numbers in DATA-SUM and a count of how many numbers were processed in DATA-COUNT. The next step is to compute the average of the numbers.

```
COMPUTE DATA-AVERAGE = DATA-SUM * 100.00   / DATA-COUNT
```

Suppose, that in a particular run, no numbers were accepted, i.e. DATA-COUNT has a value of zero. The COMPUTE statement above cannot perform a divide-by-zero and the program will abort. We can anticipate this situation with:

```
COMPUTE DATA-AVERAGE = DATA-SUM * 100.00   / DATA-COUNT
    ON SIZE ERROR MOVE 0.00 TO DATA-AVERAGE
END-COMPUTE
```

Note the use of the scope-delimiters in the second examples in (a) and (b). The ON SIZE ERROR and the NOT ON SIZE ERROR clauses are conditional and therefore need to be terminated before the statement that follows those which are to be executed if the condition arises.

c) Violation of the rules of exponentiation cause a size error condition. These rules are:
   1) The result must be a real number. Attempting to compute the square root of an arithmetic expression with a negative value is an example of a violation of this rule.
   2) When the arithmetic expression evaluates to zero, the exponent must be greater than zero. For example, consider COMPUTE Z = (A - B) ** C. If the values happen to be such that A = B and C is 0 or negative, then the rule is violated.

19.8 Review Questions

1. What is the purpose of the ON SIZE ERROR phrase in the arithmetic statement?

2. When is an END-ADD needed in an ADD statement?

3* Without using COMPUTE, write code to calculate the expression $x = \dfrac{3y + 7.5}{k}$.

4. Give two reasons why some programmers avoid using COMPUTE when possible.

5* The identifier LENGTH defined with the picture PIC 999 stores a value representing a measurement in feet. You wish to display this value in feet and inches. Write the code. (12 inches = 1 foot).

6* Write a COMPUTE statement to evaluate the mathematical expression $d = \sqrt{b^2 - 4ac}$. Why would it be prudent to use the ON SIZE ERROR phrase with this statement?

20
Sequential Files

Objectives

▸ Know the entry needed in the INPUT OUTPUT SECTION for file access.
▸ Know the entry needed in the FILE SECTION for file definition.
▸ Know the use of the four options in the OPEN statement and the use of the CLOSE statement.
▸ Know the syntax of the READ and WRITE verbs.
▸ Be familiar with the LINAGE clause.
▸ Understand the INITIAL READ method.

20.1 Introduction

Standard ANSI COBOL supports three types of file organizations:

SEQUENTIAL   The records in a sequential file may be accessed only in the order in which they were written to the file. Thus to process, say, the tenth record we must first read records 1 through 9.

INDEXED   The records in an indexed file may be processed sequentially or randomly, i.e. a record may be located based on its key.

RELATIVE   The records in a relative file may be processed sequentially or randomly, i.e. a record may be located by specifying its absolute position in the file.

This chapter discusses sequential files; indexed files are covered in Chapter 26 and relative files in Chapter 27. Sequential files are the simplest to code but are frequently not the most efficient for the task on hand.

A program which is syntactically correct (i.e. compiles without error) may fail when you attempt to run it. Conditions that cause this are called run-time errors. When the problem is related to a file operation the error is called an I-O error. The error message displayed depends on the application you are running. Micro Focus error messages are fairly easy to decipher. For example, a program which attempts to read or write to a file which has not been opened will result in the message 002 File not open when access attempted. *One message which can be misleading is* 009 No room in directory. *This can also mean that your program names a directory that does not exist. RM/COBOL-85 uses more cryptic messages. For example, attempting to read a file that has not been correctly opened will give the message* `COBOL I/O error 47`. *To find the meaning of this type of message you should refer to the table in Chapter 32. In both applications, I/O errors can be trapped by the program as shown in Chapter 32.*

20.2 Sample Program

The sample program shown below (which is not on the disk) is very simple; it reads each record in a file, displays it on the screen and sends a copy to the printer.

```
1     identification division.
2     program-id.          chap20-a.
3     environment division.
4     input-output section.
5     file-control.
6         select in-file assign to "chap20-1.dat"
7             organization line sequential.
8         select out-file assign to printer          <Micro Focus>
9             organization line sequential.
10    *    select out-file assign to printer "printer"        <RM>
11    data division.
12    file section.
13    fd in-file.
14    01 in-rec   pic x(80).
15    fd out-file.
16    01 out-rec  pic x(80).
17    working-storage section.
18    01 work-items.
19        02 file-flag    pic x value "n".
20    procedure division.
21    main-para.
22        open input in-file
23             output out-file
24        read infile at end move "y" to file-flag end-read
25        perform until file-flag = "y"
26            display in-rec
27            write out-rec from in-rec
28            read infile at end move "y" to file-flag end-read
29        end-perform
30        close in-file out-file
31        stop run.
```

This example demonstrates:

1) Each file used in a program must have:
   a) A SELECT entry in the FILE-CONTROL paragraph of the Environment Division
   b) A file description (FD) and a record description in the FILE SECTION paragraph of the Data Division.

2) Before we can read or write to a file it must be opened. The wording of an OPEN statement depends on how we wish to use the file records: read or write them.

3) A file record is read into memory using a READ statement. We often need to code this in a manner which detects if we have read the last record.

4) A record is written to the file (disk or printer) using a WRITE statement.

5) When we have finished using a file, we should close it.

We will study each of these topics in this chapter. For now, note the difference in the syntax of the READ and WRITE statements. Whereas we use READ `file-name` for reading, we use WRITE `record-name` for writing. If you remember the adage *Read a file, write a record* you will save yourself many complier errors.

20.3 The FILE-CONTROL Entry

For a sequential file the FILE-CONTROL entry for the Micro Focus COBOL and RM/COBOL-85 implementations is the SELECT entry with the format:

```
SELECT [OPTIONAL] file-name ASSIGN TO external-file-name
                          ( LINE   )
    [ [ ORGANIZATION IS ] { RECORD } SEQUENTIAL ]
                          ( BINARY )
    [ ACCESS MODE IS SEQUENTIAL ]
    [ FILE STATUS IS identifier-2 ]
```

The distinction between *file-name* and *external-file-name* is explained in Chapter 5. The reader is encouraged to review that chapter before proceeding.

Three clauses (PADDING, RESERVE AREA and RECORD-DELIMITER) have been omitted because they are advanced features, so we are not concerned with them.

The optional OPTIONAL clause may be used to indicate that the file does not currently exist. The presence of this clause affect the behaviour of the OPEN statement as discussed in Table 20-2. The FILE STATUS clause is discussed in Chapter 32 "I-O Exceptions".

The ACCESS clause is redundant for sequential files, being the only possible mode. It may be included for documentary purposes.

There are two formats of sequential files. They differ in the manner in which the records are delimited — how the system recognizes where one record ends and the next begins. The LINE sequential format is identical to the way an editor (not a word processor) program stores a file. Each record ends with a record delimiter consisting of the line-feed and carriage-return ASCII character. You should use this format when you wish to view your data files using an editor or with a DOS command such as TYPE and PRINT.

The other format for sequential files is called RECORD in Micro Focus COBOL and BINARY in RM/COBOL-85. The latter name indicates that this type of sequential file may contain binary data, i.e. data-names defined with USAGE COMP, BINARY or INDEX. This is true with both implementations. Line sequential files may not contain binary data; the data in these files is limited to the printable ASCII characters.

RECORD/BINARY files may have records of fixed or variable length. We shall limit the discussion to fixed length records.

If the ORGANIZATION phrase is omitted, the two implementations will normally default to the RECORD/BINARY sequential file format. This default may be changed using compiler directives.

20.4 The FILE SECTION Entry

The syntax for the FD entry of a sequential file is shown below. The clauses expected to be deleted in the next version of COBOL have been omitted.

```
    FD file-name

        [ IS EXTERNAL ]
        [ IS GLOBAL   ]

        [ BLOCK CONTAINS integer-1 { RECORDS    } ]
                                   { CHARACTERS }

        [ RECORD CONTAINS integer-2 CHARACTERS ]

        [ LINAGE  { identifier-2 }
                  { integer-3    }

            [ WITH FOOTING AT  { identifier-3 } ]
                               { integer-4    }

            [ LINES AT TOP     { identifier-4 } ]
                               { integer-5    }

            [ LINES AT BOTTOM  { identifier-5 } ]
                               { integer-6    }

        [ CODE-SET IS alphabet-name ]●
```

The GLOBAL and EXTERNAL clauses are used with subprograms; see Chapter 29.

The BLOCK clause is important with large files. It can save magnetic tape space, and improve the speed of input-output operations. The form for fixed-length records is shown; the full syntax supports variable length records.

The RECORD clause specifies the length of the file record. The syntax shown has been simplified for a file with fixed-length records. This clause is mainly for documentation but may also be used as an internal check on your coding. For example, if you code RECORD CONTAINS 80 CHARACTERS but your record-description entry specifies 70 bytes, then a compiler error occurs; you may have omitted an item in the record-description.

The LINAGE clause, used for printer files, is described in detail below.

The CODE-SET clause is discussed later in this chapter.

20.5 The Record Description

A record-description in the File Section of the Data Division may consist of an 01-level item with or without groups and elementary items. A file record-description may not use the VALUE clause, other than for 88-level items. The use of REDEFINES at the 01 level in the File Section is invalid and unnecessary. If a file contains records with two or more layouts we may include as many record descriptions as are needed.

20.6 The OPEN Verb

```
          ┌ INPUT    filename-1… ┐
          │ OUTPUT   filename-2… │
   OPEN   │ I-O      filename-3… │ …
          └ EXTEND   filename-4… ┘
```

For simplicity, certain phrases used with magnetic tape files have been omitted from the syntax above.

Before file records can be read or written, the file must be opened with the correct mode. The OPEN mode must match the input-output verb(s) which will be used with the file. When records are to be READ from a file, the file should be opened for INPUT meaning that the program gets input from the file. Conversely, when we wish to WRITE to a file, the file should be opened for OUTPUT meaning that the program sends output to the file. The direction of flow of data is from the program's point of view, not from the file's. Table 20-1 shows which I-O verbs are allowed for each open mode. If a program attempts to use an I-O verb that is inappropriate for the current open mode (for example, WRITE to a file opened for INPUT), a run-time error will result.

Table 20-1 OPEN modes and permitted I-O verbs for sequential files

I-O Verb	OPEN Mode			
	INPUT	OUTPUT	I-O	EXTEND
READ	Y		Y	
WRITE		Y		Y
REWRITE			Y	

If our program begins, for example, with an OPEN OUTPUT statement to enable records to be created with the WRITE verb and, at a later stage in the program, we wish to use the READ verb to process these records then we must first CLOSE the file and reopen it with an OPEN INPUT statement. This will also serve to position the file pointer to the first record in the file.

When we need to add records to an existing file, we open it with the EXTEND mode. This places the pointer at the end of the file. We may now write new records; these will be added to the existing records. The EXTEND mode is meaningful only with files having sequential organization. The educational version of RM/COBOL-85 will write only 100 records to a file opened in EXTEND mode.

The I/O open mode is used when we wish both to read and write to a file. Normally this occurs when we wish to update records in an existing file — see REWRITE verb below.

Examples of the OPEN verb:
```
    a)   OPEN INPUT FILE-A.
    b)   OPEN INPUT FILE-A FILE-B.
    c)   OPEN INPUT FILE-A FILE-B  OUTPUT FILE-C.
```

The success, or otherwise, of an OPEN statement depends on several factors:

    a)   Whether or not the file already exists.
    b)   OPEN mode used.
    c)   Whether or not the SELECT paragraph for the file contains the OPTIONAL clause.
    d)   The attributes of the file, if it already exists, compared with those declared in the program.

Table 20-2 shows the interrelationship between these factors. When the OPEN statement is not successful, an I-O exception is said to occur. Unless the programmer has provided for this, a fatal run-time error will occur. Procedures for handling I-O exceptions are described in Chapter 32, as is the topic of *attributes* of a file.

Table 20-2 Factors affecting the OPEN statement

OPEN mode	File exists	File does not exist	
		SELECT	SELECT OPTIONAL
OUTPUT	If the attributes of the existing file match those declared in the program, the OPEN statement is successful — see(d) below. Otherwise, an I-O exception occurs — see Chapter 32.	File is created	File is created; see a) below
INPUT		I-O exception	See b) below
EXTEND		I-O exception; see c) below	File is created
I-O		I-O exception; see c) below	File is created; b) applies if READ occurs before data is written to the file

a) The OPTIONAL clause is redundant with the OPEN OUTPUT mode.
b) The first READ statement returns an end-of-file condition
c) Micro Focus COBOL will create a file even when the OPTIONAL clause is missing. RM/COBOL-85 will give an errror message.
d) When the mode OUTPUT and the file exists, most compilers will cause the data in the old file to be overwritten; some systems create a new version of the file.

NOTE for RM/COBOL-85 users: If a program terminates with a run-time I-O error, the table in Chapter 32 may be helpful in discovering the cause of the problem. Micro Focus I-O error messages are self-explanatory.

20.7 The CLOSE Verb

At the termination of a program, any open file is automatically closed. Thus, it is not essential to close a file at the end of a program; however, it is good programming style to do so. If we open a file for output and then wish to use the file for input, we must first close that file. Closing a file also ensures the pointer is at the first record. The syntax for the CLOSE verb is simply:

```
CLOSE filename-1 [filename-2]...
```

For simplicity, we have omitted the optional phrases used with magnetic tape files and the LOCK option that prevents the program from reopening the file.

20.8 The WRITE Verb

Data is written to a file, one record at a time, using a WRITE statement with the syntax:

```
WRITE record-name-1 [ FROM identifier-2 ]

   [ {AFTER }  ADVANCING  { {identifier-1}  [LINE ] } ]
   [ {BEFORE}              { {integer-1   }  [LINES] } ]
   [                       { {PAGE        }          } ]
   [                       { {mnemonic-name-1}        } ]

   [ AT {END-OF-PAGE}  imperative-sentence-1 ]
   [    {EOP        }                        ]

   [ NOT AT {END-OF-PAGE}  imperative-sentence-2 ]
   [        {EOP        }                        ]
   [ END-WRITE ]
```

The statement WRITE MY-REC will be valid code provided MY-REC is the name of the record (or one of the records) associated with a file in an FD entry in the FILE SECTION and that this file has been opened appropriately with OPEN OUTPUT or EXTEND.

The single statement: WRITE MY-REC FROM ANOTHER-RECORD.
is equivalent to the two statements: MOVE ANOTHER-RECORD TO MY-REC
                                     WRITE MY-REC.

The optional ADVANCING phrase and the optional conditional phrases with END-OF-PAGE are used to format printed reports. These will be fully examined later in this chapter. The END-WRITE phrase is required only when a conditional phrase is used.

20.9 The REWRITE Verb

```
REWRITE record-name [ FROM identifier-1 ]
```

The REWRITE verb is used to update records. The file must be opened with I-O mode and the record must first be READ and modified with verbs such as MOVE and ADD. The existing record is then replaced by the new one with the REWRITE verb. Do not use the WRITE verb to update a record; this would overwrite the record following the last record read. This verb may be used with disk files but not with tape files. Magnetic tape files are updated by creating a new file with the updated records.

20.10 The READ Verb

The READ verb, clearly, is used to read a file record. Before a file can be read, it must have been opened with either OPEN INPUT or OPEN I-O. The syntax for a sequential file is:

```
READ file-name [ NEXT ] READ [ INTO identifier-1 ]
     [ AT END imperative-sentence-1 ]
     [ NOT AT END imperative-sentence-2 ]
     [END-READ ]
```

Carefully note that a WRITE statement names a *record*, while a READ names a *file*. When the programmer is about to code a WRITE, he/she knows which record is to be written. A file, however, may contain records of different types, i.e. it may have multiple record descriptions in its FD entry. The programmer does not necessarily know the type of the next record to be read. When there are multiple record descriptions, they share the same memory area. Multiple record descriptions are akin to REDEFINES in Working Storage. Once the data is read, we may use any of the record descriptions. There is usually a field in each description to tell the programmer which type of record has been read.

The single statement   `READ X-FILE INTO ANOTHER-REC`
                                     `AT END … END-READ`
is equivalent to the two statements   `READ X-FILE AT END … END-READ`
                                       `MOVE X-REC TO ANOTHER-REC.`

The optional word RECORD is there for clarification, it shows that a record is being read rather than an entire file. READ X-FILE is the same as READ X-FILE RECORD. The NEXT phrase in the READ format is optional for sequentially organized files.

The AT END phrase provides program control when the file pointer reaches the end of the file. Generally the statement associated with the AT END is one that moves a certain value to an identifier — we call this "setting a flag". Since AT END is a conditional phrase we need to use END-READ to terminate it. The AT END phrase is required in a sequential read unless a USE procedure is specified for the file-name — see Chapter 32. The converse phrase, NOT AT END, is optional and may be used to code instructions that are to be executed when the file-pointer is not at the end of the file.

20.10.1 The initial read method

We need to be clear about what is meant by "the file-pointer reaching the end of the file". The *file-pointer* is a conceptual entity. When a file is opened, the pointer is at the start of the first record. When this record is read, the pointer moves on to the next record. Suppose that we have a program which is designed to read all the records. Eventually the file pointer will be pointing to the last record, and our program will then read the last record. Carefully note that COBOL does not detect the end of-file condition at this point. After the last record has been read, the file pointer moves on to the end-of-file marker. It is the READ statement *after* the one that read the last record that detects the end-of-file marker. In other languages, such as BASIC, the instruction that reads the last record also detects the end-of-file marker. This has an important implication on how we read a file.

Consider a program which is designed to read and display all the records in a file of 20 records. Would this code be suitable?

```
MOVE "N" TO FILE-FLAG                    < incorrect code >
PERFORM UNTIL FILE-FLAG = "Y"
    READ X-FILE
        AT END      MOVE "Y" TO FILE-FLAG
    END-READ
    DISPLAY X-REC
END-PERFORM.
```

The answer is a resounding No! Consider what happens after the last record has been read and displayed. The value of FILE-FLAG is still "N" since the end-of-file marker has not been detected. Therefore the PERFORM loop continues. The next read finds the end-of-file marker so FILE-FLAG is set to "N". However, this last READ did not change the data in X-REC so the DISPLAY statement will display the existing data in that record. This means that the last record will be displayed twice!

We could rectify this using the code shown below. However it is not very efficient in that a condition (NOT AT END) must be tested for all the records read.

```
MOVE "N" TO FILE-FLAG
PERFORM UNTIL FILE-FLAG = "Y"
    READ X-FILE
        AT END       MOVE "Y" TO FILE-FLAG
        NOT AT END   DISPLAY X-REC
    END-READ
END-PERFORM.
```

The alternative is to use the Initial Read Method. In pseudocode we may represent this by:

> Read the first record — the "priming" read
> Do while not end-of file
>   Process the current record
>   Read the next record
> End do-while

This method is used in the sample program later in this chapter. The code for our present example would be:

```
MOVE "N" TO FILE-FLAG
READ X-FILE      AT END    MOVE "Y" TO FILE-FLAG    END-READ
PERFORM UNTIL FILE-FLAG = "Y"
    DISPLAY X-REC
    READ X-FILE   AT END    MOVE "Y" TO FILE-FLAG    END-READ
END-PERFORM.
```

In a subsequent chapter we shall learn to use *condition-names*. This makes the coding for the file-flag a little neater. For example:

```
02 FILE-FLAG   PIC X  VALUE "N"
   88 EOF   VALUE "Y".
......
READ X-FILE      AT END  SET EOF TO TRUE    END-READ
   PERFORM UNTIL EOF
   DISPLAY X-REC
   READ X-FILE  AT END  SET EOF TO TRUE    END-READ
END-PERFORM.
```

20.11 Printer Output

In COBOL, the printer device is treated as a file. Of course, it is a write-only file and must be opened with an OPEN OUTPUT statement. To designate a file as a printer file we need a SELECT clause. See also section 5.4.

```
Micro Focus COBOL        SELECT PRINTFILE ASSIGN TO PRINTER
                            ORGANIZATION LINE SEQUENTIAL.
RM/COBOL-85              SELECT PRINTFILE ASSIGN TO PRINTER   "PRINTER".
```

When you are in the debugging stage, it can be a waste of paper and time to send the output of trial runs to the printer. Instead the output can be sent to a disk file. To accomplish this use an entry such as: SELECT PRINTFILE ASSIGN TO PRINTER   "OUTPUT.DAT". When this code is used, the data is sent to a file called OUTPUT.DAT. Note that even when the output is redirected to a file we still use the word PRINTER as the unit-name. This ensures that the logical file is treated as if it were referencing the physical printer. However, some applications may not give the expected results when the LINAGE clause (see below) is used.

When we are writing a report, the lines of data sent to the printer will often have a variety of formats. We may have a header, a detail and a summary line in our report. For this reason we generally use an unstructured record for the printer-file. We may use, for example:

```
FD PRINT-FILE    LINAGE 66 FOOTING 66.
01 PRINT-REC     PIC X(80).
```

To print a report heading named HEAD-REC we would use:

```
WRITE PRINT-REC FROM HEAD-REC
```

Clearly the size of the record sent to the printer should be such that all the data will fit on one line. If you are using 8½"×11" (or European A4) paper and normal Courier font, a printer record may have of a size of 80. With compressed print or a wide-format printer 132 is a reasonable value. Normal Courier font prints at 10 characters to the inch.

If we wish to space records on the page, we use the ADVANCING phase of the WRITE verb. For example, to print RECORD-A followed by RECORD-B with double spacing we could use:

```
WRITE PRINT-REC FROM RECORD-A
WRITE PRINT-REC FROM RECORD-B AFTER 2
```

The reader may have a number of questions at this point. How can I "jump" to a new printer page? How can I print a heading at the top of each page? How do I tell the program I am using a 4" deep form? To answer these questions it is necessary to understand the LINAGE clause in the FD entry. Before proceeding to that topic we need to introduce the concepts of *physical page* and *logical page*. First, the reader should know that normally a printer gives 6 lines to the inch.

What would your output look like if you printed 100 records on a printer holding continuous 8½"×11" paper? How many records would there be to a page? As an exercise, and to test how your printer behaves, write a program that uses the PERFORM loop below. Define the ITEM-N with: 01 ITEM-N PIC 99.

```
PERFORM VARYING ITEM-N FROM 1 BY 1 UNTIL ITEM-N > 100
    WRITE PRINT-REC FROM ITEM-N
END-PERFORM
```

On a Hewlett-Packard LaserJet III, with paper 11" long, this program segment wrote 59 lines on the first page. The printer leaves top and bottom margins on the page — areas that cannot be written to. Although the paper was long enough for 66 lines, the maximum number of lines COBOL can use is 59. The *physical page* is 66 lines long, the *logical page* is 59 lines long. Computer programs "think" of the printer having sheets of paper with the *logical length*. A dot-matrix printer using continuous paper may be set up to leave white space on each side of the perforations.

20.11.1 The LINAGE clause

The LINAGE clause is an optional part of the FD (file description found in the File Section of the Data Division) for a sequential file. The syntax is:

```
LINAGE IS page-size
       [ WITH FOOTING AT footing-line ]
       [ LINES AT TOP top-lines ]
       [ LINES AT BOTTOM bottom-lines ]
```

Note that each data item in the clause may be either an identifier-name or an integer numeric literal. In all examples we will use integers.

Assuming we are using paper with a physical size of 11" long we could code

```
FD PRINT-FILE   LINAGE  60    FOOTING  60   TOP  3   BOTTOM  3.
```

The TOP 3 phrase would add an additional 3 lines (½ ") to the top margin, so the first line would follow 1" of white space. Similarly the bottom of the page will have 1" of white space.

The rules for the LINAGE clause are:

1) The size of the logical page is the sum of page-size, top-lines and bottom-lines. Note carefully that footing-line is NOT included in the sum. In our example, the size of the logical page is 60 + 3 + 3 = 66 lines. This is the size of the logical page.

2) TOP and BOTTOM define the top and bottom margins, respectively. The default values, operative when the phrase is omitted, are zero for each margin.

3) The page-size integer must be greater than zero; that is fairly obvious.

4) The footing-lines integer must be positive and not greater than page-size. When the program is printing a series of lines and LINAGE-COUNTER (see below) becomes equal to or greater than footing-lines, the WRITE statement is executued and the END-OF-PAGE condition becomes true.

The program CHAP20-P may be used to test the behaviour of your printer. It should give you two pages of output with a header at the top of each page The DISPLAY statements are included so that you may observe the action of the program and modify it to suit *your* printer. Modification will be needed if your printer always gives a top margin. Line 36 ejects a page from the printer; it will not be needed in a networking environment. The version of the program shown here is applicable for Micro Focus COBOL. An RM/COBOL-85 version is available on the disk.

```
1     identification division.
2     program-id. chap20-p.
3   * To demonstrate  LINAGE, LINAGE-COUNTER, WRITE-AFTER
4     select print-file
5         assign to printer
6         organization is line sequential.
7     data division.
8     file section.
9     fd print-file linage 60 footing 60 top 3 bottom 3.
10    01 print-rec    pic x(80).
11    working-storage section.
12    01 x-rec.
13        02  j        pic 99      value 0.
14        02           pic xx      value spaces.
15        02           pic x(20)   value "text text text".
16        02           pic x(20)   value spaces.
17        02           pic x(20)   value "more more more".
18        02           pic x(20)   value all "x".
19    01 h-rec.
20        02           pic x(10)   value "Heading".
21        02           pic x(62)   value spaces.
22        02           pic x(6)    value "Page ".
23        02 h-page    pic zz.
24    01 b-rec         pic x       value spaces.
25    01 page-no       pic 99      value 0.
26    procedure division.
```

```
27    main-para.
28       open output print-file
29       perform page-heading
30       perform varying j from 1 by 1 until j > 72
31          write print-rec from x-rec
32             at eop perform page-heading
33          end-write
34          display "j = " j  " linage-counter = " linage-counter
35       end-perform
36       write print-rec from b-rec after page
37       stop run.
38    page-heading.
39       display "Page-heading  j = " j
40             " linage-counter = " linage-counter
41       add 1 to page-no
42       move page-no to h-page
43       if page-no = 1
44          write print-rec from h-rec
45       else
46          write print-rec from h-rec after page
47       end-if
48       write print-rec from b-rec.
```

You may also experiment with this program by changing line 31 to WRITE...AFTER ADVANCING 2; this will give you double spacing. Micro Focus COBOL users should note that a WRITE ... AFTER ADVANCING 1 will also give double spacing if the previous WRITE statement had no ADVANCING phrase.

20.11.2 LINAGE-COUNTER

When a file is declared with a LINAGE clause, a counter called LINAGE-COUNTER is maintained by the program. This counter is given a value of 1 when the file is opened and is reset to 1 when a WRITE ... ADVANCING PAGE statement is executed. This counter must not be declared in the data division. No statement may attempt to explicitly change its value but one may find its value with statements such as:

```
MOVE LINAGE-COUNTER TO MY-LINE-COUNTER
IF LINAGE-COUNTER >= 20 THEN …
```

If more than one file contains the LINAGE clause, it is necessary to qualify the LINAGE-COUNTER reference to show which one is being referred to. If FILE-ONE and FILE-TWO each have a LINAGE clause, then we would use, for example, statements such as:

```
IF LINAGE-COUNTER OF FILE-ONE > 50 THEN …
```

The item LINAGE-COUNTER may be displayed directly in Micro Focus COBOL; in RM/COBOL-85 it must be moved to a data item if you wish to display the value.

20.11.3 Printer control commands

This section answers questions such as: " How can we programmatically set the printer to print at 8 lines per inch when it normally uses 6 lines per inch" and "How can we print italics?" These printer features are set by sending printer control commands or sequences. Printer manuals list the available features and the commands needed to set them. Listed below are some randomly selected examples for typical printers.

Printer	Print Feature	Escape Sequence or Control Code	ASCII Decimal Equivalent
Hewlett-Packard	Italic ON	ESC (s1S	27, 40, 115, 49, 83
	Italic OFF	ESC (s0S	27, 40, 115, 49, 83
IBM Proprinter	Condensed ON	SI	15
	Condensed OFF	DC4	20
Epson	6 lpi	ESC 2	27, 50
	8 lpi	ESC 0	27, 48
Digital	10 cpi	ESC [0w	27, 91, 48, 119
	12 cpi	ESC [2w	29, 91, 50, 119

While some printer manuals kindly show how to send these sequences to a printer using a BASIC program, the COBOL programmer is left wondering how to send the nonprintable characters such as ESC, SI and DC4. The program CHAP20-C shown below prints three lines to a Hewlett-Packard printer. The second line will be printed in italics. The BEFORE 0 phrases are used to prevent blank lines being printed.

To send the printer control string "ESC(s1S", the ESC (escape) character was sent as a signed binary number. The remainder of the string consists of "printable" characters so they were sent in an alphanumeric field. Other printer control sequences beginning with ESC may be sent in the same manner.

We may prefer to send all the characters as numeric items. For example, to set an Epson printer to 8 lines per inch we could use:

```
01 PRINT-EPSON-8LPI.
   02 ESKAPE  PIC S99 BINARY VALUE 27.
   02 FILLER  PIC 9         VALUE ZERO.
```

Similarly, to set condensed mode printing on with an IBM printer we would use :

```
01 PRINT-IBM-CONDENSED PIC S99 BINARY VALUE 15.

   IDENTIFICATION DIVISION.
   PROGRAM-ID. CHAP20-C.
 * Program to send printer control sequences
   ENVIRONMENT DIVISION.
   INPUT-OUTPUT SECTION.
   FILE-CONTROL.
       SELECT PRINTFILE ASSIGN TO PRINTER. (Add "PRINTER"for RM)
```

```
            DATA DIVISION.
            FILE SECTION.
            FD PRINTFILE LINAGE 66 FOOTING 66.
            01 PRINT-REC    PIC X(78).
            WORKING-STORAGE SECTION.
            01 SAMPLE-REC   PIC X(40)
                VALUE "abcdefghijklmnopqrstuvwxyz".
            01 PRINT-ITALIC-ON.
               02 ESKAPE   PIC S99 BINARY VALUE 27.
               02 FILLER   PIC X(4)       VALUE "(s1S".
            01 PRINT-ITALIC-OFF.
               02 ESKAPE   PIC S99 BINARY VALUE 27.
               02 FILLER   PIC X(4)       VALUE "(s0S".

            PROCEDURE DIVISION.
            MAIN-PARA.
               OPEN OUTPUT PRINTFILE
               WRITE PRINT-REC FROM SAMPLE-REC
               WRITE PRINT-REC FROM PRINT-ITALIC-ON  BEFORE 0
               WRITE PRINT-REC FROM SAMPLE-REC
               WRITE PRINT-REC FROM PRINT-ITALIC-OFF BEFORE 0
               WRITE PRINT-REC FROM SAMPLE-REC
               CLOSE PRINTFILE
               STOP RUN.
```

There are several alternative methods but we shall look at only two.

a) As an extension to ANSI COBOL, many compilers allow one to use the hexadecimal value of an ASCII character in a VALUE clause. We could use the following data definitions for the two ESKAPE identifiers — recall that decimal 27 equals 1B hexadecimal. The picture has a single X since it will hold just one character — the ESCAPE character. Since "ESCAPE" is a reserved word our program code uses ESKAPE as an identifier.

```
    02 ESKAPE        PIC X VALUE x"1B".     Micro Focus
    02 ESKAPE        PIC X VALUE H"1B".     RM/COBOL-85
```

b) ANSI COBOL allows for user-defined figurative constants. Within the ENVIRONMENT DIVISION, we include a SYMBOLIC CHARACTER definition within SPECIAL-NAMES.

```
    CONFIGURATION SECTION.
    SPECIAL-NAMES.
        SYMBOLIC CHARACTERS ESCAPE-CHAR IS 28.
```

Note that the ordinal position of the character is specified; since ESCAPE has the ASCII value of 27, it must be the 28th ASCII character, since the first character has a value of zero. We then replace our data definitions by:

```
    02 ESKAPE        PIC X VALUE ESCAPE-CHAR.
```

20.12 Sample Program 1

We are now in a position to write a simple program that will write and read file records. The program CHAP20-1 will accept the 10 names. When all 10 have been accepted, the program will read all the records and write them to a printer file.

Note the use of blank lines to help make the program more readable. This simple program has been written with one procedural paragraph (MAIN-PARA). We have chosen to divide the material in this paragraph into seven sentences (count the periods.) We could have chosen to have only one sentence. What is essential is the period following STOP RUN.

1) In the first sentence (line 28) X-FILE is opened to receive output from the program.
2) The next sentence (lines 29 TO 36) is an "in-line" PERFORM. The block of statements between PERFORM and END-PERFORM (lines 30 TO 35), is executed 10 times. When this sentence is completed, we will have 10 records in the file.
3) The file is now closed (line 37) and reopened to allow records to be used as data input to the program.The printer file is also opened for program output.
4) The first record in the file is READ (lines 39 to 41). We are using the "initial read" method as discussed above.
5) Another in-line PERFORM begins. The record just read is written to the printer and the next record is read. The two steps WRITE and READ are repeated until the READ statement detects the end of the file (line 45) and sets a flag.
6) Control passes to the next sentence. The two open files are CLOSED in line 49.

```
 1      IDENTIFICATION DIVISION.
 2      PROGRAM-ID.  CHAP20-1.
 3      ENVIRONMENT DIVISION.
 4      INPUT-OUTPUT SECTION.
 5      FILE-CONTROL.
 6          SELECT X-FILE ASSIGN TO DISK "XFILE.DAT"
 7              ORGANIZATION LINE SEQUENTIAL.
 8          SELECT PRINTFILE ASSIGN TO PRINTER
 9              ORGANIZATION LINE SEQUENTIAL.
10
11      DATA DIVISION.
12
13      FILE SECTION.
14      FD X-FILE.
15      01 X-REC.
16          03 X-LAST-NAME      PIC X(20).
17          03 X-FIRST-NAME     PIC X(20).
18
19      FD PRINTFILE.
20      01 PRINT-REC            PIC X(80).
21
22      WORKING-STORAGE SECTION.
23      01 WORK-ITEMS.
24          03 FILE-FLAG        PIC X   VALUE "N".
25
26      PROCEDURE DIVISION.
27      MAIN-PARA.
```

```
28          OPEN OUTPUT X-FILE
29          PERFORM 10 TIMES
30              MOVE SPACES TO X-REC
31              DISPLAY "Give first name > " NO ADVANCING
32              ACCEPT X-FIRST-NAME
33              DISPLAY "Give last name  > " NO ADVANCING
34              ACCEPT X-LAST-NAME
35              WRITE X-REC
36          END-PERFORM
37          CLOSE  X-FILE   OPEN INPUT X-FILE  OUTPUT PRINTFILE.
38          DISPLAY "Printing file..." NO ADVANCING
39          READ X-FILE
40              AT END   MOVE "Y" TO FILE-FLAG
41          END-READ
42          PERFORM UNTIL FILE-FLAG = "Y"
43              WRITE PRINT-REC FROM X-REC
44              READ X-FILE
45                  AT END   MOVE "Y" TO FILE-FLAG
46              END-READ
47          END-PERFORM
48          DISPLAY SPACES
49          CLOSE X-FILE PRINTFILE
50          STOP RUN.
```

The 10 lines will readily fit on a single page. We shall need to provide a way of going to a new page at the appropriate time when larger amounts of data are printed. We could modify the program:

```
FD PRINTFILE LINAGE 60.
...

WRITE PRINT-REC
   AT END-OF-PAGE   MOVE SPACES TO PRINT-REC
                    WRITE PRINT-REC AFTER PAGE END-WRITE
END-WRITE
```

A more usual approach would be to write a heading on the new page.

```
WRITE PRINT-REC
   AT END-OF-PAGE   PERFORM  REPORT-HEADING
END-WRITE
```

The REPORT-HEADING paragraph would look something like:

```
REPORT-HEADING.
   ADD 1 TO PAGE-NUMBER.
   WRITE PRINT-REC FROM HEADING-REC AFTER PAGE
   MOVE SPACES TO PRINT-REC
   WRITE PRINT-REC AFTER 2 LINES.
```

20.13 Sample Program 2

The program CHAP20-2 shows how to use various records in a printed report and the use of END-OF-PAGE (EOP) and LINAGE-COUNTER.

The program reads a file (CHAP20-2.DAT) containing records that represent a company's data on long distance phone charges. The data in the first record is shown in (a) below. This represents a call to London on 7 Jan. 1995 for which the cost was $8.04. This record is to be printed as shown in (b) below.

```
(a) input:    950107 0804 LONDON
(b) output:   95/01/07    LONDON                        8.04
```

```
 1        IDENTIFICATION DIVISION.
 2        PROGRAM-ID.     CHAP20-2.
 3        ENVIRONMENT DIVISION.
 4        INPUT-OUTPUT SECTION.
 5        FILE-CONTROL.
 6            SELECT DATAFILE   ASSIGN TO DISK "CHAP20-2.DAT"
 7                ORGANIZATION LINE SEQUENTIAL.
 8            SELECT PRINTFILE  ASSIGN TO PRINTER
 9                ORGANIZATION LINE SEQUENTIAL.
10        DATA DIVISION.
11        FILE SECTION.
12        FD DATAFILE.
13        01 DATA-REC.
14            02 DATA-DATE        PIC X(6).
15            02                  PIC XX.
16            02 DATA-COST        PIC 99.99.
17            02                  PIC XX.
18            02 DATA-CITY        PIC X(15).
19        FD PRINTFILE LINAGE 66 FOOTING 66.
20        01 PRINT-REC            PIC X(80).
21
22        WORKING-STORAGE SECTION.
23        01 WORK-ITEMS.
24            02 FILE-FLAG        PIC XXX VALUE SPACES.
25            02 BLANK-LINE       PIC X   VALUE SPACES.
26            02 PAGE-NO          PIC 99  VALUE 0.
27            02 PHONE-COST       PIC 99V99.
28            02 COST-SUM         PIC 9(5)V99 VALUE 0.
29        01 LINE-REC.
30            02 LINE-DATE        PIC 99/99/99.
31            02                  PIC X(4).
32            02 LINE-CITY        PIC X(16).
33            02 LINE-COST        PIC Z9.99.
34        01 HEAD-REC.
35            02 HEAD-TITLE       PIC X(40) VALUE "Telephone report".
36            02 HEAD-DATE        PIC 99/99/99.
37            02                  PIC X(15) VALUE SPACES.
```

```
38          02                    PIC X(5)  VALUE "Page".
39          02 HEAD-PAGE          PIC Z9.
40      01 UNDER-LINE             PIC X(70) VALUE ALL "-".
41      01 TOTAL-REC.
42          02                    PIC X(5)  VALUE "Total".
43          02                    PIC X(35) VALUE SPACES.
44          02 TOTAL-COST         PIC $Z,ZZZ,ZZ9.99.
45
46      PROCEDURE DIVISION.
47      MAIN-PARA.
48          OPEN INPUT DATAFILE OUTPUT PRINTFILE
49          ACCEPT HEAD-DATE FROM DATE
50          PERFORM NEW-PAGE
51          PERFORM READ-DATA
52          PERFORM TOTAL-PARA
53          CLOSE DATAFILE PRINTFILE
54          STOP RUN.
55
56      READ-DATA.
57          READ DATAFILE AT END MOVE "END" TO FILE-FLAG END-READ
58          PERFORM UNTIL FILE-FLAG = "END"
59              MOVE DATA-COST   TO PHONE-COST
60              ADD  PHONE-COST  TO COST-SUM
61              MOVE SPACES      TO LINE-REC
62              MOVE DATA-DATE   TO LINE-DATE
63              MOVE DATA-COST   TO LINE-COST
64              MOVE DATA-CITY   TO LINE-CITY
65              WRITE PRINT-REC  FROM LINE-REC
66                  AT EOP PERFORM NEW-PAGE
67              END-WRITE
68              READ DATAFILE AT END MOVE "END" TO FILE-FLAG END-READ
69          END-PERFORM.
70
71      NEW-PAGE.
72          ADD 1 TO PAGE-NO
73          MOVE PAGE-NO TO HEAD-PAGE
74          WRITE PRINT-REC FROM HEAD-REC AFTER PAGE
75          WRITE PRINT-REC FROM BLANK-LINE.
76
77      TOTAL-PARA.
78          PERFORM UNTIL LINAGE-COUNTER > 60
79              WRITE PRINT-REC FROM BLANK-LINE
80          END-PERFORM
81          WRITE PRINT-REC FROM UNDER-LINE
82          MOVE COST-SUM TO TOTAL-COST
83          WRITE PRINT-REC FROM TOTAL-REC.
```

20.14 Review Questions

1. You are writing a program that will create a file which you later wish to view in an editor. What type of sequential file will you use?

2* Your program is running in the directory C:\COBOL. The data for the program was generated with an editor in the file PROG-20.DAT. This is stored in the directory BOOK\DATA, which is on the F drive of your network. The logical name of the file is to X-FILE. Write the complete SELECT entry.

3. You have a file with 20 records. A program using OPEN OUTPUT file-name writes 8 records to the file. Is it now possible to access the 12 old records?

4. Assuming your program has defined the file-name SALES, write an OPEN statement that will permit your program to read, modify and rewrite its records.

5. Your dot matrix printer is loaded with 14" long paper. Assuming 6 lines per inch printing, what LINAGE value will you use?

6. What is wrong with this code?
```
    PERFORM UNTIL FILE-FLAG = "N"
        READ DATA-REC
            AT END MOVE "N" TO FILE-FLAG
            NOT AT END
                WRITE PRINT-REC FROM DATA-REC
                    AT EOP WRITE DATA-REC FROM HEAD-REC AFTER PAGE
                    DISPLAY DATA-REC
        END-READ
    END-PERFORM.
```

21
Transfer of Control

Objectives

- Understand the three control structures used in programming.
- Know the five relational conditions.
- Know the three arithmetic conditions.
- Know the use of the SIGN condition and the NUMERIC test.
- Know the use of condition-names.
- Know how to form compound conditions.

21.1 Program Control Structures

Three basic control structures, or logical constructs, are used in designing and coding programs: selection, sequence and repetition.

A sequence is the execution of instructions in the order that they appear in the program code independent of any conditions. A program may contain both micro or macro sequential structures.

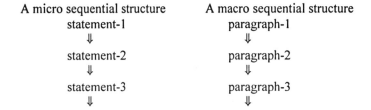

When a sequence is broken we speak of a transfer of control. Selection and repetition are examples of transfer of control.

A selection (or decision) construct is one where there are two or more possible paths for the program to follow depending on the truth value of a logical expression. The commonest selection structure is the IF construct which we represent in pseudocode by:

        IF condition-1 THEN
            sequential-block-1

ELSE
    sequential-block-2
END IF

The statements in sequential-block-1 are executed if condition-1 is true. If it is false, sequential-block-2 statements are executed. We may omit the ELSE phrase in cases where we wish only to do something when the condition is true and nothing when it is false.

Repetition is the construct in which a sequence of instructions is repeatedly executed. This construct is also called a loop or an iteration construct. Each time the code in the loop is executed we say it has performed one iteration. A repetition construct may be designed to be executed a pre-determined number of iterations. In pseudocode we write this as LOOP N TIMES or REPEAT N TIMES or DO N TIMES. Alternatively, the construct may be designed to loop until some condition is satisfied: LOOP UNTIL condition-1 is true (or false), or LOOP WHILE condition-1 is true (or false). For more on this topic see Chapter 22.

21.2 Verbs Used for Transfer of Control

The COBOL verbs which result in a transfer of control (a break in a sequence structure) are:

IF	The simplest selection structure is the IF...ELSE construct. This is very similar to the IF found in other languages.
EVALUATE	A useful alternative selection structure uses the EVALUATE verb, which emulates the CASE construct of other languages.
PERFORM	A major use of PERFORM is to modularize a program — break it into manageable blocks. A PERFORM statement, with appropriate phrases, may also be used for repetition structures of the type LOOP N TIMES, LOOP UNTIL or LOOP WHILE.
GO TO	The GO TO verb, which transfers control to another statement, is normally avoided since it leads to unstructured programming. As an exception, we may use it within the procedure set of a PERFORM THROUGH clause. This will be our only use of GO TO. We will not look at the GO TO DEPENDING construct.
EXIT	The EXIT statement may be used as the only statement in the last paragraph of a procedure set.
SEARCH	The SEARCH statement directs the program to examine a table. The WHEN phrase (selection) executes a block of statement if a specified condition is true. The optional AT END phrase (selection) may be used to execute other statements if none of the specified conditions were true.
Exceptions	A number of verbs contain "exception conditions". The READ verb used with a sequential file requires an AT END phrase. This directs the program to execute a statement if the end of file is encountered while

reading the file. Similarly, there is provision in the WRITE statement to execute a statement when END-OF-PAGE is encountered. The forms of the READ and WRITE verbs used with indexed and relative files have exception conditions that apply when an invalid key is encountered. The arithmetic verbs contain the ON SIZE ERROR exception condition. All these exception conditions, which are covered with their respective verbs in other chapters, are further examples of selection structures.

CALL

The CALL verb is an extreme example of transfer of control. This directs the computer to execute another program and then return to the calling program.

STOP RUN
EXIT
  PROGRAM

This is the ultimate transfer of control; the program (or subprogram) is terminated. The last logical statement in a program must be STOP RUN; subprograms must terminate with EXIT PROGRAM. Additional STOP RUN (or EXIT PROGRAM) statements may be used to terminate the program (or subprogram) when certain conditions are encountered.

21.3 Conditions

Before we can use a conditional verb, we must be familiar with how to code a condition.

An example in pseudocode: `IF  condition-1    THEN do-something.`
A specific example :   `IF    X > 3       THEN PERFORM PARA-A`

This example specifies that PARA-A is to be performed if X has a value greater than 3.

The syntax of other verbs also contains *condition-1*. For example:

PERFORM procedure-1   UNTIL   condition-1

SEARCH TABLE-ITEM   WHEN   condition-1 imperative-statement-1

EVALUATE   TRUE   WHEN   condition-1 imperative-statement-1

The four types of conditions are enumerated below with examples.

```
Type of Condition          Example of use

Relational                 IF X > 3  .....
Sign                       IF X - Y IS NEGATIVE ....
Class                      IF ITEM-N IS NUMERIC .....
Condition-name             IF FRESHMAN ....
```

21.4 Relation Condition

In a relation condition the *values* of two data items are compared. The relation condition may be considered to have three parts: <subject-operand><relational-operator><object-operand>. The options for the three components are shown below. The reader will see that while there are 10 relational-operators listed, functionally there are only five. The relational-operator is written either in words or in words and symbols. The first two relational-operators (IS [NOT] LESS THAN and IS [NOT] <) are equivalent, as are subsequent pairs.

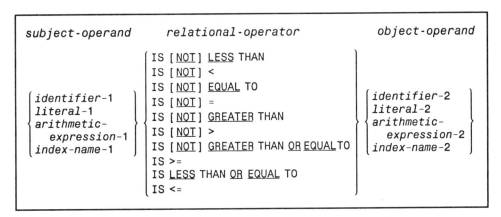

```
subject-operand        relational-operator            object-operand

                    ⎧ IS [NOT] LESS THAN      ⎫
                    ⎪ IS [NOT] <              ⎪
                    ⎪ IS [NOT] EQUAL TO       ⎪
  ⎧ identifier-1 ⎫ ⎪ IS [NOT] =              ⎪  ⎧ identifier-2 ⎫
  ⎪ literal-1    ⎪ ⎨ IS [NOT] GREATER THAN   ⎬  ⎪ literal-2    ⎪
  ⎨ arithmetic-  ⎬ ⎪ IS [NOT] >              ⎪  ⎨ arithmetic-  ⎬
  ⎪   expression-1⎪⎪ IS [NOT] GREATER THAN OR EQUAL TO ⎪ expression-2⎪
  ⎩ index-name-1 ⎭ ⎪ IS >=                   ⎪  ⎩ index-name-2 ⎭
                    ⎪ IS LESS THAN OR EQUAL TO ⎪
                    ⎩ IS <=                   ⎭
```

The format of the relation condition has four types of operands. For a given type of subject operand only some of the object operand types are valid. Obviously, it would be meaningless to compare, for example, an alphanumeric operand with an arithmetic expression. These rules apply:

a)   Two numeric operands may be compared even if they have different USAGE. It is therefore valid, for example, to compare an integer data item of DISPLAY USAGE with a data item of USAGE COMP, or with an index name.

b)   When one operand is numeric, it may not have a USAGE other than DISPLAY (implicit or explicit). Complications can occur when comparing a signed numeric item with a nonnumeric item. Thus, if ITEM-A is alphanumeric, (i) is acceptable, (ii) should be avoided:

   (i)   IF   ITEM-A > 4 ...   (ii)   IF   ITEM-A < −4 ...

c)   When one, or both, of the operands is nonnumeric, both are treated as strings for the purpose of comparison.

   The comparison of strings is based on the computer's collating sequence. Generally this is ASCII (or EBCDIC for IBM mainframe machines). The collating sequence may be altered by an entry in the OBJECT COMPUTER paragraph in the ENVIRONMENT DIVISION, or by defining an alphabet — see Appendix C. The collating sequence for the printable ASCII characters is given in Table 21-1.

Table 21-1 Printable ASCII character set

	30	40	50	60	70	80	90	100	110	120
0		(	2	<	F	P	Z	d	n	x
1		)	3	=	G	Q	[	e	o	y
2	space	*	4	>	H	R	\	f	p	z
3	!	+	5	?	I	S	]	g	q	{
4	"	,	6	@	J	T	^	h	r	|
5	#	-	7	A	K	U	_	i	s	}
6	$	.	8	B	L	V	`	j	t	~
7	%	/	9	C	M	W	a	k	u	
8	&	0	:	D	N	X	b	l	v	
9	'	1	;	E	O	Y	c	m	w	

Examples: the @ character is ASCII 64, the letter A is ASCII 65.
The printable characters are from 32 (space) to 126.
The first ASCII character is ASCII 0 (NULL), so the *ordinal* position of each character is one more than its ASCII value.

In ASCII, the exclamation point (!) has the sequence number 33. The character "A" is 65, etc. The space character is number 32. Thus, all printable characters are GREATER THAN SPACE; "A" is LESS THAN "B"; "A" is LESS THAN "a"; digits are LESS THAN all alphabetic characters. Note that there are four groupings of special characters. Many of the special characters are not members of the COBOL character set.

The string "ABCD" is greater than "ABC", the fourth character of the former, "D", has a higher ASCII value than the implied space in the fourth place in "ABC".

The reader who wishes to work with extended ASCII (characters with an ASCII value greater than 127) or with nonprintable characters, should become familiar with the SYMBOLIC CHARACTERS entry in SPECIAL-NAMES. This is discussed in Chapter 6 under user-defined figurative constants and in Appendix C.

21.5 Sign Condition

In a sign condition, the subject is compared with zero, using the format:

```
                                         ( POSITIVE )
              arithmetic-expression      { NEGATIVE }
                                         ( ZERO     )
```

The pairs of statements in each line below are equivalent:

```
IF X POSITIVE …           IF X > 0 …
IF X NEGATIVE …           IF X < 0 …
IF X - Y ZERO …           IF X = Y …
IF 2 * X - 5 POSITIVE …   COMPUTE Z = 2 * X - 5, IF Z > 0 …
```

21.6 Class Condition

The class condition tests the class type of its operand. The format is:

$$
identifier\text{-}1 \text{ IS } [\underline{NOT}]
\begin{cases}
\underline{NUMERIC} \\
\underline{ALPHABETIC} \\
\underline{ALPHABETIC\text{-}LOWER} \\
\underline{ALPHABETIC\text{-}UPPER} \\
class\text{-}name\text{-}1
\end{cases}
$$

The following rules apply:

a) The NUMERIC test may be used on numeric and alphanumeric data items but not on those declared as alphabetic.
    The data item will pass the NUMERIC test if it contains a value composed of only digits (0 to 9) and a single operational sign.

b) The ALPHABETIC tests may not be used on data items described as numeric.
    The data item will pass the test if it is composed only from the English alphabetic character set, consisting of the letters "A" to "Z", and "a" to "z", and the space character.

c) The ALPHABETIC-UPPER test fails if lowercase characters are present.
    The ALPHABETIC-LOWER test fails if uppercase characters are present.

d) The class-name test is used in conjunction with class names defined in the SPECIAL-NAMES paragraph of the Environment Division.

    Example: `SPECIAL-NAMES.`
    `CLASS HEX-DIGIT IS "0" THRU "9", "A" THRU "F".`
    `....`
    `IF X-CHAR IS HEX-DIGIT ....`

    This condition will be true if X-CHAR is in the set {0,1,2,3,4,5,6,7,8,9,A,B,C,D,E,F}.

21.7 Condition-names

An identifier may be declared to be a condition-name by using level 88 in its description. Recall from Chapter 6, that a condition-name is defined in the Data Division using a data-description entry in the form:

```
88 condition-name ⎰ VALUE  IS  ⎱ ⎰ literal-1 ⎡ ⎰ THROUGH ⎱ literal-2 ⎤ ⎱ ...
                  ⎱ VALUES ARE ⎰ ⎱          ⎣ ⎱ THRU    ⎰         ⎦ ⎰
```

Consider these two examples:

```
02 X-FLAG    PIC X.           02 WHAT-NEXT PIC X.
   88 X-ON VALUE "Y".            88 WHAT-YES   VALUE "Y", "y"
```

The elementary items are called *conditional variables* since they are *condition-names* (88 level items) associated with them. The comma between the literals is optional.

The following pairs of statements are equivalent:

```
(a) IF X-FLAG = "Y" ...         IF X-ON ...
(b) IF WHAT-NEXT = "Y" OR "y" ...  IF WHAT-YES ...
(c) MOVE "Y" TO X-FLAG          SET X-ON TO TRUE
(d) MOVE "Y" TO WHAT-NEXT       SET WHAT-YES TO TRUE
```

The SET is used in the last two pairs of statements to give the conditional variable the value of the condition-name. From the second of these we see that when the condition-name has more than one value, it is the left-most value that is assigned to the conditional variable. Many compilers also support a SET ...TO FALSE statement but we will not investigate this nonstandard feature.

In the code below, we compare two equivalent program segments.

```
            (a)                         (b)
DISPLAY "Print report? "        DISPLAY "Print report? "
ACCEPT WHAT-NEXT                ACCEPT WHAT-NEXT
IF WHAT-NEXT = "Y" OR "y"       IF WHAT-YES
    PERFORM REPORT-PARA             PERFORM REPORT-PARA
...                            ...
```

We can use condition-names to ensure that the program user inputs a valid reply.

```
        02 REPORT-CODE      PIC X  VALUE SPACES.
           88 REPORT-WEEK       VALUE "W", "w".
           88 REPORT-MONTH      VALUE "M", "m".
           88 REPORT-QUARTER    VALUE "Q", "q".
           88 REPORT-VALID      VALUE "W" "w", "M" "m", "Q" "q".
        ...
    PERFORM UNTIL REPORT-VALID
        DISPLAY "Which report do you require?"
        DISPLAY "Weekly, Monthly, or Quarterly? Reply: W/M/Q "
                NO ADVANCING
        ACCEPT REPORT-CODE
    END-PERFORM
```

Condition-names are particularly useful when we are processing data which is numerically coded. To keep the example brief we will use a few codes; the same principles apply when there are many codes, but the usefulness increases. A chemical manufacturing company keeps employer data in a file which uses these codes for job titles:

1	Engineer	2	Chemist
3	Plumber	4	Electrical
5	Mechanic	5	Clerical

You are writing a program for the personnel manager; it is difficult to remember the codes all the time. To make life more complicated some jobs are unionized and parts of your program must treat them differently. Condition-names help.

```
02 JOB-CODE      PIC 9.
   88 ENGR       VALUE 1.
   88 CHEM       VALUE 2.
   88 PLUM       VALUE 3.
   88 ELECT      VALUE 4.
   88 MECH       VALUE 5.
   88 CLERIC     VALUE 6.
   88 UNIONIZED  VALUE 3 THRU 5.
```

It is much easier to remember, for example, to code IF PLUM ..., than it is to remember that the code for plumber is 3. You no longer need to recall which jobs are unionized and the code can be shorter: IF UNIONIZED ... rather than IF JOB-CODE = 3 OR 4 OR 5 ... The data-entry clerk can also be relieved of the chore of remembering the numeric codes. We can let the clerk enter more intuitive alphanumeric code:

```
DISPLAY "Enter job title " NO ADVANCING
ACCEPT INPUT-CODE
IF INPUT-CODE = "ENGR" SET ENGR TO TRUE...
```

The last statement is more likely to be an EVALUATE which we investigate in a later chapter.

In the next example a condition-name is used within a table:

```
01 THIS-TABLE.
   02 THIS-ITEM  PIC X(8)  OCCURS 10 TIMES INDEXED BY TX.
      88 THIS-TEST   VALUE "ABC".
```

Just as we must use an index-name or a subscript to refer to a specific element in the table, so we must also use an index-name or subscript to test a condition-name:

```
IF THIS-TEST (TX) THEN .......
```

21.8 Compound Conditions

A *compound condition* is formed by:

a) negating a simple condition using NOT: NOT condition-1
b) combining simple conditions :   condition-1 AND condition-2
    condition-3 OR condition-4
c) a combination of a) and b):   condition-5 AND NOT condition-6
    NOT condition-7 AND condition-8

A compound condition is evaluated using the following rules:
   a) The order of precedence is NOT, AND, OR
   b) The order of precedence is overridden by parentheses
   c) Conditions at the same hierarchical level are evaluated left to right
   d) When a simple condition is evaluated as "false" no further evaluation of the compound condition is made.

21.8.1 Negation

As we have seen above, some of the conditions have NOT as part of their formats. For example:

```
IF X NOT EQUAL TO Y
IF ITEM-A NOT NUMERIC
```

Other simple conditions are negated by the use of the word NOT. Thus we can use condition-names in a statement such as: `IF NOT FRESHMAN`. Double negatives in COBOL, as in English, should be avoided, e.g. `IF NOT X NOT = Y`.

21.8.2 Combinations of conditions

We may combine two or more conditions; these in turn may be simple, combined or negated. Parentheses may be used in such combinations.

```
IF X = 4 AND Y = 2 …
IF X = 4 AND NOT FRESHMAN …
IF (X = 4 OR Y = 5) AND ( J NOT > 4 ) AND NOT SENIOR …
```

Unless the programmer is an expert in logic, compound conditions which combine NOT with AND/OR are best avoided. An EVALUATE statement, used in place of an IF statement, frequently makes compound conditions unnecessary.

21.8.3 Abbreviation of conditions

With relational conditions, we may use an abbreviated format:

relation-condition-1 { {<u>AND</u> / <u>OR</u>} [*relational-operator*] *object-operand* }...

In each of the following examples (a) and (b) are equivalent.

```
        (a)                              (b)
IF X = 3 OR X = 4               IF X = 3 OR 4
IF X = 3 OR X > 5 AND X < 20    IF X = 3 OR > 5 AND < 20
IF (NOT (X = Y)) OR (X = Z)     IF NOT X = Y OR Z
                                       <not recommended>
```

21.8.4 Some pitfalls to avoid

Even when we are telling the truth we do not always say what we mean. The supervisor who asks an assistant to "Get me a list of all customers who live in Halifax and Sydney" would be shocked to be given a blank page. Code such as:

```
IF   CUSTOMER-CITY = "HALIFAX" AND "SYDNEY" ...
```

will not select any records! How can an identifier have two values at the same time? The supervisor meant to say "or" rather than "and". The divergence between logic and conversational English usage gets greater when we add NOT to the statement.

Care be must exercised when coding a compound negation condition. If we wish to execute a statement when both X and Y have non-zero values, the condition will be:

```
X IS NOT ZERO AND Y IS NOT ZERO.
```

An alternative would be `NOT (X = 0 AND Y = 0)`. Will omitting the parentheses change the operation of your program? To answer that question you need to understand rule (a) above.

Be careful with compound conditions:
- use parentheses liberally
- think twice when using AND; should it be OR?
- avoid very complex conditions
- CONTINUE (Chapter 23) may sometimes be used to avoid compound NOT conditions
- use an EVALUATE rather than IF statement to simplify the conditions.

21.9 Review Questions

1* You wish to calculate FRACTION using `DIVIDE A-COUNT BY TOTAL-COUNT GIVING FRACTION`. If TOTAL-COUNT happens to have a zero value, the result of the division is undefined and FRACTION should be given a value of zero. Write code using: a)   a DIVIDE statement enclosed within an IF structure, and
            b)   using the ON SIZE ERROR phrase.

2. Give the output for the code

```
IF ITEM-A > ITEM-B
   THEN DISPLAY "True"
   ELSE DISPLAY "False"
END-IF
```

When ITEM-A has the value "SMITH" and ITEM-B has the values a) "Smith", b) "JOHNSTON", and c) SPACES.

3. Your program requires the user to type in a two-digit number. You wish to ensure that a number was, in fact, keyed in. Code the following algorithm:

> Display "Enter a two-digit number"
> Accept the reply into Item-A (PIC XX)
> Test to see if a number was entered; if so move Item-A to Item-N (PIC 99)

4* Enclose the code you wrote in question 3 within a PERFORM structure such that the program loops until the user does enter a number.

5* Modify your answer to question 4 using condition-names with ITEM-N such that the code loops until a value in the range 5 to 15 is entered.

6. Are these two statements equivalent?
    a) `IF NOT X > 5 AND < 8` do-something
    b) `IF X < 5 OR > 8 CONTINUE`
        `ELSE` do-something `END-IF`.

22
The PERFORM Verb

Objectives

- ▸ Understand the difference between an in-line and out-line PERFORM.
- ▸ Know the syntax of the four formats of the PERFORM statement.
- ▸ Understand the nesting of PERFORM statements.

22.1 Introduction

There are two types of PERFORM statements; the in-line and the out-line. Each may use one of the phrases: UNTIL, TIMES or VARYING. The forms of the two types are:

in-line: PERFORM optional-phrase
          statement-1
          statement-2
          ...
      END-PERFORM

out-line: PERFORM *procedure-name* optional-phrase

The in-line PERFORM executes the block of statements between PERFORM and END-PERFORM as many times as required by the optional phrase. Control then passes to the statement following END-PERFORM.

The out-line PERFORM verb causes transfer of control to *procedure-name*. A procedure-name may denote a single paragraph or a block of consecutive paragraphs; it may also denote a section or a block of sections. If no optional phrase is coded, control returns to the statement immediately following the current PERFORM statement when the named paragraph(s) has been executed. This is similar to GOSUB in BASIC, and to the calling of a procedure in Pascal/Modula-2. Unlike in BASIC, there is no need for a return statement at the end of the procedure; control is automatically transferred back when the end of the procedure is encountered. The PERFORM... TIMES format is like a FOR or DO loop in other languages, while PERFORM... UNTIL allows us to code DO... UNTIL and DO... WHILE constructs. ANSI COBOL does not permit recursive calls meaning that a procedure may not call itself. Some implementations of COBOL (Micro Focus COBOL, for example) do permit recursion but recursion is outside the scope of this book.

The choice of in-line or out-line format, and the optional phrase to use with it, will depend on the problem at hand and, in part, on the programmer's style. Generally, the in-line PERFORM is more appropriate when the code to be executed is short and simple. More complicated code is best put in an out-line PERFORM. When the same code is to be executed at different stages in the program, it is better to use out-line PERFORM.

The program CHAP20-1 uses two in-line performs. To demonstrate what is meant by an "out-line" perform, we will re-code the procedure division of that program.

```
PROCEDURE DIVISION.
MAIN-PARA.
    OPEN OUTPUT X-FILE.
    PERFORM REQUEST-DATA 20 TIMES
    CLOSE X-FILE    OPEN INPUT X-FILE    OUTPUT PRINTFILE
    READ X-FILE
        AT END   MOVE "Y" TO FILE-FLAG
    END-READ
    PERFORM READ-AND-WRITE UNTIL FILE-FLAG = "Y"
    CLOSE X-FILE PRINTFILE
    STOP RUN.

REQUEST-DATA.
    MOVE SPACES TO X-REC
    DISPLAY "Give first name " NO ADVANCING ACCEPT X-FIRST-NAME
    DISPLAY "Give last name "  NO ADVANCING ACCEPT X-LAST-NAME
    WRITE X-REC.
                    <there must be a period at the end of each paragraph>

READ-AND-WRITE.
    WRITE PRINT-REC FROM X-REC
    READ X-FILE
        AT END   MOVE "Y" TO FILE-FLAG
    END-READ.
```

22.2 Syntax of the PERFORM Verb

The following applies to all formats:

procedure-1 and procedure-2	Are names of procedures (paragraphs or sections) in the Procedure Division of the program in which the PERFORM occurs. A PERFORM in the main program may not reference procedures in a subprogram. The consecutive code between *procedure-1* and *procedure-2* is called the procedure set. An in-line PERFORM does not name a procedure set; the procedure set is the block of statements between PERFORM and END-PERFORM.
identifier-1, etc.	Are numeric identifiers.

literal-1, etc.   Are numeric literals.

condition-1, etc.   Are valid COBOL conditions.

THRU   May be replaced by THROUGH.

END-PERFORM   Terminates an in-line PERFORM statement. An in-line PERFORM is a PERFORM statement containing one or more imperative statements.

22.2.1 Format-1: PERFORM

```
                        Format-1:  PERFORM

    PERFORM [ procedure-name-1  [ THRU procedure-name-2 ]]
        [ imperative-statement-1  END-PERFORM ]
```

This format is generally used only for an out-line perform. For example: PERFORM PARA-A. It would be redundant to use it for an in-line perform. There is no functional difference between (a) and (b):

(a)	(b)
statement-1	PERFORM
statement-2	statement-1
	statement-2
	END-PERFORM

22.2.2 Format-2: PERFORM ... TIMES

```
                        Format-2:  PERFORM … TIMES

    PERFORM [ procedure-name-1  [ THRU procedure-name-2 ]]
        ⎰ identifier-1 ⎱ TIMES
        ⎱ integer-1    ⎰
        [ imperative-statement-1  END-PERFORM ]
```

1) If identifier-1 is negative or zero when the PERFORM is about to be executed, the procedure set is not executed. Control passes immediately to the statement which follows the PERFORM statement.

2) If identifier-1 is altered within the procedure set the number of iterations is not affected.

22.2.3 Format-3: PERFORM ... UNTIL

```
                    Format-3:  PERFORM … UNTIL

PERFORM [ procedure-name-1  [ THRU procedure-name-2 ]]
  ⎡          ⎧ BEFORE ⎫ ⎤
  ⎢ WITH TEST ⎨ AFTER  ⎬ ⎥        UNTIL condition-1
  ⎣          ⎩        ⎭ ⎦
  [ imperative-statement-1  END-PERFORM ]
```

1) The procedure set is performed whilst condition-1 is false. Care must be exercised to ensure that condition-1 will eventually become true.

2) If the TEST clause is omitted, a TEST BEFORE is implied; i.e. TEST BEFORE is the default. The TEST BEFORE clause causes the condition to be checked before each iteration. If the condition is true when the PERFORM is first entered, the procedure set is not executed.

3) When TEST AFTER is specified, the condition is checked after each iteration. The procedure set is performed at least once. With appropriate coding of the *condition-1*, the test after phrase allows us to code a DO...WHILE construct.

22.2.4 Format-4: PERFORM ... VARYING

```
                    Format-4:  PERFORM … VARYING

PERFORM [ procedure-name-1  [ THRU procedure-name-2 ]]
  ⎡          ⎧ BEFORE ⎫ ⎤
  ⎢ WITH TEST ⎨ AFTER  ⎬ ⎥
  ⎣          ⎩        ⎭ ⎦
                                    ⎧ identifier-2  ⎫
          ⎧ identifier-1 ⎫          ⎪               ⎪
  VARYING ⎨ index-name-1 ⎬  FROM    ⎨ index-name-2  ⎬
          ⎩             ⎭          ⎪ literal-2      ⎪
                                    ⎩               ⎭
     ⎧ identifier-3 ⎫
  BY ⎨ literal-2     ⎬        UNTIL condition-1
     ⎩             ⎭
  [ imperative-statement-1  END-PERFORM ]
```

1) If an index-name is used as identifier-2 in the VARYING clause then:
    a)   the FROM clause must use an integer data item or a positive numeric literal
    b)   the BY clause must use an integer data item or a nonzero literal.

2) If an index-name is used in the FROM clause then:
    a)   the VARYING clause must use an integer data item
    b)   the BY clause must use an integer data item or a positive integer literal.

3) The comments concerning TEST made in Format-3 apply. However, any change made during the execution of the procedure set to the variables of the VARYING, FROM or

BY clauses will affect the PERFORM statement.

4) This format also has an optional AFTER phrase which has been omitted from the syntax diagram because the same result can be achieved using the more intuitive method of nesting PERFORM statements.

22.3 Examples

We have seen that there are 4 formats for the PERFORM statement and that each may be used in-line or out-line. However, the reader should note that it is redundant to use Format-1 in an in-line mode. So there are 7 basic constructions. We shall look at examples of some of these.

a) Let us define GAUSS-SUM and the sum of the first 10 integers;

GAUSS-SUM = 1+2+3+4+5+6+7+8+9+10

Our task is to compute GAUSS-SUM. The following examples are used to demonstrate the PERFORM verb, some may not be ideal ways of achieving our goal. Our program code assumes these identifiers are declared:

```
03 GAUSS-SUM   PIC 999 VALUE ZERO.
03 COUNTER-N   PIC 99  VALUE ZERO.
```

(i)
```
PERFORM 10 TIMES
ADD 1 TO COUNTER-N
  ADD COUNTER-N TO GAUSS-SUM
END-PERFORM
```

(ii)
```
PERFORM UNTIL COUNTER-N > 10
  ADD 1 TO COUNTER-N
  ADD COUNTER-N TO GAUSS-SUM
END-PERFORM
```

(iii)
```
PERFORM VARYING COUNTER-N
  FROM 1 BY 1 UNTIL COUNTER-N > 10
    ADD COUNTER-N TO GAUSS-SUM
END-PERFORM
```

(iv)
```
DISPLAY "GIVE FIRST NUMBER "
ACCEPT FIRST-N
DISPLAY "GIVE LAST NUMBER "
ACCEPT LAST-N
PERFORM GAUSS-PARA
    VARYING COUNTER-N
    FROM FIRST-N
    UNTIL COUNTER-N > LAST-N.
. . . .

GAUSS-PARA.
    ADD COUNTER-N TO GAUSS-SUM
```

Clearly, example (iii) is the neatest. The first two are offered as examples of the other PERFORM formats. Example (iv) does something a little different. It is left as a task for the reader to say what it does and what problems may arise. The reader may also wish to devise a method of finding the sum of the first 100 even (or odd) integers.

b) Our next examples will perform calculations on a table. We will use the table defined by:

```
03 X-TABLE.
   05 X-ROW OCCURS 12 TIMES INDEXED BY XRX.
      07 X-COLUMN OCCURS 10 TIMES INDEXED BY XCX.
         09 X-ITEM PIC 99.
```

We may find the sum of all the X-ITEM values in the table using:

```
PERFORM VARYING XRX FROM 1 BY 1 UNTIL XRX > 12
   PERFORM VARYING XCX FROM 1 BY 1 UNTIL XCX > 10
      ADD X-ITEM (XRX XCX) TO ITEM-TOTAL
   END-PERFORM
END-PERFORM
```

The following code will find the row-total for each of the 12 rows.

```
PERFORM VARYING XRX FROM 1 BY 1 UNTIL XRX > 12
   MOVE ZERO TO ROW-TOTAL
   PERFORM VARYING XCX FROM 1 BY 1 UNTIL XCX > 10
      ADD MY-ITEM (XRX XCX) TO ROW-TOTAL
   END-PERFORM
   SET ROW-N TO XRX
   DISPLAY "Total for row " ROW-N " is " ROW-TOTAL
END-PERFORM
```

The column totals may be found using this code.

```
PERFORM VARYING MCX FROM 1 BY 1 UNTIL MCX > 10
   MOVE ZERO TO COL-TOTAL
   PERFORM VARYING MRX FROM 1 BY 1 UNTIL MRX > 12
      ADD MY-ITEM (MRX MCX) TO COL-TOTAL
   END-PERFORM
   SET COL-N TO MCX
   DISPLAY "Total for column " COL-N " is " COL-TOTAL
END-PERFORM
```

There are various algorithms for sorting a table. The simplest is the "bubble sort" which is demonstrated in the program CHAP22-1 which is on the disk. While the bubble sort is less efficient than some other methods, it is generally easier to code and fast enough for most applications.

22.4 Nesting of PERFORM Statements

If within the set of procedures of one PERFORM statement, there is another PERFORM, then the set of procedures of the second PERFORM must be totally included in, or totally excluded from, the procedures of the first. The diagrams below illustrate three valid nesting constructs. Although in the last example, m THRU p overlaps with o THRU q, the construction is valid because the first PERFORM is no longer active when the second executes.

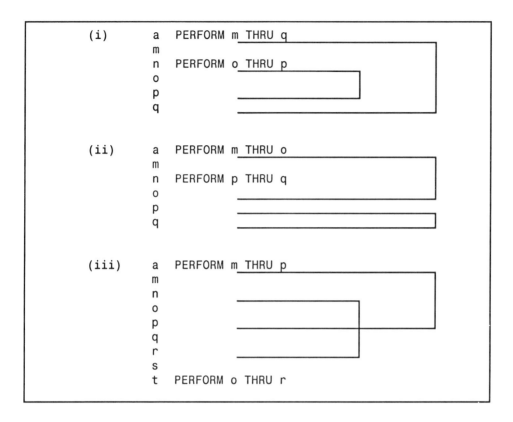

22.5 Using GO TO and EXIT

In the next example we shall break the golden rule which states "Never use a GO TO statement". Suppose we have code that executes a series of paragraphs but we needed to terminate the procedure set whenever certain conditions were true. Consider the sample code shown below. All the GO TO statements must transfer control to PARA-D such that there is a single exit point. The only statement permitted in that paragraph is the single EXIT. Even authors, such as the current one, who abhor the GO TO verb, will concede that is a valid use of that dreaded verb! Generally, however, alternative coding can be used to avoid this construction.

```
PERFORM PARA-A THROUGH PARA-D
.....

PARA-A.
    ....
    IF condition-1  THEN GO TO PARA-D END-IF
    ....

PARA-B.
    ....
```

```
IF condition-2  THEN GO TO PARA-D END-IF
   ....

PARA-C.
   ....

PARA-D.
   EXIT.
```

The programmer who codes a GO TO which transfers control anywhere outside the set of procedures of a PERFORM may be in for a nasty surprise. The compiler will not flag an error but on run-time the results can be unpredictable. The rule to remember is: "one entry point and one exit point".

COBOL also provides a GO TO ... DEPENDING ON statement, but the author does not wish to encourage the reader to use GO TO and hence provides no further details!

In Micro Focus COBOL, the EXIT PERFORM statement may be used within in an in-line PERFORM structure to terminate the perform prematurely. Similarly, an EXIT PARAGRAPH statement may be used within a paragraph to terminate that paragraph.

22.6 Review Questions

1* Given the table: MONTHLY-SALES OCCURS 12 TIMES PIC 9(4) INDEXED BY MSX
    write code to display this type of output:

    Sales for Month 1   3256
    Sales for Month 2   2467
    . . . .
    Sales for Month 12   1298

    You will need to define some more data-names.

2* Your program has the data-definition-entries
    ```
    02 EVEN-VALUE OCCURS 10 TIMES INDEXED BY EVEN-X   PIC 99
    02 LOOP-COUNTER                                   PIC 99
    ```
    Write a PERFORM structure to fill the table with the even numbers 2, 4, ... , 20.

3* Write code, without using the IF structure, for the algorithm:
    Keep adding 5 to ITEM-N until it is equal to or greater than 25. If ITEM-N is equal to or greater than 25 before the loop, add 5 anyway.

23
The IF and EVALUATE Verbs

Objectives

▸ Know the syntax of both verbs.
▸ Understand what is meant by the scope of a verb.
▸ Know the difference between NEXT SENTENCE and CONTINUE.
▸ Know the five types of subjects and objects of the EVALUATE statement and the valid combinations.

23.1 The IF Statement

The IF statement tests a condition and determines the subsequent action of the program depending upon the true value of the condition.

```
IF condition-1 THEN

    { (statement-1)... }    { ELSE (statement-2)... [END-IF] }
    { NEXT SENTENCE   }    { ELSE NEXT SENTENCE             }
                           { END-IF                         }
```

a)   Statement-1 and statement-2 may be one or more imperative or conditional statements or a combination of both.

b)   Condition-1 is any valid COBOL condition; simple or compound.

c)   The use of NEXT SENTENCE in place of sentence-1 is discussed below.

d)   ELSE NEXT SENTENCE is totally redundant and should be avoided. ANSI COBOL does not permit the use of ELSE NEXT SENTENCE and END-IF in the same statement; most compilers relax this rule.

e)   Note that the keyword THEN is optional.

f)   In some languages the IF statement has one syntax for a single-line statement and another for a multiple-line statement. This is not true of COBOL — there is one syntax.

However, the reader is encouraged to adopt a style for coding IF statements. For example:

Single statement: `IF X NOT = 0 THEN PERFORM PARA-A END-IF`

Code with one THEN and one ELSE statement is easy to understand with this style:

```
IF X = 0
    THEN PERFORM PARA-A
    ELSE PERFORM PARA-B
END-IF
```

For longer, more complex statements the following style may be used:

```
IF ITEM-X  > 0
    statement-1
    statement-2
    statement-3
ELSE
    statement-4
    statement-5
END-IF
```

23.1.1 Scope and transfer of control

The scope of an IF statement is terminated by one of:
 a) An END-IF phrase at the same level of nesting; this is the preferred method.
 b) A separator period; this is not recommended.

Transfer of control occurs as shown in Table 23-1 below:

Table 23-1 Transfer of control in an IF structure

Condition-1 is true	Condition-1 is false
Statement-1 is executed and control is then passed to the end of the IF statement.	If there is no ELSE clause, control is passed to the next executable statement following END-IF.
Or, when NEXT SENTENCE is used, control is passed directly to the next *sentence*.	If ELSE NEXT SENTENCE is used, control is passed to the next *sentence*. Otherwise, statement-2 is executed and control is then passed to the end of the IF statement.

If statement-1 or statement-2 contains a verb which causes transfer of control (IF, EVALUATE, PERFORM, etc.), then the appropriate scope-terminator (END-IF, etc.) is required.

23.1.2 NEXT SENTENCE and CONTINUE

The word CONTINUE is a special case of statement-1. One may think of it as a *do-nothing* or null statement. CONTINUE passes control to the next *statement*. NEXT SENTENCE, which is also non-operational, passes control to the next *sentence.*

Suppose we wish to execute a statement when X has a non-zero value. Two ways to code this are:

```
(a)     IF X NOT 0            (b)     IF X = 0
            THEN statement-x               THEN CONTINUE
        END-IF                             ELSE statement-x
                                       END-IF
```

The reader will now understand why ELSE NEXT SENTENCE and ELSE CONTINUE are redundant. In the author's opinion, CONTINUE is preferred over NEXT SENTENCE since the action of the latter depends very much on the placement of terminal periods. There will be occasions when NEXT SENTENCE will produce simpler code. However, if (when!) the program is later modified, one will need to be careful if new sentences are added. Conversely, when the IF statement is contained within another statement (e.g. within a PERFORM or EVALUATE), it may be most inappropriate to use NEXT SENTENCE. To avoid complications it is better to adopt a programming standard. Since CONTINUE may always be used, let us agree to abandon NEXT SENTENCE with all its complications.

23.1.3 Nesting of IF statements

Since statement-1 and statement-2 may be conditional statements, it follows that the IF statement may be nested as shown in example (iii). However, it is generally better to use the EVALUATE verb rather than nested IFs since the code is more readable and hence less prone to logic errors. The action of Example (iii) is duplicated in Example (x) using EVALUATE.

```
Example (iii)    IF X = 0
                     THEN    IF Y = 0
                                 THEN    DISPLAY "X = 0 and Y = 0"
                                 ELSE    DISPLAY "X = 0 but Y <> 0"
                             END-IF
                     ELSE    IF Y = 0
                                 THEN    DISPLAY "X <> 0 but Y = 0"
                                 ELSE    DISPLAY "Neither X nor Y is zero"
                             END-IF
                 END-IF
```

23.2 The EVALUATE Statement

The EVALUATE statement is a very flexible and useful alternative to complex and nested IF statements. The programmer should become familiar with all its features. To get an appreciation of how EVALUATE works, look through the examples which follow before studying the syntax and rules. EVALUATE is similar to the CASE construct of other languages.

The syntax of the EVALUATE statement may be written as:

```
EVALUATE  subject-1 [ALSO  subject-2 ]…
   WHEN     object-1  [ALSO object-2]…imperative statement-1
   [WHEN    object-3  [ALSO object-4]…imperative statement-2 ]…
   [WHEN OTHER         imperative-statement-3 ]
[END-EVALUATE ]
```

The six formats for subjects and the seven for objects are:

Subject format	Object format
(1) identifier-1	(a) [NOT] identifier-1 [THRU identifier-3]
(2) literal-1	(b) [NOT] literal-2 [THRU literal-3]
(3) arithmetic- expression-1	(c) [NOT] arithmetic-expression-2 [THRU arithmetic-expression-3]
(4) TRUE	(d) TRUE
(5) FALSE	(e) FALSE
(6) condition-1	(f) condition-2
	(g) ANY

However, for any given choice of subject type, not all object types are appropriate. The valid combinations of subject/object pairs are:

Subject types	Valid Object types
(1) identifier-1	(a) [NOT] identifier-1 [THRU identifier-3] (b) [NOT] literal-2 [THRU literal-3] (c) [NOT] arithmetic-expression-2 [THRU arithmetic-expression-3]
(2) literal-1	(a) [NOT] identifier-1 [THRU identifier-3] (c) [NOT] arithmetic-expression-2 [THRU arithmetic-expression-3]
(3) arithmetic- expression-1	(a) [NOT] identifier-1 [THRU identifier-3] (b) [NOT] literal-2 [THRU literal-3]
(4) TRUE	(f) condition-2
(5) FALSE	(f) condition-2
(6) condition-1	(d) TRUE (e) FALSE
all subject types	(g) ANY

The following rules apply; they will become clearer as we use the EVALUATE statement.

1) Identifiers, literals and arithmetic expressions must yield valid operands for a comparison of the subject/object pair. Thus, for example, a numeric identifier as a subject cannot be compared with an alphanumeric object. The figurative constant ZERO may be used as either a numeric or an alphanumeric item.

2) The word ANY may be used as an object item of a subject of any type. In this case the test of subject against object is always satisfied.

3) When the ALSO phrase is used, the number of objects must match the number of subjects.

23.2.1 Transfer of control in an EVALUATE statement

The scope of an EVALUATE statement is terminated by either an END-EVALUATE or a separator period. It is important to understand when control is transferred out of the EVALUATE statement. As soon as the first subject/object match has been found, its associated imperative statement is executed, the EVALUATE statement is terminated. There could be subsequent matches but these will not be tested. Thus in Example (vi) below, if both X and Y have a value of zero, only PARA-A will be performed. For PARA-B to be performed, X must be other than zero and Y must equal zero. It is crucial that the programmer carefully thinks out the correct order in which to code the WHEN phrases.

23.2.2 Examples of EVALUATE statements

Let ITEM-N be a numeric identifier. We wish to perform different statements depending on the value of ITEM-N. We could, of course, use a series of nested IF..ELSE statements. EVALUATE provides a more flexible alternative to IF statements. The following statement is self explanatory. In this example the subject (ITEM-N) is a numeric identifier. The objects in the first three WHEN phrases are literals. The object in the third is a range of values.

```
Example (iv) EVALUATE  ITEM-N
             WHEN   1          DISPLAY "ITEM-N = 1"
             WHEN   2          DISPLAY "ITEM-N = 2"
             WHEN   3 THRU 5   DISPLAY "ITEM-N is between 3 and 5"
             WHEN   OTHER      DISPLAY "ITEM-N = 0 or ITEM-N > 5"
           END-EVALUATE
```

When the subject is a nonnumeric identifier we must use nonnumeric object literals. Let ITEM-A have a picture of X.

```
Example (v) EVALUATE   ITEM-A
            WHEN   "A" THRU "C" DISPLAY "ITEM-A is A or B or C"
            WHEN   "D"          DISPLAY "ITEM-A is D"
            WHEN   "E" THRU "Z" DISPLAY "ITEM-A has E through Z"
            WHEN   OTHER DISPLAY "ITEM-A is not uppercase letter"
          END-EVALUATE
```

The object (OTHER) in the final phrase, is a "catch-all" object. The statement associated with this phrase is performed only when no match is found in any preceding WHEN phrases. Note that the WHEN OTHER phrase is syntactically optional.

The subject in Example (vi) is "TRUE". The objects are conditions. If one wishes to use a condition as an object, the subject must be TRUE or FALSE; the converse is also true. Example (vii) is invalid.

```
Example (vi)    EVALUATE   TRUE
                    WHEN   X = ZERO   PERFORM   PARA-A
                    WHEN   Y = 0      PERFORM   PARA-B
                    WHEN   X > 5      PERFORM   PARA-C
                END-EVALUATE
```

```
Example (vii)   EVALUATE   ITEM-N
                    WHEN   > 1    PERFORM   PARA-A      <invalid>
```

Recall that an "imperative-statement" may be a series of imperative statements. So we could code:

```
Example (viii)   EVALUATE   TRUE
                     WHEN   END-OF-FILE
                               DISPLAY "At end of file"
                               CLOSE MY-FILE
                     WHEN   STUDENT-NAME = "MACDONALD"
                               IF STUDENT-GNAME = "JOHN"
                                   THEN DISPLAY "Found JOHN MACDONALD"
                               END-IF
                 END-EVALUATE
```

In the first comparison we have two imperative statements. In the second we make the otherwise conditional IF statement to be imperative by using an END-IF.

There may be occasions when you wish no further comparisons to be made when a specified match is found but you also need the program to take no action at that point other than to pass control to the statement following the EVALUATE. This may be achieved by using CONTINUE as the imperative statement. In the next example the program will inform the user that $X = Y$ only when they are equal and non-zero.

```
Example (ix)    EVALUATE   TRUE
                    WHEN   X = 0 AND Y = 0   CONTINUE
                    WHEN   X = Y             DISPLAY "X equals Y"
                END-EVALUATE
```

Example (x) Compare this EVALUATE statement with the nested IFs in Example (iii) above.

```
                EVALUATE   X       ALSO   Y
                    WHEN   0       ALSO   0     DISPLAY "X = 0   and Y = 0 "
                    WHEN   0       ALSO   ANY   DISPLAY "X = 0   but Y <> 0"
```

```
        WHEN   ANY    ALSO   0      DISPLAY "X <> 0 but Y = 0 "
        WHEN   OTHER              DISPLAY "Neither X nor Y is zero"
    END-EVALUATE
```

This code is much easier to follow than that in (iii). It is therefore more likely that the programmer will achieve the desired logic using this construction rather than nested IFs.

Arithmetic expressions are composed of numeric identifiers, numeric literals and arithmetic symbols. Some examples are:

```
(i)    X + 4
(ii)   (ITEM-N - 5) / (ITEM-NN * 3)
(iii)  ITEM-N ** 2                    < ITEM-N squared >
```

Example (xi) These examples show the use of arithmetic expressions. The (a) form with an arithmetic expression as the object is less likely to be used than the (b) form where the subject is an arithmetic expression.

```
(a) EVALUATE ITEM-N
        WHEN  (X + 3) / 4    DISPLAY "ITEM-N equals (X+3)/4"
        ...
```

```
(b) EVALUATE (X + 3) / 4
        WHEN  5              DISPLAY "Expression = 5"
        WHEN  10 THRU 15     DISPLAY "Expression has value 10 to 15"
        WHEN  ITEM-N         DISPLAY "Expression = ITEM-N"
        WHEN  ZERO           DISPLAY "Expression has value of zero"
        ...
```

Note the use of the figurative constant ZERO in the last WHEN clause. We could have used this in all previous examples in place of "0", the zero digit.

Example (xii) Suppose we have the data description ITEM-N PIC 9. We expect ITEM-N to have a value in the range 1 to 9 and we code this EVALUATE statement as:

```
    EVALUATE  ITEM-N
        WHEN   1 THRU 5  DISPLAY "ITEM-N in range 1 to 5"
        WHEN   6 THRU 9  DISPLAY "ITEM-N in range 6 to 9"
    END-EVALUATE
```

What will happen if ITEM-N has the value 0? This case is not covered by any WHEN clause. In some languages a CASE construction generates a run-time error when no case is true. These languages require an explicit ELSE to handle unexpected values. In COBOL, we may include a WHEN OTHER clause but it is not required by the syntax. In the example, since no case is true with ITEM-N = 0, no statement within the EVALUATE construction will be executed. The program will continue at the statement following END-EVALUATE.

23.3 Review Questions

1* Correct this code:
```
IF MONTH < 4
    DISPLAY "First Quarter"
    IF MONTH = 1    DISPLAY "First Month of Quarter"
ELSE IF MONTH < 7
    DISPLAY "Second Quarter"
    IF MONTH = 4    DISPLAY "First Month of Quarter"
ELSE IF MONTH < 10
    DISPLAY "Third Quarter"
    IF MONTH = 7    DISPLAY "First Month of Quarter"
ELSE
    DISPLAY "Fourth Quarter"
    IF MONTH = 10   DISPLAY "First Month of Quarter"
END-IF.
```

2* Compare these two segments of code; note the period on the sixth line of each. What will be the output in each case if X has a value of 5?

```
        A.                          B.
IF X > 0                    IF X > 0
    CONTINUE                    NEXT SENTENCE
ELSE                        ELSE
    DISPLAY "X is 0"            DISPLAY "X is 0"
END-IF                      END-IF
DISPLAY "X = " X.           DISPLAY "X = " X.
DISPLAY "All done"          DISPLAY "All done"
```

3* Redo the corrected code in question 1 using one or two EVALUATE statements.

4* In an application, only certain values for ITEM-1, ITEM-2 and ITEM-3, and combinations thereof, are valid. These are:

ITEM-1	ITEM-2	ITEM-3
-20 to 0	"COLD"	0
1 to 20	"WARM"	1
21 to 40	"HOT"	any number

Write an EVALUATE statement to display "Valid" or "Invalid" as appropriate.

24
The SEARCH Verb

Objectives

▸ Know the use of the sequential SEARCH statement.
▸ Understand the need to use a SET statement before a SEARCH.

24.1 Introduction

In section 18.5 of Chapter 18 we had a table called MONTH-TABLE. Since the months of the year have a defined sequence (January = 1 , February = 2, etc.), it is very easy to generate the name of the month from a data item's numeric value. Thus, for example: DISPLAY MONTH (3) will display "March". Generally, there is not a unique ordinal position for each member of a set of data items. For example, which is the fifth province? Even if we arranged the names of the 50 U.S. States alphabetically, who could recall which was, say, the 18th state. Clearly, we need another way to handle data like this.

In Example 3 of section 18.6 in Chapter 18, we used a PERFORM loop together with an IF statement, to find a province name from its abbreviation. We could also have used an EVALUATE statement with twelve WHEN clauses. Either approach is fairly efficient for such a small table, but not for a long table such as one containing the 50 U.S. States. The following example shows a third method: the SEARCH statement. This is a more efficient method for short or long tables. Note that when the SEARCH statement is used, the table must define an index-name.

```
Example 1:  01 PROVINCES-OF-CANADA.
               03 PROVINCE-VALUES.
                  05    PIC X(30) VALUE "NF Newfoundland".
                  05    PIC X(30) VALUE "NS Nova Scotia".
                  05    PIC X(30) VALUE "PE Prince Edward Island".
                  05    PIC X(30) VALUE "NB New Brunswick".
                  05    PIC X(30) VALUE "PQ Quebec".
                  05    PIC X(30) VALUE "ON Ontario".
                  05    PIC X(30) VALUE "MN Manitoba".
                  05    PIC X(30) VALUE "SK Saskatchewan".
                  05    PIC X(30) VALUE "AB Alberta".
                  05    PIC X(30) VALUE "BC British Columbia".
                  05    PIC X(30) VALUE "YK Yukon".
                  05    PIC X(30) VALUE "NT North West Territories".
```

```
03 PROVINCE-TABLE REDEFINES PROVINCE-VALUES.
   05 PROVINCE OCCURS 12 TIMES INDEXED BY PX.
      07 PROV-ABREV   PIC X(2).
      07              PIC X.
      07 PROV-NAME PIC X(27).


SET PX TO 1                        < carefully note this statement >
SEARCH  PROVINCE
   AT END
      DISPLAY "Not found in table " ADDRESS-PROV
   WHEN ADDRESS-PROV = PROV-ABREV (PX)
      MOVE PROV-NAME (PX) TO OUTPUT-PROVINCE
END-SEARCH
```

Using the same table, the following code may be used to check that a value in ADDRESS-PROV is valid.

Example 2:
```
SET PX TO 1
SEARCH  PROVINCE
   AT END   DISPLAY "Not found in table " ADDRESS-PROV
   WHEN     ADDRESS-PROV = PROV-ABREV (PX) CONTINUE
END-SEARCH
```

The following should be noted:

a) We start by setting the table index to 1 to specify that we wish to search the entire table. If we wish to search only part we could set the index to the starting position.

b) *The data item we searched was the one with the OCCURS phrase.* This is the only case when we may reference such an item without the use of an index or subscript. We could not use the SEARCH statement if the INDEX BY phrase had been omitted from the table definition.

c) The AT END clause is optional. It should be used when it is important to know that the search failed to locate a match.

d) The WHEN clause operates similarly to the WHEN in an EVALUATE statement. Thus once a match is found, the search is terminated and control passes to the next statement. It is permitted to include more than one WHEN clause in the SEARCH statement; this would not be appropriate in our example.

In Example 1 we have used the *serial* format of the SEARCH verb. The search begins by comparing ADDRESS-PROV with the first value of PROV-ABREV (it started here because we set PX to 1 just before the SEARCH statement). Comparison is made with the second, the third, etc. entry until either a match is found or the end of the table is encountered. The *binary* search will be considered later.

24.2 Format-1: Serial SEARCH

```
                        Format-1: Serial SEARCH

        SEARCH identifier-1

            ⎡           ⎧ index-name-1 ⎫ ⎤
            ⎢ VARYING   ⎨              ⎬ ⎥
            ⎣           ⎩ identifier-2 ⎭ ⎦

            [ AT END imperative-statement-1 ]

            ⎧                ⎧ imperative-statement-2 ⎫ ⎫
            ⎨ WHEN condition-1 ⎨                      ⎬ ⎬ ...
            ⎩                ⎩ NEXT SENTENCE          ⎭ ⎭

            [ END-SEARCH ]
```

It can be seen that there must be at least one WHEN clause. If NEXT SENTENCE is used, control passes to the next *sentence*; if the imperative statement is CONTINUE, then control passes to the next *statement*. See the comments in Chapter 18 on the use of NEXT SENTENCE and CONTINUE.

index-name   It was noted in the Chapter 18 (Tables), that an OCCURS phrase may have one or more index-names. In a serial search, the first (or only) index-name is incremented with each comparison. When the search is terminated by a successful WHEN, this index-name has a value equal to the occurrence number of the table item which satisfied the condition. If a search terminates without satisfying a condition, the value in the index-name is out of range.

VARYING   The VARYING clause causes both the first index-name in the table and another index, or identifier, to be incremented. If another index-name is used, it may be an index-name associated with the table being searched or with another table. If an identifier is varied, it may be an integer numeric data item or an index data item (i.e. one with USAGE INDEX). When VARYING is used, the first index name associated with the searched table is incremented at the same time as the "varied" item.

The following example will demonstrate the use of VARYING in the SEARCH statement and the use of two index-names.

Suppose we have a table which is only partially full — elements with an occurrence number greater than N contain only spaces. We need to know the occurrence number N, perhaps so that later in the program we can print out the first N elements in the table.

Example 3:   B-ITEM OCCURS 10 TIMES INDEXED BY BX1 BX2 PIC X(10).

To locate the first blank entry we may use code such as given in (a) or (b).

```
        (a)                           (b)

SET BX1 TO 1                  SET BX1 BX2 TO 1
SEARCH B-ITEM                 SEARCH B-ITEM   VARYING BX2
   WHEN B-ITEM (BX1) = SPACES    WHEN  B-ITEM  (BX1)  =  SPACES
            CONTINUE                      CONTINUE
END-SEARCH                    END-SEARCH
SET BX2 TO BX1                SET BX2 DOWN BY 1
SET BX2 DOWN BY 1
```

Later in the program, we may use the value of BX2, the occurrence number of the last non-blank entry.

```
PERFORM VARYING BX 1 FROM 1 BY 1 UNTIL BX1 > BX2
   DISPLAY B-ITEM (BX1)
END-PERFORM
```

The next example shows a use for varying the index name of a second table. In place of PROVINCE-TABLE shown above, suppose that we had two tables:

```
01 TABLE-A.
   03 PROV-ABREV OCCURS 12 TIMES INDEX BY PAX PIC X(2).
01 TABLE-B.
   03 PROV-NAME  OCCURS 12 TIMES INDEX BY PNX PIC X(23).
```

There is a correspondence between the two tables such that the value in the Nth occurrence number in TABLE-A is the abbreviation of the province names in the Nth occurrence number in TABLE-B.

Example 4 will produce the same results as Example 1. Please note that this is only a simple example to show a use of the VARYING clause: it is not a recommended way of doing things.

```
Example 4:  SET PAX PNX TO 1
            SEARCH  PROV-ABREV VARYING PNX
               AT END
                      DISPLAY "Not found in table " ADDRESS-PROV
               WHEN ADDRESS-PROV = PROV-ABREV (PAX)
                      MOVE PROV-NAME (PNX) TO OUTPUT-PROVINCE
            END-SEARCH
```

To search completely a multidimensional table, it is necessary to execute the search within a perform-loop or within a search. Thus with a two dimensional table, the first search will vary the first dimension (i.e. the index name associated with the table item with the lower level number). The second search will vary the index name of the subordinate identifier.

The table below shows part of the data in TABLE-STORE.

Department	List of employees			
Shipping	Mike	John	Mary	Elizabeth
Sales	Roseanne	Jennifer	Frank	Harry
Bookkeeping	Alice	Paul	Douglas	George

```
01 TABLE-STORE.
   03 TABLE-DEPARTMENT OCCURS 8 TIMES INDEXED BY DEPTX.
    05 DEPARTMENT PIC X(20).
    05 EMPLOYEE   PIC X(20) OCCURS 10 TIMES INDEXED BY EMPX.
```

Example 5:   In this example we need to know the department in which an employee works.

```
DISPLAY "Enter employee name " NO ADVANCING
ACCEPT ASK-EMPLOYEE
MOVE "N" TO GOT-IT
PERFORM VARYING DEPTX FROM 1 BY 1
                  UNTIL DEPTX > 8 OR GOT-IT = "Y"
    SET EMPX TO 1
    SEARCH EMPLOYEES
       WHEN EMPLOYEE (DEPTX EMPX) = ASK-EMPLOYEE
                  MOVE "Y" TO GOT-IT
    END-SEARCH
END-PERFORM
IF GOT-IT = "Y"
    DISPLAY ASK-EMPLOYEE " works in " DEPARTMENT (DEPTX)
ELSE
    DISPLAY ASK-EMPLOYEE " not found in table"
END-IF
```

Example 6:   Perhaps we need to know if an employee works in a certain department.

```
DISPLAY "Enter employee name " NO ADVANCING
ACCEPT ASK-EMPLOYEE
DISPLAY "Enter department " NO ADVANCING
ACCEPT ASK-DEPARTMENT
SET DEPTX
SEARCH TABLE-DEPARTMENT
    AT END       DISPLAY ASK-DEPARTMENT " is invalid"
    WHEN ASK-DEPARTMENT = DEPARTMENT (DEPTX)
        SET EMPX TO 1
        SEARCH EMPLOYEES
           AT END
               DISPLAY ASK-EMPLOYEE " not located in table"
           WHEN EMPLOYEE (DEPTX EMPX) = ASK-EMPLOYEE
               DISPLAY
                 "Employee works in " DEPARTMENT (DEPTX)
        END-SEARCH
END-SEARCH
```

Example 7:   You are running a small store in a Canadian airport where customers pay using various currencies. You need a program to convert, for example, 5 UK pounds to Canadian dollars. Since the rate of exchange varies daily, you have placed the exchange data in a file which you update daily. The file format with some sample data is shown below. The first record indicates that one US dollar is worth $1.4037 Canadian.

Currency code	Rate PIC 9V999	Blank space	Text
US	14037		US dollars
UK	21778		UK pounds

The program below shows how this file can be read into a table and used in a simple program.

```
1     IDENTIFICATION DIVISION.
2     PROGRAM-ID.      CHAP24-1.
3   * Program to compute value of foreign currency
4     ENVIRONMENT DIVISION.
5     INPUT-OUTPUT SECTION.
6     FILE-CONTROL.
7         SELECT RATE-FILE ASSIGN TO DISK "CHAP24-1.DAT"
8             ORGANIZATION LINE SEQUENTIAL.
9
10    DATA DIVISION.
11    FILE SECTION.
12    FD RATE-FILE.
13    01 RATE-REC.
14        02 RATE-CODE      PIC X(5).
15        02 RATE-NOTE      PIC X(24).
16        02 RATE-RATE      PIC 9V9(6).
17    WORKING-STORAGE SECTION.
18    01 FLAG-ITEMS.
19        02 FILE-FLAG      PIC X VALUE "N".
20            88 EOF   VALUE "Y".
21    01 INPUT-ITEMS        VALUE SPACES.
22        02 INPUT-CODE     PIC X(4).
23        02 INPUT-AMOUNT   PIC 9999.
24    01 OUTPUT-ITEMS.
25        02 OUTPUT-AMOUNT  PIC ZZZZ9.
26        02               PIC X         VALUE SPACES.
27        02 OUTPUT-NOTE    PIC X(25).
28        02               PIC X(10)   VALUE " is worth ".
29        02 OUTPUT-CANADA  PIC ZZZZ9.99.
30        02               PIC X(17)   VALUE " Canadian dollars".
31    01 EXCHANGE-TABLE     VALUE SPACES.
32        02 EXCHANGE-DATA OCCURS 50 TIMES INDEXED BY EX.
33            03 EXCHANGE-CODE      PIC X(5).
34            03 EXCHANGE-NOTE      PIC X(24).
35            03 EXCHANGE-RATE      PIC 9V9(6).
```

```
36
37    PROCEDURE DIVISION.
38    MAIN-PARA.
39        PERFORM INITIALIZE-TABLE
40        PERFORM PROCESS-PARA TEST AFTER UNTIL INPUT-CODE = SPACES
41        STOP RUN.
42
43    INITIALIZE-TABLE.
44        OPEN INPUT RATE-FILE
45        SET EX TO 1
46        READ RATE-FILE AT END SET EOF TO TRUE END-READ
47        PERFORM UNTIL EOF
48            MOVE RATE-REC TO EXCHANGE-DATA (EX)
49            SET EX UP BY 1
50            READ RATE-FILE AT END SET EOF TO TRUE END-READ
51        END-PERFORM
52        CLOSE RATE-FILE.
53
54    PROCESS-PARA.
55        INITIALIZE INPUT-ITEMS
56        DISPLAY "Enter currency code > " NO ADVANCING
57        ACCEPT INPUT-CODE
58        IF INPUT-CODE NOT = SPACES
59            PERFORM LOOKUP-PARA
60        END-IF.
61
62    LOOKUP-PARA.
63        SET EX TO 1
64        SEARCH EXCHANGE-DATA
65            AT END      DISPLAY "Invalid code"
66            WHEN EXCHANGE-CODE (EX) = INPUT-CODE
67                PERFORM REPORT-PARA
68        END-SEARCH.
69
70    REPORT-PARA.
71        DISPLAY "Enter amount        > " NO ADVANCING
72        ACCEPT INPUT-AMOUNT
73        COMPUTE OUTPUT-CANADA ROUNDED =
74                INPUT-AMOUNT * EXCHANGE-RATE (EX)
75        MOVE INPUT-AMOUNT      TO OUTPUT-AMOUNT
76        MOVE EXCHANGE-NOTE (EX) TO OUTPUT-NOTE
77        DISPLAY OUTPUT-ITEMS.
```

Example 8: You are conducting a study on fish catches. Your data file for the year contains thousands of records. A typical record looks like this:

```
01/01/94  YARMOUTH  COD          1000
01/01/94  YARMOUTH  HADDOCK      0500
```

The first record shows that on certain day at one port, 1000 pounds of cod was landed. You wish to summarize the data giving the total catch for the year for each fish species. For the sake of brevity, we will assume there are 5 species involved. We will need a table in the form:

```
01 TOTAL-INFO.
   02 TOTAL-FILLER.
      03 PIC X(15)    VALUE "COD       000000".
      03 PIC X(15)    VALUE "MACKEREL 000000".
      03 PIC X(15)    VALUE "HALIBUT  000000".
      03 PIC X (15)   VALUE "HAKE      000000".
      03 PIC X(15)    VALUE "HERRING  000000".
   02 TOTAL-TABLE REDEFINES TOTAL-FILLER
      03 TOTAL-DATA OCCURS 5 TIMES INDEXED BY TX.
         04 TOTAL-TYPE   PIC X(9).
         04 TOTAL-LAND   PIC 9(6).
```

Let the fields in the file containing the type and amount of fish have the names FISH-TYPE and FISH-LAND, respectively. For each record read we will process this paragraph:

```
SET TX TO 1
SEARCH TOTAL-DATA
   AT END    DISPLAY "Invalid type " FISH-TYPE
   WHEN TOTAL-TYPE (TX) = FISH-TYPE
        ADD FISH-LAND TO TOTAL-LAND (TX)
END-SEARCH
```

Example 9:   Consider this problem: We have a file containing data on phone calls made in a certain time period. We wish to know which cities were called and how many calls were made to each. It would be impractical to code a table with all possible cities. So we use a different approach. We start with a blank table and add the data as needed.

```
1    IDENTIFICATION DIVISION.
2    PROGRAM-ID.    CHAP24-2.
3  *    Program to report phone calls by city
4
5    ENVIRONMENT DIVISION.
6    INPUT-OUTPUT SECTION.
7    FILE-CONTROL.
8        SELECT PHONE-FILE ASSIGN TO DISK "CHAP24-2.DAT"
9              ORGANIZATION LINE SEQUENTIAL.
10   DATA DIVISION.
11   FILE SECTION.
12   FD PHONE-FILE.
13   01 PHONE-REC.
14       02 PHONE-DATE      PIC 9(6).
15       02                 PIC XX.
16       02 PHONE-COST      PIC 99V99.
17       02                 PIC XX.
18       02 PHONE-CITY      PIC X(14).
19   WORKING-STORAGE SECTION.
20   01 FLAG-ITEMS.
21       02 FILE-FLAG       PIC X VALUE "N".
```

```
22              88 EOF   VALUE "Y".
23  01 STAT-TABLE    VALUE SPACES.
24      02 STAT-DATA OCCURS 1000 TIMES   INDEXED BY SX.
25          03 STAT-CITY        PIC X(20).
26          03 STAT-COUNT       PIC 9(4).
27          03 STAT-COST        PIC 9(4)V99.
28  01 CITY-COUNT               PIC 999 VALUE 0.
29  01 OUTPUT-REC.
30      02 OUTPUT-CITY          PIC X(20).
31      02                      PIC XX        VALUE SPACES.
32      02 OUTPUT-COUNT         PIC ZZZ9.
33      02                      PIC XX        VALUE SPACES.
34      02 OUTPUT-COST          PIC $$$,$$9.99.
35
36  PROCEDURE DIVISION.
37  MAIN-PARA.
38      PERFORM FILL-TABLE
39      PERFORM REPORT-PARA
40      STOP RUN.
41
42  FILL-TABLE.
43      INITIALIZE STAT-TABLE
44      OPEN INPUT PHONE-FILE
45      READ PHONE-FILE AT END SET EOF TO TRUE END-READ
46      PERFORM UNTIL EOF
47          PERFORM LOOKUP-PARA
48          READ PHONE-FILE AT END SET EOF TO TRUE END-READ
49      END-PERFORM
50      CLOSE PHONE-FILE.
51
52  LOOKUP-PARA.
53      SET SX TO 1
54      SEARCH STAT-DATA
55          AT END      DISPLAY "Table is full !!!"
56          WHEN STAT-CITY (SX) = PHONE-CITY
57                  ADD 1            TO STAT-COUNT (SX)
58                  ADD PHONE-COST   TO STAT-COST(SX)
59          WHEN STAT-CITY (SX) = SPACES
60                  MOVE PHONE-CITY  TO STAT-CITY (SX)
61                  ADD  1           TO STAT-COUNT (SX) CITY-COUNT
62                  MOVE PHONE-COST  TO STAT-COST(SX)
63      END-SEARCH.
64
65  REPORT-PARA.
66      PERFORM VARYING SX FROM 1 BY 1 UNTIL SX > CITY-COUNT
67          MOVE STAT-CITY (SX)   TO OUTPUT-CITY
68          MOVE STAT-COUNT (SX)  TO OUTPUT-COUNT
69          MOVE STAT-COST (SX)   TO OUTPUT-COST
70          DISPLAY OUTPUT-REC
71      END-PERFORM.
```

Let the city in the first record be LONDON. Since the table is empty at this point, the first WHEN clause in LOOKUP-PARA cannot be true but the second one will be. This will add that city name to the table and increment the count by one. Every new city will be handled the same way. When a city occurs the second and subsequent times in the file, the first WHEN clause will process the record. The AT END clause will be executed only if we have more cities than the table size (1000) permits.

The output would be more useful if we first sorted the data file, this is covered in the next chapter.

24.3 Format-2: Binary Search

```
                        Format-2:  Binary SEARCH

 SEARCH ALL identifier-1

     [ AT END imperative-statement-1 ]


              ⎧           ⎧ IS EQUAL TO ⎫  ⎧ identifier-1            ⎫ ⎫
     WHEN ⎨ data-name-1 ⎨ IS =        ⎬  ⎨ literal-1               ⎬ ⎬
              ⎩           ⎩             ⎭  ⎩ arithmetic-expression-1 ⎭ ⎭
              ⎩ condition-name-1


      ⎡      ⎧           ⎧ IS EQUAL TO ⎫  ⎧ identifier-2            ⎫ ⎫ ⎤
      ⎢ AND ⎨ data-name-2 ⎨ IS =        ⎬  ⎨ literal-2               ⎬ ⎬ ⎥ ...
      ⎢      ⎩           ⎩             ⎭  ⎩ arithmetic-expression-2 ⎭ ⎭ ⎦
      ⎣      ⎩ condition-name-2

     ⎧ imperative-statement-2 ⎫
     ⎨ NEXT SENTENCE          ⎬
     ⎩                        ⎭

     [ END-SEARCH ]
```

data-name-1 data-name-2	each must be indexed by the first index-name associated with identifier-1.
identifier-1 identifier-2	must not be referenced in the KEY IS clause of identifier-1 or indexed by the first index-name associated with identifier-1.
condition-name-1 condition-name-2	must be single valued condition-names (level 88) associated with identifier-1.
Binary Search	In a binary search, the table is successively divided into two parts until a match is found. Just as a binary sort is more efficient than a bubble sort when a large number of items are involved, a binary search is faster, on average, than a serial search. To use a binary search the searched item in the table must be a key and the values of this item must be in order, ascending or descending.

```
Example 10:    01 PROVINCES-OF-CANADA.
                  03 PROVINCE-VALUES.
                     05    PIC X(30) VALUE "AB Alberta".
                     05    PIC X(30) VALUE "BC British Columbia".
                     05    PIC X(30) VALUE "MN Manitoba".
                     05    PIC X(30) VALUE "NB New Brunswick".
                     05    PIC X(30) VALUE "NF Newfoundland".
                     05    PIC X(30) VALUE "NS Nova Scotia".
                     05    PIC X(30) VALUE "NT North West Territories".
                     05    PIC X(30) VALUE "ON Ontario".
                     05    PIC X(30) VALUE "PE Prince Edward Island".
                     05    PIC X(30) VALUE "PQ Quebec".
                     05    PIC X(30) VALUE "SK Saskatchewan".
                     05    PIC X(30) VALUE "YK Yukon".
                  03 PROVINCE-TABLE REDEFINES PROVINCE-VALUES.
                     05 PROVINCE OCCURS 12 TIMES
                        ASCENDING KEY IS PROV-ABREV INDEXED BY PX.
                           07 PROV-ABREV  PIC X(2).
                           07 FILLER      PIC X.
                           07 PROV-NAME   PIC X(27).

               SEARCH ALL PROVINCE
                   AT END
                       DISPLAY "Not found in table " ADDRESS-PROV
                   WHEN PROV-ABREV (PX) = ADDRESS-PROV
                       MOVE PROV-NAME (PX) TO OUTPUT-PROVINCE
               END-SEARCH
```

A binary search can be more efficient than a serial search especially when the table is large — 50 or more elements. However, it is less flexible. The data must be stored in ascending or descending order. This is not always convenient or possible. There can be but one WHEN clause in a binary search, and the condition is limited to an equality. Furthermore, one must be careful to correctly code the equality. Whereas in Example 1, we had the option to use:

either   (a) WHEN PROV-ABREV (PX) = ADDRESS-PROV
or   (b) WHEN ADDRESS-PROV = PROV-ABREV (PX)

in Example 10, the syntax requires we use (a) since PROV-ABREV is the KEY data item associated with the identifier PROVINCE.

24.4 Review Questions

1. What is the advantage of a Binary Search over a Serial Search?

2. State what must be present in the data-description-entry of a table if we wish to use a SEARCH statement with it?

3. A table is defined by:

```
02  COUNTRY-TABLE OCCURS 50 TIMES INDEXED BY CX.
    03  COUNTRY-CODE     PIC XX.
    03                   PIC X(5).
    03  COUNTRY-CAPITAL  PIC X(20).
```

and contains data such as:

```
        UK      LONDON
        FR      PARIS
        CH      BERN
```

Write a serial SEARCH statement that will check that TEST-CODE is in the table and that TEST-CAPITAL correctly corresponds with TEST-CODE. Display "Valid" or "Invalid" as appropriate.

25
The SORT and MERGE Verbs

Objectives

▸ Know the SD entry required in the FILE SECTION for a sort-file.
▸ Understand the concept of primary, secondary, etc. keys.
▸ Know the four forms of the SORT verb.

25.1 The SORT Verb

The purpose of the SORT verb is to sort file records into a defined order. Within the SORT statement, one or more of the data items of the record are declared to be *keys*; the records are sorted according to the value of the keys. The first key is the primary key, the second is the secondary key, etc. We can require that the sort place the records in ascending or descending order of each key.

```
SORT file-name-1

   { ON { ASCENDING  } KEY { data-item-1 }... }...
   {      DESCENDING                          }

   [ WITH DUPLICATES IN ORDER ]

   [ COLLATING SEQUENCE IS alphabet-name ]

   { INPUT PROCEDURE IS procedure-name-1  [ THRU procedure-name-2 ] }
   { USING { file-name-2 }...                                       }

   { OUTPUT PROCEDURE IS procedure-name-3  [ THRU procedure-name-4 ] }
   { GIVING { file-name-3 }...                                       }
```

We may write four skeleton formats for the SORT statement:

1) SORT...USING...GIVING
2) SORT...INPUT PROCEDURE...GIVING
3) SORT...USING...OUTPUT PROCEDURE
4) SORT...INPUT PROCEDURE...OUTPUT PROCEDURE.

file-name-1	This is the name of a temporary file to be created when the SORT statement is executed. We shall call this the *sortfile*.

The sortfile must be declared in the FILE-CONTROL paragraph and described by an SD entry in the FILE SECTION. Its file record description should match that of file-name-2; see program CHAP25-1 below. It is not legal to attempt to OPEN or CLOSE a sortfile; the SORT verb manages the opening and closing of this file.

file-name-2	This is the input file which is to be sorted when the SORT statement has the form: SORT...USING file-name-2. This file may be a sequential, relative, or indexed file. It will have an FD description in FILE SECTION. The size of the record must be exactly the same as that for file-name-1. Generally there is a one-to-one correspondence between the elementary data items of these two records, but this is not required.

file-name-3	Is the output file which results when the SORT has the form SORT....GIVING. The comments for file-name-2 apply to this file.

NOTE: When the SORT statement is executed neither file-name-2 nor file-name-3 may be open. These files must not be referenced by OPEN or CLOSE statements within the input or output procedures.

data-name-1	This identifier (and all other identifiers used as keys) must be one of the data items in the record description of file-name-1 (the sortfile). Data items used as keys may not contain an OCCURS clause nor may they be subordinate to an identifier with that clause.

procedure-name-1 procedure-name-2	The names of the first (and, optionally, the last) paragraph or section in the input procedure, when SORT... INPUT PROCEDURE... is used.

procedure-name-3 procedure-name-4	The names of the first (and, optionally, the last) paragraph or section in the output procedure, when SORT... OUTPUT PROCEDURE... is used.

25.1.1 DUPLICATES phrase

The DUPLICATES phrase is best explained with an example. Suppose we have a file of names and addresses and we wish to sort this file alphabetically by the names in the records. Thus we will sort by REC-SURNAME and REC-GIVEN. There may be records in the file with identical values for each of these keys respectively. For example we could have records such as:

MACDONALD   MARY   OTTAWA

MACDONALD MARY   SASKATOON
MACDONALD MARY   ANTIGONISH

These records need not be consecutive; there could be records with other names between them. If the DUPLICATES phrase is specified, then after the sort the Mary MacDonalds will be in the same order with respect to each other as they were before the sort. Note that in this example we are not sorting by city. In the absence of the DUPLICATES phrase, the order of the various Mary MacDonalds will be undefined.

25.1.2 SEQUENCE phrase

The sorting of the records normally follows the collating sequence that is native to the compiler being used. On a PC this will be the ASCII collating sequence — see Chapter 20. The SEQUENCE phrase is used when we wish to use a sorting order which differs from the native order. We would need to define *alphabet-name* in SPECIAL-NAMES paragraph of the CONFIGURATION SECTION. This topic is covered in Appendix B.

25.2 The RELEASE and RETURN Verbs

When an input procedure is used in a SORT statement we need to be able to write a sort-file record. The RELEASE verb replaces the WRITE verb when the file is an SD (sortfile) type.

```
RELEASE record-name-1 RECORD [ FROM identifier-1]
```

record-name-1   must be the name of the record used by sortfile
identifier-1   may be any identifier in the program other than record-name-1.

When an output procedure used in a SORT statement we need to be able to read a sort-file record. The RETURN verb replaces the READ verb when the file is a sortfile.

```
RETURN file-name-1 RECORD [ INTO identifier-1 ]
       AT END imperative-statement-1 ]
       [NOT AT END imperative-statement-2 ]
       [ END-RETURN ]
```

file-name-1   the name of the sortfile
identifier-1 may be any identifier in the program other than record-name-1.

25.3 Examples of the Use of SORT

In our two examples we shall look at programs which use forms (1) and (4) of the SORT verb. The reader is encouraged to run these two programs and to examine the output files using an editor, or by adding code, that will either display the sorted file records on the screen or on the printer. The programs will be similar to the example in Chapter 20. Ten names and ages will be entered in file records. We then sort the resulting file. The sort will put the records in order by names and by ages. The primary key will be the surname, the secondary key the given-name, and age will be the third key. The first two keys will be in ascending order, the third in descending order. If we use the names Abigail Aalto and William Zwicker more than once, the oldest person called Abigail Aalto will be first and the youngest called William Zwicker will be last in our sorted file. Please note that these are hardly "real life" programs, they merely highlight the operation of the SORT statement.

The program CHAP25-1 uses SORT... USING... GIVING. If we wished we could have only one file (oldfile) and changed the sort to SORT... USING OLDFILE GIVING OLDFILE. In a business application one generally avoids using the same file in the two phrases. If the program is interrupted, perhaps by a power failure, the oldfile may be lost or corrupted.

The second program, CHAP25-2, uses SORT... INPUT PROCEDURE... OUTPUT PROCEDURE. This program performs the same function as the first. Carefully note that there are no OPEN or CLOSE statements referencing the sortfile.

```
1       IDENTIFICATION DIVISION.
2       PROGRAM-ID.  CHAP25-1.
3
4       ENVIRONMENT DIVISION.
5       INPUT-OUTPUT SECTION.
6       FILE-CONTROL.
7           SELECT OLDFILE ASSIGN TO DISK "CHAP25-1.OLD"
8                   ORGANIZATION LINE SEQUENTIAL.
9           SELECT NEWFILE ASSIGN TO DISK "CHAP25-1.NEW"
10                  ORGANIZATION LINE SEQUENTIAL.
11          SELECT SORTFILE ASSIGN TO "SORTFILE".
12      DATA DIVISION.
13
14      FILE SECTION.
15      FD OLDFILE.
16      01 OLD-REC.
17          03 OLD-LAST-NAME        PIC X(20).
18          03 OLD-FIRST-NAME       PIC X(20).
19          03 OLD-AGE              PIC 99.
20
21      FD NEWFILE.
22      01 NEW-REC.
23          03 NEW-LAST-NAME        PIC X(20).
24          03 NEW-FIRST-NAME       PIC X(20).
25          03 NEW-AGE              PIC 99.
26
27      SD SORTFILE.
```

```
28    01 SORT-REC.
29        03 SORT-LAST-NAME        PIC X(20).
30        03 SORT-FIRST-NAME       PIC X(20).
31        03 SORT-AGE              PIC 99.
32
33    WORKING-STORAGE SECTION.
34    01 MESSAGE-REC    PIC X(50) VALUE "SORTING WILL NOW BEGIN".
35
36    PROCEDURE DIVISION.
37    MAIN-PARA.
38        PERFORM PARA-A
39        PERFORM PARA-B
40        STOP RUN.
41
42    PARA-A.
43        OPEN OUTPUT OLDFILE
44        PERFORM 10 TIMES
45           MOVE SPACES TO OLD-REC
46           DISPLAY "Give first name "  NO ADVANCING
47           ACCEPT OLD-FIRST-NAME
48           DISPLAY "Give last name   "  NO ADVANCING
49           ACCEPT OLD-LAST-NAME
50           DISPLAY "Give age         "  NO ADVANCING
51           ACCEPT OLD-AGE
52           WRITE OLD-REC
53        END-PERFORM
54        CLOSE OLDFILE.
55        DISPLAY MESSAGE-REC.
56
57    PARA-B.
58        SORT SORTFILE
59           ASCENDING KEY SORT-LAST-NAME   SORT-FIRST-NAME
60           DESCENDING KEY SORT-AGE
61           USING OLDFILE    GIVING NEWFILE
62        DISPLAY "Use an Editor to view:"
63        DISPLAY "   a) unsorted file CHAP25-1.OLD"
64        DISPLAY "   b) sorted file CHAP25-1.NEW".

 1    IDENTIFICATION DIVISION.
 2    PROGRAM-ID.  CHAP25-2.
 3
 4    ENVIRONMENT DIVISION.
 5    INPUT-OUTPUT SECTION.
 6    FILE-CONTROL.
 7        SELECT NEWFILE ASSIGN TO DISK "CHAP25-2.NEW"
 8             ORGANIZATION LINE SEQUENTIAL.
 9        SELECT SORTFILE ASSIGN TO "SORTFILE".
10    DATA DIVISION.
11
12    FILE SECTION.
13    FD NEWFILE.
14    01 NEW-REC.
```

```
15          03 NEW-LAST-NAME        PIC X(20).
16          03 NEW-FIRST-NAME       PIC X(20).
17          03 NEW-AGE              PIC 99.
18
19     SD SORTFILE.
20     01 SORT-REC.
21          03 SORT-LAST-NAME       PIC X(20).
22          03 SORT-FIRST-NAME      PIC X(20).
23          03 SORT-AGE             PIC 99.
24
25     WORKING-STORAGE SECTION.
26     01 OLD-REC.
27          03 OLD-LAST-NAME        PIC X(20).
28          03 OLD-FIRST-NAME       PIC X(20).
29          03 OLD-AGE              PIC 99.
30
31     01 MESSAGE-REC    PIC X(50) VALUE "SORTING WILL NOW BEGIN".
32     01 FILE-FLAG      PIC X     VALUE SPACES.
33          88 EOF            VALUE "Y".
34
35     PROCEDURE DIVISION.
36     MAIN-PARA.
37         SORT SORTFILE
38              ASCENDING  KEY SORT-LAST-NAME  SORT-FIRST-NAME
39              DESCENDING KEY SORT-AGE
40              INPUT  PROCEDURE PARA-A1 THRU PARA-A2
41              OUTPUT PROCEDURE PARA-B
42         STOP RUN.
43
44     PARA-A1.
45         PERFORM 10 TIMES
46            MOVE SPACES TO OLD-REC
47            DISPLAY "Give first name " NO ADVANCING
48            ACCEPT OLD-FIRST-NAME
49            DISPLAY "Give last name  " NO ADVANCING
50            ACCEPT OLD-LAST-NAME
51            DISPLAY "Give age        " NO ADVANCING
52            ACCEPT OLD-AGE
53            RELEASE SORT-REC FROM OLD-REC
54         END-PERFORM.
55
56     PARA-A2.
57         DISPLAY MESSAGE-REC.
58
59     PARA-B.
60         OPEN OUTPUT NEWFILE
61         PERFORM UNTIL EOF
62            RETURN SORTFILE INTO NEW-REC
63                  AT END     SET EOF TO TRUE
64                  NOT AT END  WRITE NEW-REC
65                              DISPLAY NEW-REC
66            END-RETURN
67         END-PERFORM.
```

25.4 The MERGE Verb

The MERGE statement is used to combine two or more files with similar record structure and records that are similarly ordered. The result is one large file with the records of all the input files ordered with respect to the merge key.

```
MERGE file-name-1

   { ON { ASCENDING  } KEY { data-item-1 }... }...
   {      DESCENDING }

   [ COLLATING SEQUENCE IS alphabet-name ]

   USING file-name-2 { file-name-3 }...

   { OUTPUT PROCEDURE IS procedure-name-1  [ THRU procedure-name-2 ]
   { GIVING { file-name-4 }...
```

```
MERGE MERGEFILE
    ASCENDING KEY MERGE-LAST-NAME  MERGE-FIRST-NAME
    USING FILE-A FILE-B    GIVING FILE-C
```

The file called MERGEFILE must be declared with an SD entry as with a sort-file. The two files FILE-A and FILE-B should have identical record structures and be sorted in the way specified by the ASCENDING KEY phrase. The output file, FILE-C, will contain the records of FILE-A and FILE-B. Note that the statement

```
SORT SORTFILE
    ASCENDING KEY SORT-LAST-NAME SORT-FIRST-NAME
    USING FILE-A FILE-B        GIVING FILE-C
```

would give the same result. However, if the input files are already sorted, it would be less efficient.

25.5 Review Questions

1* The record description for the file DATA-FILE includes the data-names CUST-ACCT, CUST-NAME, CUST-BALANCE. You wish to write a report in which those who owe the most are printed first. Those with the same BALANCE are to be listed in alphabetical order. Write a SORT-USING-GIVING statement to be used at the start of the program.

2. You have two files with identical data structures. You need the data to be in one file sorted by a certain key. Can this be done with one SORT statement?

3* The record desciption for the file DATA-FILE contains the fields CUST-ACC-NO, CUST-NAME and CUST-CITY. It is currently sorted by CUST-ACC-NO. Your program will accept a value for TEST-CITY. It will then display, in alphabetical order, all customers for whom TEST-CITY = CUST-CITY. You do not wish to modify the existing file, nor do you wish to create a new one. Write the required code.

26
Indexed Files

Objectives

- ▸ Know the advantage of an indexed file over a sequential file.
- ▸ Understand the concept of a primary key.
- ▸ Be able to code the SELECT entry for the three ACCESS modes.
- ▸ Know how to OPEN an indexed file for each mode.
- ▸ Know the syntax of the random READ, WRITE and REWRITE verbs.
- ▸ Know how to process an indexed file in sequential mode.

26.1 Introduction

In an indexed file each record has a key field which may be used to access the record randomly; i.e. we can locate a record without reading all the records that precede it as is required with sequential files. Indexed files may be processed sequentially when that mode is more applicable for the task.

Unlike a sequential file, which may be on disk or on tape, an indexed file must be a disk file when it is being processed. An indexed file, of course, may be archived on tape. When an indexed file is created, the program automatically creates an index to the data in the file. In some implementations, including RM/COBOL-85, the index forms part of the indexed file. In other implementations, such as Micro Focus COBOL, the index is kept in a secondary file, which may not be accessed directly. Micro Focus uses the extension IDX for the file containing the indexing data. When an indexed file is updated with WRITE or DELETE statements, the file's index is also updated. An entry in this index contains the key value and a pointer to the corresponding record in the main indexed file. For example, if there is a record in the indexed file with a key value of 881919 and this is the 20th record in the file, then the index entry will contain an entry which is equivalent to "881919 20", the "20" is a pointer to the location of the 20th record.

An indexed file is often initially created from data existing in a sequential file; in this case the indexed file must be used in sequential mode. When an indexed file is created in direct mode, the SELECT clause will require the OPTIONAL phrase.

Before we continue, we must be familiar with the idea of a KEY. In a Student Information System, each student has an identification number. Similarly in a banking or commercial system each customer has a unique account number. In an inventory system, each item has a unique product code. These unique items (id number, account number, product code) are examples of keys. When we speak of a "customer number" we are referring to a string of digits and not a number in the mathematical sense; one does not perform arithmetic operations on customer "numbers". Keys composed of digits are the most common, but other keys are used. For example, in an inventory system a "part number" may have a value such as B123. The ANSI COBOL standard requires the key data item to be of alphanumeric category (i.e. it should have a PICTURE composed only of Xs or be a group item). Most compilers also allow a PICTURE composed of 9s for the key's description. If your key is composed of digits it is best to use this type of PICTURE; this may prevent users from miss-keying data.

The key data item must be part of the record description of the indexed file. Most programmers make it the first item in the record although this is not a requirement. For example:

```
01 STU-REC.
   03 STU-ID          PIC X(9).    <<the primary KEY>>
   03 STU-LAST-NAME   PIC X(20).
   etc.
```

26.2 The SELECT Entry for an Indexed File

```
SELECT [ OPTIONAL ] file-name ASSIGN TO external-file-name

     ORGANIZATION IS INDEXED

                   ⎧ SEQUENTIAL ⎫
     ACCESS MODE IS ⎨ RANDOM     ⎬
                   ⎩ DYNAMIC    ⎭

     RECORD KEY IS primary-key

     [ ALTERNATE RECORD KEY IS alternate-key [ WITH DUPLICATES ]  ]…

     [ FILE STATUS IS file-status-identifier ]
```

The identifier *external-file-name* is explained in Chapter 5. The OPTIONAL and FILE STATUS clauses are described in Chapter 32.

There are three choices for the ACCESS MODE. The first is used when the file is processed sequentially, for example when it is created, or sequentially printed. When we wish to access a record directly by its key value, the RANDOM mode is used. When a program uses sequential access in one procedure and random in another, the mode is DYNAMIC. In our example the "primary-key" would be STU-ID since for each record this will have a unique value. We may wish to make STU-LAST-NAME an alternate-key to be able to process the records in the order of the students' last names. The use of FILE STATUS is shown in the sample programs at the end of the chapter.

26.3 The FD Entry and Record Description

The FD entry and record descriptions for indexed files are the same as for sequential files (Chapter 20). Of course, any keys specified in the SELECT entry must be included in the record description.

26.4 The OPEN Verb for Indexed Files

```
        ⎧⎧ INPUT  ⎫      ⎫
  OPEN  ⎨⎨ OUTPUT ⎬ file-name-1... ⎬...
        ⎩⎩ I-O    ⎭      ⎭
```

Table 26-1 shows the valid combinations of ACCESS mode and OPEN mode for the five input-output statements used with indexed files.

Table 26-1 Valid statements for indexed files

File Access Mode	I-O Verb	OPEN mode		
		INPUT	OUTPUT	I-O
Sequential	READ	Y		Y
	WRITE		Y	
	REWRITE			Y
	START	Y		Y
	DELETE			Y
Random	READ	Y		Y
	WRITE		Y	Y
	REWRITE			Y
	START			
	DELETE			Y
Dynamic	READ	Y		Y
	WRITE		Y	Y
	REWRITE			Y
	START	Y		Y
	DELETE			Y

26.5 The READ Verb for Indexed Files

When an indexed file is accessed sequentially the READ syntax is similar to that for sequential files (READ `file-name` AT END...); refer to Chapter 20. *Note that the NEXT phrase is required in the READ statement when sequentially reading an indexed file with access mode DYNAMIC:* READ `file-name` NEXT... Most compilers also allow READ `file-name` PREVIOUS...

To read randomly a record in an indexed file, the READ statement has the form:

```
READ  file-name  RECORD  [ INTO identifier-1 ]
    [ KEY IS key-identifier ]
    [ INVALID KEY  imperative-statement-1 ]
    [ NOT INVALID KEY imperative-statement-2 ]
    [ END-READ ]
```

To use a random read statement it is required that:
   a)   ACCESS MODE IS RANDOM (or DYNAMIC) be used
   b)   the file be opened for INPUT or I-O
   c)   the RECORD KEY be initialized before the READ.

Example 1: To read the record for a given id number.

```
SELECT STUDENT-FILE  ASSIGN TO DISK "STUFILE.DAT"
    ORGANIZATION IS INDEXED
    ACCESS MODE IS RANDOM
    RECORD KEY IS   STU-ID.
....
FD STUDENT-FILE.
01 STU-REC.
    03 STU-ID          PIC X(6).
    03 STU-LAST-NAME   PIC X(20).  etc.
....
OPEN INPUT STUDENT-FILE.
DISPLAY "Give student ID "  NO ADVANCING
ACCEPT STU-ID                           < initialize the key >
READ STUDENT-FILE
    INVALID KEY
        DISPLAY "ID not found in file"
    NOT INVALID KEY
        DISPLAY "Student's name is " STU-LAST-NAME SPACE STU-GNAMES
END-READ.
```

If there is no record with the specified value of the KEY then the INVALID KEY clause is executed.

The KEY IS phrase may be used to establish the key of reference. The primary key is the key of reference when the phrase is omitted. If STU-LAST-NAME had been declared to be an alternative key and we wished to find the first record with a STU-LAST-NAME value of SMITH, we would code:

```
MOVE "SMITH" TO STU-LAST-NAME
READ STUDENT-FILE
KEY IS STU-LAST-NAME  ....
```
One might expect there to be duplicate records with the same last name value; a sample program at the end of the chapter shows how these may be accessed.

26.6 The WRITE Verb for Index Files

```
WRITE record-name [ FROM identifier-1 ]
     [ INVALID KEY imperative-statement-1 ]
     [ NOT INVALID KEY imperative-statement-2 ]
     [ END-WRITE ]
```

This is always the format of the WRITE statement for an indexed file regardless of the access mode used. Note that the invalid key clause is optional but it is always advisable to use it. The WRITE verb will fail and the imperative-statement-1 will be executed when the value of the primary key-identifier:
   a)   Is blank.
   b)   Duplicates the value of an existing key.
   c)   Is not greater than the value of the value of the key in the previous record and the file is being processed in sequential mode.

26.7 The REWRITE Verb

When an indexed file is updated randomly the steps executed are:
   1)   Access mode is random, or dynamic.
   2)   The file is opened for I-O.
   3)   The appropriate record is located by:
            a) moving the value of its key to key-identifier, and
            b) reading the record using READ...INVALID KEY.
   4)   The field to be updated is given a new value, for example by using MOVE or an arithmetic verb.
   5)   The new record is placed over the old using REWRITE.

```
REWRITE  record-name [ FROM identifier-1 ]
     [ INVALID  KEY  imperative-statement-1 ]
     [ NOT INVALID  KEY  imperative-statement-2 ]
     [ END-REWRITE ]
```

The REWRITE fails and the imperative-statement-1 is executed when the value of the key does not match the key of any existing record in the file. This form of the REWRITE verb may also be used with indexed files accessed in sequential mode and opened for I-O.

26.8 The START Verb

The START verb is used with an indexed file accessed in sequential or dynamic mode. It serves to position the file pointer at a record and to establish the key of reference. The verb may also be used with relative files; the notes here apply to indexed files.

```
START  [ file-name KEY relation-condition data-name-1 ]
           [ INVALID KEY imperative-statement-1 ]
           [ NOT INVALID KEY imperative-statement-2 ]
           [ END-START ]
```

where the relational condition may be one of:
a) IS EQUAL TO   or   IS =
b) IS GREATER THAN   or   IS >
c) IS NOT LESS THAN   or   IS NOT <
d) IS GREATER THAN OR EQUAL TO or   IS >=

file-name   An indexed file opened for INPUT or I-O, and accessed in SEQUENTIAL or DYNAMIC mode.

data-name-1 May be the primary or an alternative key of the file. It may also be an alphanumeric data item subordinate to such a key provided its leftmost character corresponds with the leftmost character of the key.

      For example, if MY-KEY is the primary key for the file and it is defined by:
```
        02 MY-KEY.
            03 MY-KEY-ALPHA     PIC X(3).
            03 MY-KEY-BETA      PIC X(17).
```
then data-name-1 may be MY-KEY or MY-KEY-ALPHA but it may not be MY-KEY-BETA.

Example (a):
```
MOVE "B123" TO MY-KEY
START MY-FILE  KEY >= MY-KEY
    INVALID KEY ...
```

A subsequent sequential READ will read the record with key equal to B123 or the next record with a value of MY-ITEM greater than B123

Example (b): The KEY phrase may be omitted from the START statement provided the primary key item for the file contains a valid value.
```
        MOVE "B123" TO MY-KEY
        START MY-FILE
            INVALID KEY ....
```

This is equivalent to specifying an EQUAL TO <primary-key> in the statement; thus the statement above is equivalent to START MY-FILE KEY = MY-KEY START KEY = MY-KEY .....

Example (c):   MOVE "SMITH" TO MY-ALT-KEY
              START MY-FILE KEY >= ALT-KEY

In this example, an alternative key is specified. If we now read the file sequentially the records will be read in the order specified by the alternate key. The alternate key is now the *key of reference* until another START statement is executed.

26.9 The DELETE Verb

Occasions arise when one needs to delete a record from a file. For example, when a bank customer closes an account. See Table 26-1 for valid access and open modes for this statement.

```
DELETE file-name RECORD
    [ INVALID KEY imperative-statement-1 ]
    [ NOT INVALID KEY imperative-statement-2 ]
    [ END-DELETE ]
```

26.10 Indexed Files with Primary Key

We will start by looking at indexed files with only a primary key. In the next section we explore the use of alternate keys.

26.10.1 Creating the indexed file

In the first example we will create an indexed file from the data in a sequential file. The indexed file will be processed in sequential mode; this requires the input data to be sorted in the ascending order by the data item to be used as the primary key. The program CHAP26-1 uses the data in a sequential file (CHAP26-1.DAT) to generate an indexed file (CHAP26–1.INX). The two files contain similar fields but have different record structures. We have used a single MOVE CORRESPONDING statement rather than a series of MOVE statements. This requires the fields in the two files to have the same names. Hence the data name CUSTOMER-KEY is not unique, requiring us to use a qualified name CUSTOMER-KEY OF CUSTOMFILE in line 12 of the program. Since it is a simple program we will code it in one paragraph.

For this program to be successful the data used to create the indexed file must be sorted by the field being used as the key. Note the use of the initial-read method to process the input file.

```
1    IDENTIFICATION DIVISION.
2    PROGRAM-ID. CHAP26-1.
3  * Create an indexed file from data in a sequential file
4    ENVIRONMENT DIVISION.
5    INPUT-OUTPUT SECTION.
```

```
 6    FILE-CONTROL.
 7        SELECT OLDFILE ASSIGN TO DISK "CHAP26-1.DAT"
 8            ORGANIZATION LINE SEQUENTIAL.
 9        SELECT CUSTOMFILE  ASSIGN TO DISK "CHAP26-1.INX"
10            ORGANIZATION IS INDEXED
11            ACCESS MODE  IS SEQUENTIAL
12            RECORD KEY   IS CUSTOMER-KEY OF CUSTOMFILE.
13        SELECT SORTFILE ASSIGN TO "SORTFILE".
14    DATA DIVISION.
15    FILE SECTION.
16    FD OLDFILE.
17    01 CUSTOMER-REC.
18        02 CUSTOMER-GIVEN         PIC X(20).
19        02 CUSTOMER-LAST          PIC X(20).
20        02 FILLER                 PIC X.
21        02 CUSTOMER-KEY           PIC X(4).
22        02 FILLER                 PIC X(4).
23        02 CUSTOMER-AMT           PIC 99V99.
24    SD SORTFILE.
25    01 SORT-REC.
26        02 SORT-GIVEN             PIC X(20).
27        02 SORT-LAST              PIC X(20).
28        02 FILLER                 PIC X.
29        02 SORT-KEY               PIC X(4).
30        02 FILLER                 PIC X(4).
31        02 SORT-AMT               PIC 99V99.
32    FD CUSTOMFILE.
33    01 CUSTOM-REC.
34        02 CUSTOMER-KEY           PIC X(4).
35        02 FILLER                 PIC XX.
36        02 CUSTOMER-LAST          PIC X(20).
37        02 CUSTOMER-GIVEN         PIC X(20).
38        02 FILLER                 PIC XX.
39        02 CUSTOMER-AMT           PIC S9(4)V99
40                                      SIGN IS LEADING SEPARATE.
41
42    WORKING-STORAGE SECTION.
43    01 WORK-ITEMS.
44        02 FILE-FLAG              PIC X   VALUE "N".
45            88 EOF   VALUE "Y".
46    PROCEDURE DIVISION.
47    MAIN-PARA.
48        SORT SORTFILE  ASCENDING KEY SORT-KEY
49                            USING OLDFILE GIVING OLDFILE
50
51        OPEN INPUT   OLDFILE
52            OUTPUT   CUSTOMFILE
53
54        READ OLDFILE AT END SET EOF TO TRUE END-READ
55        PERFORM  UNTIL EOF
56            MOVE SPACES TO CUSTOM-REC
57            MOVE CORRESPONDING CUSTOMER-REC TO CUSTOM-REC
```

```
58          WRITE CUSTOM-REC
59            INVALID KEY
60                DISPLAY "Invalid " CUSTOMER-KEY OF CUSTOM-REC
61          END-WRITE
62          DISPLAY CUSTOM-REC
63          READ OLDFILE AT END SET EOF TO TRUE END-READ
64        END-PERFORM
65
66        CLOSE OLDFILE CUSTOMFILE
67        DISPLAY "Indexed file created"
68        STOP RUN.
```

26.10.2 Random locating and updating a record

In our next sample program (CHAP26-2) we will use the indexed file created by the program CHAP26-1. We may think of CUSTOMER-AMT in this file as the credit balance for a group of customers. This field will be updated as customers make additional purchases or make payments on their accounts.

The output from such a program would normally be to a printer; companies like to keep hardcopy reports of transactions. A display routine is used in the sample program for simplicity.

Before we can update a record we must first locate it in the file. This is achieved in LOCATE-PARA using the random mode format of the READ statement. Having located the record, we ask the user, in GET-DATA-PARA, to supply the new information; this is used to calculate the customer's new balance. The manipulation of the numeric input data is not very elegant. This could be improved using enhanced DISPLAY and ACCEPT statements if we are coding in RM/COBOL-85 or Micro Focus COBOL. When the data for a particular customer has been entered we update the record with a REWRITE statement in UPDATE-PARA. A sample of typical output is shown after the program listing.

```
1     IDENTIFICATION DIVISION.
2     PROGRAM-ID. CHAP26-2.
3     * This program updates an indexed file interactively
4     ENVIRONMENT DIVISION.
5     INPUT-OUTPUT SECTION.
6     FILE-CONTROL.
7           SELECT CUSTOMFILE  ASSIGN TO DISK "CHAP26-1.INX"
8               ORGANIZATION IS INDEXED
9               ACCESS MODE  IS RANDOM
10              RECORD KEY   IS CUSTOM-KEY.
11
12    DATA DIVISION.
13    FILE SECTION.
14    FD CUSTOMFILE.
15    01 CUSTOM-REC.
16        02 CUSTOM-KEY      PIC X(4).
17        02 FILLER          PIC XX.
18        02 CUSTOM-LAST     PIC X(20).
```

```
19        02 CUSTOM-GIVEN    PIC X(20).
20        02 FILLER          PIC XX.
21        02 CUSTOM-AMT      PIC S9(4)V99 SIGN IS LEADING SEPARATE.
22
23    WORKING-STORAGE SECTION.
24    01 TRANS-ITEMS.
25        02 TRANS-KEY       PIC X(4).
26           88 TRANS-QUIT   VALUE "QUIT" "EXIT".
27        02 TRANS-AMT       PIC ZZZZ.ZZ.
28        02 TRANS-SIGN      PIC XX.
29           88 TRANS-DB     VALUE "DB".
30           88 TRANS-CR     VALUE "CR".
31           88 TRANS-VALID  VALUE "DB" "CR".
32        02 HOLD-AMT        PIC S9999V99.
33        02 SHOW-BALANCE    PIC ZZZ9.99DB.
34
35    01 WORK-ITEMS.
36        02 LYNE            PIC 99 VALUE 5.
37
38    PROCEDURE DIVISION.
39    MAIN-PARA.
40        DISPLAY SPACES LINE 1 ERASE
41        DISPLAY "Program to update customer's balance"
42        DISPLAY "To end program type EXIT or QUIT for key value"
43        DISPLAY SPACES
44        OPEN I-O CUSTOMFILE
45        PERFORM LOCATE-PARA UNTIL TRANS-QUIT
46        CLOSE CUSTOMFILE
47        STOP RUN.
48
49    LOCATE-PARA.
50        DISPLAY "Enter KEY > " LINE LYNE POSITION 1
51        MOVE SPACES TO TRANS-KEY
52        ACCEPT TRANS-KEY  LINE LYNE POSITION 13
53        MOVE TRANS-KEY TO CUSTOM-KEY
54        IF NOT TRANS-QUIT
55          READ CUSTOMFILE
56            INVALID KEY
57                DISPLAY "Customer not found" LINE LYNE POSITION 30
58            NOT INVALID KEY
59                MOVE CUSTOM-AMT TO SHOW-BALANCE
60                DISPLAY CUSTOM-LAST  LINE LYNE POSITION 30
61                       ", " CUSTOM-GIVEN
62                DISPLAY SHOW-BALANCE LINE LYNE POSITION 70
63                PERFORM GET-DATA-PARA
64                PERFORM UPDATE-PARA
65                ADD 2 TO LYNE
66          END-READ
67        END-IF.
68
69    GET-DATA-PARA.
70        ADD 1 TO LYNE
```

```
71          MOVE ZERO TO TRANS-AMT
72          DISPLAY "Enter amount > " LINE LYNE POSITION 1
73          ACCEPT TRANS-AMT LINE LYNE POSITION 16
74          MOVE TRANS-AMT TO HOLD-AMT
75          MOVE SPACES TO TRANS-SIGN
76          PERFORM UNTIL TRANS-VALID
77              DISPLAY "Enter DB or CR > " LINE LYNE POSITION 26
78              ACCEPT TRANS-SIGN LINE LYNE POSITION 43
79          END-PERFORM
80
81          IF TRANS-DB
82              SUBTRACT HOLD-AMT FROM CUSTOM-AMT
83          ELSE
84              ADD HOLD-AMT TO CUSTOM-AMT
85          END-IF
86          MOVE CUSTOM-AMT TO SHOW-BALANCE
87          DISPLAY SHOW-BALANCE LINE LYNE POSITION 70.
88
89     UPDATE-PARA.
90          REWRITE CUSTOM-REC
91            INVALID KEY   DISPLAY "File error"
92          END-REWRITE.
```

Sample output with keyed in values shown in italics:

```
Enter KEY      > A123      SMITH        , JOHN      1028.79DB
Enter amount   > 100.00    Enter DB or CR > CR       928.79DB

Enter KEY      > E455      FLOYD        , JAMES       20.00
Enter amount   > 50.50     Enter DB or CR > DB        30.50DB

Enter KEY      > QUIT
```

26.11   Indexed Files with Alternate Keys

The indexed file created by the program CHAP26-1 enabled us to find randomly the record of one customer at a time by specifying the value of the customer's account number — i.e. the file's key. This was demonstrated in program CHAP26-2. We may also wish to be able to look up customers on the basis of their name. We will see now how to generate an indexed file which has alternate keys.

26.11.1 Creating the indexed file

Assume that the input data for our new indexed file is CHAP26-1.DAT, the same file that we used in the program CHAP26-1. With a minor modification to that program we would have a program which produce an indexed file with an account number as the primary file and a name as the alternate key. The modification will be to the SELECT clause for our new file. In the program CHAP26-3 (on the accompanying disk), we have used the customer's last name for the alternate index. The SELECT entry to accomplish this is:

```
SELECT CUSTOMFILE  ASSIGN TO DISK  "CHAP26-3.INX"
    ORGANIZATION INDEXED  ACCESS MODE IS SEQUENTIAL
    RECORD KEY IS CUSTOMER-KEY OF CUSTOMFILE
    ALTERNATE RECORD KEY IS CUSTOMER-LAST OF CUSTOMFILE
        WITH DUPLICATES.
```

Note the use of WITH DUPLICATES; this is required since we will generally have more than one customer with the same last name.

If we wish to have the alternate keys for both the last and given names we could use:

```
SELECT CUSTOMFILE  ASSIGN TO DISK "CHAP26-3.INX"
    ORGANIZATION INDEXED  ACCESS MODE IS SEQUENTIAL
    RECORD KEY IS CUSTOMER-KEY OF CUSTOMFILE
    ALTERNATE RECORD KEY IS CUSTOMER-LAST  OF CUSTOMFILE
        WITH DUPLICATES
    ALTERNATE RECORD KEY IS CUSTOMER-GIVEN OF CUSTOMFILE
        WITH DUPLICATES.
```

26.11.2 Sequential processing of an indexed file

The program CHAP26-4 illustrates how we may sequentially process a file with primary and alternate keys. This program uses the index file created by CHAP26-3 — see above. The user has the choice of viewing the records in the order established either by the primary key (CUSTOMER-KEY — the customer's account number) or that set by the alternate key (CUSTOMER-LAST — the customer's last name).

When the second option is chosen, the user may select a subset of the records; for example, those with the alternate key beginning with the letters C through S. The data in the file was chosen so that one name (FLOYD) appears twice in the file. Since we indexed on only the last name not the full name, these "duplicate" records will appear with given names in the order in which they were present when the file was created. This is shown in the sample output following the program.

This program uses the "initial read" method which was discussed in Chapter 20. Note the use of the START statements. In PARA-A we "prime" the alternate key with LOW-VALUE; no key can have a value less than this by definition of LOW-VALUE. The START statement uses the KEY phrase to locate the first record and to set the key of reference to CUSTOMER-LAST. In PARA-C we may start the process at any point. If CUSTOMER-LAST is primed with a value of "C", the first record processed will be first one having a CUSTOMER-LAST value beginning with "C" — in our case this is CHISHOLM.

```
1    IDENTIFICATION DIVISION.
2    PROGRAM-ID. CHAP26-4.
3    * Program to process an indexed file sequentially
4
5    ENVIRONMENT DIVISION.
6    INPUT-OUTPUT SECTION.
7    FILE-CONTROL.
```

```
8          SELECT CUSTOMERFILE  ASSIGN TO DISK "CHAP26-3.INX"
9             ORGANIZATION IS INDEXED  ACCESS MODE IS SEQUENTIAL
10            RECORD KEY IS CUSTOMER-KEY
11            ALTERNATE RECORD KEY IS CUSTOMER-LAST WITH  DUPLICATES.
12     DATA DIVISION.
13     FILE SECTION.
14     FD CUSTOMERFILE.
15     01 CUSTOMER-REC.
16         02 CUSTOMER-KEY     PIC X(4).
17         02 FILLER           PIC XX.
18         02 CUSTOMER-LAST    PIC X(20).
19         02 CUSTOMER-GIVEN   PIC X(20).
20         02 FILLER           PIC XX.
21         02 CUSTOMER-AMT     PIC S9(4)V99 SIGN LEADING SEPARATE.
22
23     WORKING-STORAGE SECTION.
24     01 WORK-ITEMS.
25             02 FILE-FLAG     PIC X  VALUE "N".
26               88 EOF   VALUE "Y".
27             02 PROCESS-FLAG PIC X VALUE SPACES.
28                88 PROCESS-A  VALUE "A".
29                88 PROCESS-B  VALUE "B".
30                88 PROCESS-C  VALUE "C".
31                88 PROCESS-Q  VALUE "Q".
32             02 LAST-START   PIC X  VALUE SPACES.
33             02 LAST-END     PIC X  VALUE SPACES.
34             02 GO-FLAG      PIC X.
35
36     PROCEDURE DIVISION.
37     MAIN-PARA.
38        PERFORM UNTIL PROCESS-Q
39           DISPLAY "  "
40           DISPLAY "Select one of the following:"
41           DISPLAY "   A - to report by Primary Key"
42           DISPLAY "   B - to report by Secondary Key"
43           DISPLAY "   C - for partial Secondary Key report"
44           DISPLAY "   Q - to quit program"
45           DISPLAY "Type A, B, C or Q  > " NO ADVANCING
46           ACCEPT PROCESS-FLAG
47           MOVE SPACES TO CUSTOMER-REC
48           OPEN INPUT CUSTOMERFILE
49           MOVE "N" TO FILE-FLAG
50           EVALUATE TRUE
51             WHEN   PROCESS-Q       CONTINUE
52             WHEN   PROCESS-A       PERFORM PARA-A
53             WHEN   PROCESS-B       PERFORM PARA-B
54             WHEN   PROCESS-C       PERFORM PARA-C
55           END-EVALUATE
56           CLOSE CUSTOMERFILE
57        END-PERFORM
58        STOP RUN.
59
```

```
60    PARA-A.
61        DISPLAY "Sequential read by primary key"
62        READ CUSTOMERFILE
63              AT END SET EOF TO TRUE
64        END-READ
65        PERFORM READ-FILE UNTIL EOF.
66
67    PARA-B.
68        DISPLAY "Sequential read by alternate key - all records"
69        MOVE LOW-VALUE TO CUSTOMER-LAST
70        START CUSTOMERFILE
71              KEY NOT LESS CUSTOMER-LAST
72              INVALID KEY  DISPLAY "Invalid key"
73        END-START
74
75        READ CUSTOMERFILE
76              AT END SET EOF TO TRUE
77        END-READ
78        PERFORM READ-FILE UNTIL EOF.
79
80    PARA-C.
81        DISPLAY "Sequential read by alternate key - selected records"
82        MOVE "Z" TO LAST-START  MOVE "A" TO LAST-END
83        PERFORM UNTIL LAST-END >= LAST-START
84            DISPLAY "Give letter to begin > " NO ADVANCING
85            ACCEPT LAST-START
86            DISPLAY "Give letter to end   > " NO ADVANCING
87            ACCEPT LAST-END
88        END-PERFORM
89
90        MOVE LAST-START TO CUSTOMER-LAST
91        START CUSTOMERFILE
92              KEY NOT LESS CUSTOMER-LAST
93              INVALID KEY  DISPLAY "Invalid key"
94        END-START
95
96        READ CUSTOMERFILE
97            AT END SET EOF TO TRUE
98        END-READ
99        PERFORM READ-FILE UNTIL EOF.
100
101   READ-FILE.
102       DISPLAY CUSTOMER-REC
103
104       READ CUSTOMERFILE
105          AT END    SET EOF TO TRUE
106       END-READ.
107
108       IF PROCESS-C AND CUSTOMER-LAST (1:1) > LAST-END
109              SET EOF TO TRUE
110       END-IF.
```

Sample output from this program, with user input shown in italics:

```
Select one of the following:
   A - to report by Primary Key
   B - to report by Secondary Key
   C - for partial Secondary Key report
   Q - to quit program
Type A, B, C or Q  > A


Sequential read by primary key
A123  SMITH            JOHN              +001000
A234  JONES            ANNE              +005000
A799  FLOYD            ROBERT            +002000
B456  WILBERFORCE      ROBERT            +002500
B700  MACDONALD        ELIZABETH         +003550
C045  ZWICKER          JAMES             +005050
C066  WILLIAMS         ANNE              +004500
D123  CHISHOLM         BRIAN             +000500
E222  ABBOT            DAVID             +001000
E455  FLOYD            JAMES             +002000
G100  ROBERTSON        FRANCES           +001500


Select one of the following:
   A - to report by Primary Key
   B - to report by Secondary Key
   C - for partial Secondary Key report
   Q - to quit program
Type A, B, C or Q  > B


Sequential read by alternate key - all records
E222  ABBOT            DAVID             +001000
D123  CHISHOLM         BRIAN             +000500
A799  FLOYD            ROBERT            +002000
E455  FLOYD            JAMES             +002000
A234  JONES            ANNE              +005000
B700  MACDONALD        ELIZABETH         +003550
G100  ROBERTSON        FRANCES           +001500
A123  SMITH            JOHN              +001000
B456  WILBERFORCE      ROBERT            +002500
C066  WILLIAMS         ANNE              +004500
C045  ZWICKER          JAMES             +005050


Select one of the following:
   A - to report by Primary Key
   B - to report by Secondary Key
   C - for partial Secondary Key report
   Q - to quit program
Type A, B, C or Q  > C


Sequential read by alternate key- selected records
Give letter to begin > C
Give letter to end   > S
```

```
D123   CHISHOLM          BRIAN               +000500
A799   FLOYD             ROBERT              +002000
E455   FLOYD             JAMES               +002000
A234   JONES             ANNE                +005000
B700   MACDONALD         ELIZABETH           +003550
G100   ROBERTSON         FRANCES             +001500
A123   SMITH             JOHN                +001000
```

```
Select one of the following:
   A - to report by Primary Key
   B - to report by Secondary Key
   C - for partial Secondary Key report
   Q - to quit program
Type A, B, C or Q  > Q
```

26.11.3 Locating records by alternate key

The method of randomly (or, more precisely, dynamically) processing an indexed file with duplicate key values is shown in the program CHAP26-5. In our data there are two records having FLOYD as the value of CUSTOMER-LAST which is our duplicate key. The random read statement will locate only the first. We can detect the presence of duplicate keys by examining the value of the file status data item. More complete details of this topic are given in Chapter 32. We need a FILE STATUS phrase in the SELECT entry and an alphanumeric data item in WORKING-STORAGE to hold the value of the file status; in this program it is CUSTOMER-STATUS.

When the random READ statement detects duplicate key values it returns a value of "02" to CUSTOMER-STATUS. To locate the records with the duplicate key values we must switch from using a random READ statement to a sequential READ statement. This why we specify DYNAMIC ACCESS in the SELECT entry. We continue reading in this manner until no more duplicates are detected; i.e. until SALE-STATUS has a value of "00". Note the NEXT phrase in the sequential read statement; this is required when using dynamic access mode.

```
1      IDENTIFICATION DIVISION.
2      PROGRAM-ID. IND005.
3    *  Program processes indexed randomly by alternate key
4
5      ENVIRONMENT DIVISION.
6      INPUT-OUTPUT SECTION.
7      FILE-CONTROL.
8          SELECT CUSTOMERFILE  ASSIGN TO DISK "CUSTOMER.IND"
9             FILE STATUS IS CUSTOMER-STATUS
10            ORGANIZATION IS INDEXED
11            ACCESS MODE IS DYNAMIC
12            RECORD KEY IS CUSTOMER-KEY
13            ALTERNATE RECORD KEY IS CUSTOMER-LAST WITH DUPLICATES.
14
15     DATA DIVISION.
16     FILE SECTION.
17     FD CUSTOMERFILE.
```

```
18      01 CUSTOMER-REC.
19         02 CUSTOMER-KEY      PIC X(4).
20         02 FILLER            PIC XX.
21         02 CUSTOMER-LAST     PIC X(20).
22         02 CUSTOMER-GIVEN    PIC X(20).
23         02 FILLER            PIC XX.
24         02 CUSTOMER-AMT      PIC 9(4).
25
26      WORKING-STORAGE SECTION.
27      01 CUSTOMER-STATUS  PIC XX.
28              88 CUSTOMER-OK        VALUE "00".
29              88 CUSTOMER-DUPLICATE VALUE "02".
30
31      01 WORK-ITEMS.
32         02 PROCESS-FLAG  PIC X  VALUE "Y".
33           88 PROCESS-END VALUE "N".
34         02 FILE-FLAG     PIC X.
35           88 EOF   VALUE "Y".
36
37
38      PROCEDURE DIVISION.
39      MAIN-PARA.
40          OPEN INPUT CUSTOMERFILE
41          PERFORM RANDOM-READ UNTIL PROCESS-END
42
43          CLOSE CUSTOMERFILE
44          STOP RUN.
45
46      RANDOM-READ.
47          MOVE SPACES TO CUSTOMER-REC
48          DISPLAY "Enter last-name " NO ADVANCING
49          ACCEPT CUSTOMER-LAST
50          READ CUSTOMERFILE
51             KEY IS CUSTOMER-LAST
52             INVALID KEY
53               DISPLAY  "Cannot find record for " CUSTOMER-LAST
54                        " file status is " CUSTOMER-STATUS
55             NOT INVALID KEY
56               DISPLAY CUSTOMER-REC
57               PERFORM SEQUENTIAL-READ
58                       UNTIL NOT CUSTOMER-DUPLICATE
59          END-READ
60          DISPLAY SPACES
61          DISPLAY "Look for another ? > " NO ADVANCING
62          MOVE SPACES TO PROCESS-FLAG
63          ACCEPT PROCESS-FLAG.
64
65      SEQUENTIAL-READ.
66          READ CUSTOMERFILE NEXT
67             AT END CONTINUE
68             NOT AT END
69                 IF CUSTOMER-DUPLICATE
```

```
70                       DISPLAY CUSTOMER-REC
71                   END-IF
72           END-READ.
```

Sample output from CHAP26-5:

```
Enter last-name CHISHOLM
D123  CHISHOLM           BRIAN        +000500    File status is 00

Look for another ? > Y
Enter last-name FLOYD
A799  FLOYD              ROBERT       +002000    File status is 02
E455  FLOYD              JAMES        +002000    File status is 00

Look for another ? > Y
Enter last-name GEORGE
Cannot find record for GEORGE                    File status is 23

Look for another ? > N
```

26.12 Review Questions

1. What is the advantage of an indexed file over a sequential file?

2* A file was created with a program using the clauses

```
    RECORD KEY IS CUST-ACC-NO
    ALTERNATE KEY IS CUST-LAST-NAME
```

You have written another program in which the alternate key is not refernced in the Procedure Division. When this program runs a run-time error is displayed stating there is a conflict with file attributes. What is the most likely cause of the problem?

3. A program is to process an indexed file in both sequential and random modes. What ACCESS MODE will you declare?

4* The READ statement for processing an indexed file sequentially is similar to that used for sequential files. What is the important difference?

5. Explain the purpose of the START verb.

6. Your program is processing a file indexed by CUST-ACCT-NO in random mode. It contains the code:

```
        DISPLAY "Enter customer account number "
        ACCEPT CUST-ACCT-NO
        READ CUST-FILE
```

```
        AT INVALID KEY
            DISPLAY "Key is invalid"
        NOT AT INVALID KEY
            PERFORM PROCEDURE-PARA
    END-READ.
```

A user replies to the ACCEPT with "1256" and the program displays "Key is invalid". Explain what this means.

27
Relative Files

Objectives

- ▸ Know the advantage and disadvantage of a relative file over an indexed file.
- ▸ Be able to code the SELECT entry for the three ACCESS modes.
- ▸ Know how to OPEN a relative file for each mode.
- ▸ Know the syntax of the random READ, WRITE and REWRITE verbs.

27.1 Introduction

Relative files, like indexed files, provide a means of randomly accessing a specific record. They differ from index files in that a record is located by its absolute position (record number) rather than by an index value. Relative files may also be processed sequentially when this is applicable to the task.

Conceptually, a relative file is not unlike a COBOL table. Just as we can process — access or change — the data in the tenth element of a table, we can read or write the tenth record in a relative file. Of course, when the program is running, the table is stored in memory whilst the relative file is on disk.

How does a relative file differ from an indexed file? When we write a record in an indexed file the system handles all the work of maintaining the file's index. When we read such a file, we specify the value of the key and the system uses this to locate the appropriate record. All this uses "overhead" time. When a record is written to a relative file the program must specify where the record is to be placed; when a record is read from a relative file the program must know its location.

Which is the more efficient method — having the system or the program do the "housekeeping" chores? The answer will depend on the type of key being used. We shall limit the discussion to numeric keys. We will not delve too deeply into the full potential of relative files. Most modern compilers provide means by which a program can access data base management systems. For complex applications it is much more efficient to use a commercially available DBMS rather than going to the trouble of creating one.

27.2 Creating a Relative File

We will start with a very simple relative file. Suppose we have an inventory listing 100 items in a manner similar to Figure 27-1. We wish to put this data into a relative file using Part-Number as the key. We will begin by creating an empty file with room to hold all the records. If there is no possibility that the inventory will ever grow beyond 100 items, then that value will suffice. Once the file is created there is no way of extending the number of records it may hold.

Figure 27-1

Part-Number	Description	Quantity-on-hand
001	widget	100
002	rotor	080
...		
099	bodkin	075
100	whatnot	120

Even if the Part-Number range contains gaps (e.g. maybe we do not use values in the range 060 to 069), we still need 100 records since that is the largest value of Part-Number.

What if Part-Number had values in the range 1001 to 1100? It would be a waste of disk space to create a file to hold 1100 records. Since there would still be 100 items, we need only 100 records. The data for an item with Part-Number 1001 would be located in the first record. The data for a Part-Number with a value of 1020 would be in record 20. In general, we can compute the record location of any item using the expression *record location = Part-Number – 1000*. The algorithm for converting the key (here it is the Part-Number) to the record location is called the *hashing algorithm*. We will explore this topic, briefly, in a later section.

Program CHAP27-1 will create an empty file called CHAP27-1.REL. The extension REL was chosen to remind us what type a file it is. The COBOL language does not require any particular extension; we could have used DAT. The resulting file is ready to hold up to 100 records with Part-Numbers in the range 1000 to 1100. The COBOL system treats the file as if no records actually exist at this stage because we have added no data to the file.

The key features to note about this program are:
a) The SELECT entry for the relative file uses ORGANIZATION IS RELATIVE, and ACCESS MODE IS SEQUENTIAL. This mode must be used when a relative file is created.
b) The operand RECORD-LOCATION of the RELATIVE KEY clause is defined in WORKING-STORAGE, not in the file's data-description-entry as with indexed files.
c) The syntax of the WRITE statement is the same as for indexed files.

```
1    IDENTIFICATION DIVISION.
2    PROGRAM-ID.          CHAP27-1.
3    AUTHOR.              B. V. LIENGME.
```

```
 4
 5     ********************************************
 6     *     To create an 'empty' relative file
 7     ********************************************
 8
 9     ENVIRONMENT DIVISION.
10     INPUT-OUTPUT SECTION.
11     FILE-CONTROL.
12        SELECT INVENT-FILE
13              ASSIGN TO DISK "CHAP27-1.REL"
14              ORGANIZATION IS RELATIVE
15              ACCESS IS SEQUENTIAL
16              RELATIVE KEY IS RECORD-LOCATION.
17     DATA DIVISION.
18     FILE SECTION.
19     FD INVENT-FILE.
20     01   INVENT-REC.
21          03   INVENT-PART-NO  PIC 9999.
22          03   INVENT-NAME     PIC X(20).
23          03   INVENT-QUANT    PIC 999.
24     WORKING-STORAGE SECTION.
25     01 WORK-ITEMS.
26        02 RECORD-LOCATION  PIC 999.
27     PROCEDURE DIVISION.
28     MAIN-PARA.
29        OPEN OUTPUT INVENT-FILE
30        MOVE SPACES TO INVENT-REC
31        PERFORM WRITE-PARA VARYING RECORD-LOCATION
32              FROM 1 BY 1 UNTIL RECORD-LOCATION > 100
33        DISPLAY "File is created"
34        CLOSE INVENT-FILE
35        STOP RUN.
36
37     WRITE-PARA.
38        WRITE INVENT-REC
39         INVALID KEY
40              DISPLAY "Cannot make record" RECORD-LOCATION
41        END-WRITE.
```

27.3 Verbs used with Relative Files

The verbs OPEN, CLOSE, READ, WRITE, REWRITE, DELETE and START may all be used with relative files in the same way as they are with indexed files. The INVALID KEY clause is explained below.

27.4 Adding Records to the File

Whether we are adding records to a newly created file or adding additional records, there are three steps for adding a record to a relative file:

1)   move data to the record fields
2)   compute the record's location in the file
3)   write the record.

The program CHAP27-2 reads data from the sequential file CHAP27-2.DAT. This file contains only 20 records; you may view the contents of the file using an editor program but for this demonstration our program will list them on the screen as it places the records in the relative file.

You should note the following features about this program:

a)   The relative file is defined with ACCESS RANDOM in the SELECT clause.
b)   The data item RECORD-LOCATION is not part of the file's data-description-entry but is defined in WORKING-STORAGE.
c)   We compute the value of RECORD-LOCATION using the expression
        `RECORD-LOCATION = INVENT-PART-NO - 1000`
d)   The WRITE statement contains an INVALID KEY phrase. This will report any attempts we might make to write (a) to a location which is beyond the file boundary — i.e. in our case to a location greater than 100 or less than 1, or (b) to a location in the file already containing a record — i.e. if we had two items with the same Part-Number. If it is essential for the program to differentiate between these two conditions we may use FILE STATUS as described in Chapter 32.

The reader may wish to use this program as a model for another program which accepts data from the keyboard and adds new records to the file CHAP27-1.REL.

If our input file contained all of the 100 records we wished to add to the file, we could use a single program to perform the functions of both program CHAP27-1 and CHAP27-2. The relative file would be declared to have ACCESS MODE SEQUENTIAL. The data in the input file would need to be to sorted in order of Part-Number.

```
 1      IDENTIFICATION DIVISION.
 2      PROGRAM-ID.             CHAP27-2.
 3      AUTHOR.                 B. V. LIENGME.
 4
 5      ************************************************
 6      *     To load data into a relative file
 7      ************************************************
 8
 9      ENVIRONMENT DIVISION.
10      INPUT-OUTPUT SECTION.
11      FILE-CONTROL.
12          SELECT INVENT-FILE
13                 ASSIGN TO DISK "CHAP27-1.REL"
14                 ORGANIZATION IS RELATIVE
15                 ACCESS IS RANDOM
16                 RELATIVE KEY IS RECORD-LOCATION.
17          SELECT DATA-FILE
18                 ASSIGN TO DISK "CHAP27-2.DAT"
19                 ORGANIZATION IS LINE SEQUENTIAL.
20      DATA DIVISION.
21      FILE SECTION.
```

```
22    FD  INVENT-FILE.
23    01   INVENT-REC.
24         03   INVENT-PART-NO  PIC 9999.
25         03   INVENT-NAME     PIC X(20).
26         03   INVENT-QUANT    PIC 999.
27    FD DATA-FILE.
28    01   DATA-REC.
29         03   DATA-PART-NO    PIC 9999.
30         03                   PIC X.
31         03   DATA-NAME       PIC X(20).
32         03                   PIC X.
33         03   DATA-QUANT      PIC 999.
34    WORKING-STORAGE SECTION.
35    01 WORK-ITEMS.
36         02 RECORD-LOCATION   PIC 999.
37         02 FILE-FLAG         PIC X VALUE "N".
38              88 EOF VALUE "Y".
39    PROCEDURE DIVISION.
40    MAIN-PARA.
41        OPEN INPUT DATA-FILE
42             OUTPUT INVENT-FILE
43        MOVE SPACES TO INVENT-REC
44        READ DATA-FILE AT END SET EOF TO TRUE END-READ
45        PERFORM UNTIL EOF
46             PERFORM WRITE-PARA
47             READ DATA-FILE AT END SET EOF TO TRUE END-READ
48        END-PERFORM
49        CLOSE DATA-FILE INVENT-FILE
50        STOP RUN.
51
52    WRITE-PARA.
53        MOVE DATA-PART-NO TO INVENT-PART-NO
54        MOVE DATA-NAME    TO INVENT-NAME
55        MOVE DATA-QUANT   TO INVENT-QUANT
56        SUBTRACT 1000 FROM DATA-PART-NO GIVING RECORD-LOCATION
57        DISPLAY RECORD-LOCATION " -> " DATA-REC
58        WRITE INVENT-REC
59          INVALID KEY
60               DISPLAY "Cannot make record " RECORD-LOCATION
61        END-WRITE.
```

27.5 Randomly Reading and Updating a Record

The algorithm for randomly reading a particular record is:
  1)   Get the record key. This may mean that the program (i) prompts the user to give its
        value, or (ii) reads a record from a file containing input data.
  2)   Compute the value of the record location.
  3)   Read the file.

The program CHAP27-3 demonstrates an interactive look-up procedure in the paragraph

READ-PARA. The key features to note are:

a) The syntax of a random read for a relative file is the same as for an indexed file.

b) An INVALID KEY condition will exist if (i) the record location specified is beyond the file boundary — i.e. if we try to read a location 101, or (ii) the record has never been added. If it is essential for the program to differentiate between these two conditions we may use FILE STATUS as described in Chapter 32.

To update a record once we have located it, we use a REWRITE statement. This is demonstrated in paragraph UPDATE-RECORD of program CHAP27-3. The syntax of the REWRITE verb is the same as for indexed files.

```
 1     IDENTIFICATION DIVISION.
 2     PROGRAM-ID.           CHAP27-3.
 3     AUTHOR.               B. V. LIENGME.
 4
 5     **************************************************
 6     *   Random Read and Update of Relative file
 7     **************************************************
 8
 9     ENVIRONMENT DIVISION.
10     INPUT-OUTPUT SECTION.
11     FILE-CONTROL.
12        SELECT INVENT-FILE
13              ASSIGN TO DISK "CHAP27-1.REL"
14              ORGANIZATION IS RELATIVE
15              ACCESS IS RANDOM
16              RELATIVE KEY IS RECORD-LOCATION.
17     DATA DIVISION.
18     FILE SECTION.
19     FD INVENT-FILE.
20     01  INVENT-REC.
21         03  INVENT-PART-NO  PIC 9999.
22         03  INVENT-NAME     PIC X(20).
23         03  INVENT-QUANT    PIC 999.
24     WORKING-STORAGE SECTION.
25     01 WORK-ITEMS.
26         02 WHAT-ITEM        PIC 9(4).
27            88 ALL-DONE VALUE 0.
28         02 RECORD-LOCATION  PIC 999.
29     01 OUT-REC VALUE SPACES.
30         03               PIC X(10).
31         03 OUT-PART-NO    PIC 9(4).
32         03               PIC X.
33         03 OUT-NAME       PIC X(20).
34         03               PIC X.
35         03 OUT-QUANT      PIC ZZ9.
36     PROCEDURE DIVISION.
37     MAIN-PARA.
38        OPEN I-O INVENT-FILE
39        MOVE SPACES TO INVENT-REC
```

```
40          PERFORM TEST AFTER UNTIL ALL-DONE
41            DISPLAY "Enter Part-Number or 0 to exit: " NO ADVANCING
42            ACCEPT WHAT-ITEM
43            IF NOT ALL-DONE
44                PERFORM READ-PARA
45            END-IF
46          END-PERFORM
47          CLOSE INVENT-FILE
48          STOP RUN.
49
50      READ-PARA.
51          SUBTRACT 1000 FROM WHAT-ITEM GIVING RECORD-LOCATION
52          READ  INVENT-FILE
53            INVALID KEY
54                DISPLAY "Part-No "  WHAT-ITEM " is invalid"
55            NOT INVALID KEY
56                MOVE INVENT-PART-NO TO OUT-PART-NO
57                MOVE INVENT-NAME    TO OUT-NAME
58                MOVE INVENT-QUANT   TO OUT-QUANT
59                DISPLAY RECORD-LOCATION " -> " OUT-REC
60                PERFORM UPDATE-PARA
61          END-READ.
62
63      UPDATE-PARA.
64          DISPLAY "Enter new value for Quantity-on-Hand: "
65            NO ADVANCING
66          ACCEPT INVENT-QUANT
67          REWRITE INVENT-REC
68              INVALID KEY DISPLAY "Rewrite error"
69              NOT INVALID KEY
70                MOVE INVENT-QUANT   TO OUT-QUANT
71                DISPLAY RECORD-LOCATION " -> " OUT-REC
72          END-REWRITE.
```

27.6 Reading a Relative File Sequentially

In Chapter 26 we learnt how to read an indexed file sequentially using a READ file-name
NEXT ... statement and how to start this process at a given position in the file using a
START statement. These statements are also applicable with a relative file. Similarly, a
relative file may be declared with ACCESS MODE DYNAMIC and the file may be
processed sequentially and randomly in the same program.

27.7 More Complex Hashing Functions

We started this chapter by considering the problem of storing 100 records in a relative file
when the record key was a sequence of numbers going from 1 to 100. We then saw how we
could handle a sequence going from 1001 to 1100. Our programs used the hashing algorithm:
Record location = Part-number − 1000.

Could we use phone numbers as the key in a relative file? In North America phone numbers contain 10 digits and if we assume the "lowest" number is 100-100-1000 we would still need have a range of some 8 billion values. Only some of these correspond to actual phone numbers. Furthermore, even the largest of companies will never have sufficient customers to use more than a small fraction of all valid phone numbers. Hopefully, no sane programmer would waste the disk space needed for a relative file with such a range of values. There are various hashing functions which could help in this and similar situations. We will consider only two.

One such algorithm selects digits from certain positions of the key to generate the record location. For the phone number example we will use the second, fourth, ninth, and tenth.

```
02 PHONE-NUMBER       PIC 9(10).
02 REDEFINES PHONE-NUMBER.
   03 P-DIGIT OCCURS 10 TIMES PIC 9.
   .....
COMPUTE RECORD-LOCATION =
   P-DIGIT(2) * 1000 + P-DIGIT(4) * 100
   + P-DIGIT(9) * 10 + P-DIGIT(10).
```

The phone number 902-555-1212 will give a record location value of 0512. The largest possible value will be 9999 so we could store that number of records in a relative file.

The divide-and-remainder function is commonly used with relative files. Let us simplify the problem using a key with a range of values from 1 to 99,999. If we divide any of these values by 13131 and add 1 to the remainder we will get results in the range 1 to 13131.

Do these algorithms solve our problem? The answer is "Yes; however ... ". Yes, we do get a manageable range of values for the record location. The hashing function we used in our programs is said to be a *one-to-one* function; each key value results in a unique record location. However, the functions above, like complex hashing functions, produce what are called *collisions*. A collision occurs when a hashing function results in the same record location for two keys with different values. In the phone number example, 803-522-8312 would also give a location value of 0512. In the divide-and-remainder example, both 131317 and 144448 give results of 8 if we divide by 1313 and add 1. When two or more key values generate the same record location using a given hashing function they are said to be synonyms.

Of course, we cannot use the same record location for two items. In the past, programmers have produced sophisticated methods to handle synonyms. These methods are used by some data base management systems. The author feels that reinventing the wheel is not a productive exercise and, faced with a COBOL programming task involving the problems posed by the need to use other than one-to-one hashing functions, would seek a DBMS which is callable from COBOL to achieve the objective.

27.8 Review Questions

1. Explain why relative files may be more efficient than indexed files.

2. The amount of disk space occupied by a relative file is independent of the amount of data stored in it. True or false?

3. A record cannot be deleted from a relative file. True or false?

4. Explain what is meant by hashing and synonym.

5* You wish to use a relative file with a 2-character code as the key. The key can have values from AA to ZZ. This hashing function is suggested to you:

Let A = 01, B = 02, etc. For the key AA this will give the number 0101. Since this is the lowest possible value, you can subtract 0100. Now we have AA = 0001, AB = 0002, etc.

Will this function work without synonyms? Is it efficient?

28
String Operations

Objectives

▸ Know the syntax of the STRING and UNSTRING verbs.
▸ Be competent in the use of these verbs.
▸ Be familiar with the various uses of the INSPECT verb.

28.1 Introduction

A *string* is a consecutive set of characters from the COBOL character set. We have used strings, in the form of nonnumeric literals to give values to alphanumeric identifiers: 02 COMPANY-NAME VALUE "Acme Manufacturing"; MOVE "Weekly Report" TO PAGE-TITLE. Just as there are verbs to manipulate numeric data, there are also verbs that manipulate strings. These are STRING, UNSTRING and INSPECT. See also String Functions in Chapter 32.

The operation that joins two or more strings together into one concise string is called *concatenation.* The STRING verb is used to perform concatenation.

Suppose we have a file for which part of the record description is:
```
03 REC-FAMILY      PIC X(30).
03 REC-GIVEN       PIC X(30).
```

This file may have records such as:
```
SMITH           JOHN
MACDONALD       MARY ELIZABETH
```

We may wish to print names without unnecessary blanks between given names and surnames:
```
JOHN SMITH
MARY ELIZABETH MACDONALD
```
with one space between the two names. Or we may wish to print:
```
SMITH, JOHN.
MACDONALD, MARY ELIZABETH
```

We may need the converse; our input file contains records such as:
```
SMITH, JOHN
MACDONALD, MARY ELIZABETH
```

Now we wish to put JOHN in one field and SMITH in another. The UNSTRING verb will perform this function.

The INSPECT verb permits us to count selectively and/or change a character or series of characters.

These three verbs each have several possible operations. We have space to explore only their basic operations.

28.2 The STRING Verb

```
STRING
        ⎧ ⎧identifier-1⎫    ⎫       ⎧identifier-2⎫   ⎫
        ⎨ ⎨           ⎬ ... ⎬ DELIMITED BY ⎨literal-2   ⎬ ... ⎬ ...
        ⎩ ⎩literal-1  ⎭    ⎭       ⎩SIZE       ⎭   ⎭
        INTO identifier-3
        [ WITH POINTER identifier-4 ]
        [ ON OVERFLOW imperative-statement-1 ]
        [ NOT ON OVERFLOW imperative-statement-2 ]
        [ END-STRING ]
```

literal-1 literal-2	May be any nonnumeric literal, or any nonnumeric figurative constant except ALL.
identifier-1 identifier-2	May be an alphanumeric or an elementary numeric data item. May not have a USAGE clause other than USAGE DISPLAY.
identifier-3	Must be alphanumeric. May not have a JUSTIFIED clause, nor a USAGE other than DISPLAY.
identifier-4	Must be an elementary numeric item, with a size one greater than that of identifier-3 .

We will look briefly at the optional phrases; we may then ignore them in the rest of the discussion.

WITH POINTER	Suppose we are stringing a surname and a given name into identifier-3 (call this *receiver-item*). Perhaps we wish to put the string into receiver-item starting at its third character position. Then we would code WITH POINTER START-HERE; we would then ensure that START-HERE had a value of 3 before the STRING statement executed. As each character is moved to receiver-item START-HERE is incremented by 1. If we use an initial value of 1 for START-HERE, its value less 1 after the STRING statement will be a count of the

number of characters moved.

ON OVERFLOW   If the number of characters we string into receiver-item exceeds the size of its picture clause, an ON OVERFLOW condition will occur. This will cause imperative-statement-1 to be executed. In the example of stringing a surname and a given name, this statement might direct the program to perform another paragraph that would string the surname and an initial.

To aid our discussion we will re-write the format of the STRING verb as:
```
STRING { { sender-item}… DELIMITED BY delimiter }… INTO receiver-item
```

Unless receiver-item is emptied (MOVE SPACES TO receiver-item) *before the execution of the* STRING *statement, it will retain any characters that are not overwritten by the* STRING *statement. It is generally good practice to initialize receiver-item on a line in your program immediately preceding the STRING statement.*

identifer-2
literal-2

When a delimiter is specified by an identifier or literal, the characters in sender-item are moved to receiver-item one by one until the statement encounters the delimiter. The delimiter character string is not passed to receiver-item.

SIZE   When the sender-item is delimited by SIZE, every character in that item (including trailing spaces) is moved to receiver-item.

Example 1:
```
STRING    REC-GIVEN     DELIMITED BY TWO-SPACES
          SPACE         DELIMITED BY SIZE
          REC-FAMILY    DELIMITED BY TWO-SPACES
          INTO          ONE-NAME
```

Data item	Initial value	Final value
REC-FAMILY	SMITH	unchanged
REC-GIVEN	JOHN	unchanged
ONE-NAME	SPACES	JOHN SMITH

Example 2:
```
STRING    REC-FAMILY    DELIMITED BY TWO-SPACES
          ", "          DELIMITED BY SIZE
          REC-GIVEN     DELIMITED BY TWO-SPACES
          INTO          ONE-NAME
```

will give ONE-NAME a value of: SMITH, JOHN

In these examples, TWO-SPACES is defined as PIC XX VALUE SPACES. We could have used DELIMITED BY " " in the STRING statement with two spaces between the quotes. Had we delimited by a single space, then the STRING verb operating on a name such as

"JOHN XAVIER" would detect the single space between the two given names and move only the first one to the receiving item. There may be cases where this is exactly what the programmer requires, in which case DELIMITED BY SPACES would achieve the objective.

If you find yourself using a STRING statement in which the only delimiter is SIZE, you have misunderstood the purpose of the verb. Your receiving item should be a structured record and your STRING statement should be replaced by a series of MOVE statements.

28.3 The UNSTRING Verb

```
UNSTRING identifier-1
    [ DELIMITED BY [ALL] {identifier-2}... [ OR [ALL] {identifier-3} ] ]...
                         {literal-1  }              {literal-2  }
    INTO { identifier-4 [ DELIMITER IN identifier-5 ] [COUNT IN identifier-6 ] }...
    [ WITH POINTER identifier-7 ]
    [ TALLYING IN identifier-8 ]
    [ ON OVERFLOW imperative-statement-1 ]
    [ NOT ON OVERFLOW imperative-statement-2 ]
    [ END-UNSTRING ]
```

literal-1 literal-2	Must be either nonnumeric literals or figurative constants without ALL.
identifier-1 identifier-2 identifier-3 identifier-5	Must be alphanumeric data items.
identifier-4	May be an alphabetic, alphanumeric or numeric data item.
identifier-7	Must be an elementary numeric data item. Its size must be 1 greater than the size of identifier-1.
identifier-6 identifier-8	Must be elementary numeric data items.

Again, we shall rewrite this as a simplified form that facilitates discussion.

```
UNSTRING sending-item DELIMITED BY delimiter-1
         INTO   receiver-1   receiver-2...
```

The sending-item is to be "split" into several parts; these will be placed in the receivers. The "splitting", or "unstringing" will occur whenever the character(s) represented by delimiter-1 is encountered. If the receiving item is too small to contain all the characters, truncation will occur. The characters of the delimiter are not moved to a receiver. They can be placed in identifier-5 if the DELIMITER IN phrase is included in the statement.

DELIMITER	The statement: `UNSTRING ONE-NAME DELIMITED BY " "`
	                                `INTO REC-GIVEN REC-FAMILY`
	will reverse the operation we performed in the first example of the STRING verb.
	Likewise, `UNSTRING ONE-NAME DELIMITED BY ", "`
	                                `INTO REC-FAMILY REC-GIVEN`
	will reverse what occurred in the second STRING example.

OR	If we had records with names in two formats, for example JOHN, SMITH and JOHN*SMITH, we could unstring them with:
	    `UNSTRING ONE-NAME DELIMITED BY ", " OR "*"`
	          `INTO REC-FAMILY REC-GIVEN`
	
	Should the records contain a mixture of types such as "JOHN*SMITH", and "JOHN**SMITH", we might use `DELIMITED BY "*"`or `"**"`.

ALL	An alternative would be to use `DELIMITED BY ALL "*"`, then each occurrence of `"*"` will be taken as part of the delimiter.
COUNT	When the COUNT phrase is used with a receiving item, COUNT is incremented by one every time a character is moved to the receiving item. The program should initialize COUNT to zero before the UNSTRING statement.
TALLYING	If we wish to know how many receiving items had data passed to them, we use the TALLYING phrase. The data item identifier-8 requires initializing.
POINTER	If we wish to start the unstring process at some character other than the first one in the sending item, we would use the WITH POINTER phrase. If, for example, identifier-7 is given a value of 3 before the UNSTRING statement then "unstringing" will begin with the third character in identifier-1. Identifier-7 is incremented by one for each character examined.

The observant reader will note that the DELIMITED BY phrase in the syntax is optional. This seems to be a paradox since the operation of UNSTRING, as we have seen so far, appears to require a delimiter. If our task is to move a subset of the string (for example, the third and subsequent characters of sender-item are to be moved to receiver-item), then we would use WITH POINTER but would not need a DELIMITED BY phrase. Reference modification achieves the same objective, for example:

```
MOVE SENDER-ITEM (3:10) TO RECEIVER-ITEM
```

OVERFLOW   An OVERFLOW condition occurs when:

a) The initial value of identifier-7 in the POINTER phrase is either less than 1 or greater than the size of the sending item, or

b) All the receiving items are filled before all the characters in the sending items are tested.

28.4 The INSPECT Verb

In the four formats of the INSPECT verb shown below, the terms *identifier* and *literal* have been abbreviated to *ident* and *lit*, respectively.

```
INSPECT ident-1 TALLYING
  [                  [ {BEFORE}        {ident-4}  ]                 ]
  { ident-2 FOR { CHARACTERS [{AFTER } INITIAL {lit-2 }]...        }}
  {             { {ALL    } {{ident-3} [{BEFORE} INITIAL {ident-4}]...}...}...
  {             { {LEADING} {{lit-1  } {AFTER } INITIAL {lit-2  }
```

```
INSPECT ident-1 REPLACING
  {                   {ident-5} [{BEFORE}        {ident-4}]          }
  { CHARACTERS BY {lit-3  } [{AFTER } INITIAL {lit-2  }]...         }
  { {ALL    }       {ident-5}  { [{BEFORE} INITIAL {ident-4}]...}... }...
  { {LEADING} BY {lit-3  }  { {AFTER }         {lit-2  }
  { {FIRST  }
```

```
INSPECT ident-1 TALLYING
  [                  [ {BEFORE}        {ident-4}  ]                 ]
  { ident-2 FOR { CHARACTERS [{AFTER } INITIAL {lit-2 }]...        }}
  {             { {ALL    } {{ident-3} [{BEFORE} INITIAL {ident-4}]...}...}...
  {             { {LEADING} {{lit-1  } {AFTER } INITIAL {lit-2  }

REPLACING
  {                   {ident-5} [{BEFORE}        {ident-4}]          }
  { CHARACTERS BY {lit-3  } [{AFTER } INITIAL {lit-2  }]...         }
  { {ALL    }       {ident-5}  { [{BEFORE} INITIAL {ident-4  }]...}... }...
  { {LEADING} BY {lit-3  }  { {AFTER }         {literal-2}
  { {FIRST  }
```

```
INSPECT ident-1 CONVERTING {ident-6} TO {ident-7}
                           {lit-4  }    {lit-5  }
      [ {BEFORE}        {ident-4} ]
      [ {AFTER } INITIAL {lit-2  } ]
```

A full discussion of these powerful statements is beyond the scope of this book. The following examples should enable successful use of each format.

Format-1: Examples of INSPECT...TALLYING

`02 MY-STRING PIC X(20) VALUE "ABC*DEFABC"` Note that the actual value contains 6 spaces after the final "C" because of PIC X(20).

Statement	Value of X-COUNT
INSPECT X-STRING TALLYING FOR CHARACTERS	20
INSPECT X-STRING TALLYING FOR CHARACTERS BEFORE "*"	3
INSPECT X-STRING TALLYING FOR CHARACTERS AFTER "*"	16
INSPECT X-STRING TALLYING FOR ALL "*"	1
INSPECT X-STRING TALLYING FOR LEADING "*"	0
INSPECT X-STRING TALLYING FOR LEADING "ABC"	1
INSPECT X-STRING TALLYING FOR ALL "ABC" AFTER "*"	1

Format-2: Examples of INSPECT...REPLACING

`02 X-STRING PIC X(20) VALUE "ABC*DEFABC"`
This is the initial value of X-STRING for each of the following examples.

Statement	Final value of X-STRING
INSPECT X-STRING REPLACING FOR CHARACTERS BY "x" BEFORE "*"	xxx*DEFABC
INSPECT X-STRING REPLACING ALL "AB" BY "x" BEFORE "*"	xxB*DEFABC
INSPECT X-STRING REPLACING FIRST "C" BY "x"	ABx*DEFABC
INSPECT X-STRING REPLACING FIRST "C" BY "x" AFTER "*"	ABC*DEFABx
INSPECT X-STRING REPLACING LEADING "D" BY "x"	no change
INSPECT X-STRING REPLACING LEADING "D" BY "x" AFTER "*"	ABC*xEFABC

Format-3:   This format allows the programmer to combine the functions of Formats-1 and -2 into a single statement.

Format-4:   Examples using INSPECT...CONVERTING

Suppose we had a file containing names in upper case letters and that we required all but the first letter to be in lower case. We begin by defining an identifier for the characters we wish to change.

```
02 NAME-ITEM.
   03 NAME-ONE      PIC X.
   03 NAME-REST     PIC X(19).
```

We could use a Format-2 INSPECT statement with 26 ALL clauses:

```
INSPECT NAME-REST REPLACING    ALL "A" BY "a"
                               ALL "B" BY "b".
                               ...
                               ALL "Z" BY "z"
```

More simply we could use a Format-4 statement:

```
INSPECT NAME-REST
   CONVERTING    "ABCDEFGHIJKLMNOPQRSTUVWXYZ"
   TO            "abcdefghijklmnopqrstuvwxyz"
```

If we write this format as INSPECT input-string CONVERTING input-array BY output-array, this format works by looking at each character in the input-string and locating it in the input-array and replacing the character by the corresponding character from the output-array. Thus, in our example, "B" is the second letter in the input-array, so "B" will be replaced by the second letter in output-array, namely "b".

28.5 Review Questions

1. Our program will use the statement STRING . . . . . INTO OUT-REC.
    Explain why we generally need a MOVE SPACES TO OUT-REC before the STRING statement.

2. A class-mate has this code in a program:

```
01 OUT-REC       PIC X(60).
01 X-REC.
   02 X-ONE      PIC X(20).
   02 X-TWO      PIC X(20).
   02 X-THREE    PIC X(20).
MOVE SPACES TO OUT-REC
STRING X-ONE X-THREE X-TWO DELIMITED BY SIZE INTO OUT-REC.
```

Write more effective code to replace the STRING statement.

3* In a) below the identifier TWO-SPACES is defined by

```
02 TWO-SPACES    PIC XX    VALUE SPACES.
```

Which is the more appropriate code to use in a STRING statement?

    a) `CUST-CITY    DELIMITED BY TWO-SPACES`
    b) `CUST-CITY    DELIMITED BY SPACES`

4. The data-name CUST-FIRST-NAME may contain one or more names e.g. "JOHN", "MARY ELLEN", etc. Write the code needed to find how many there are.

29
Interprogram Communication

Objectives

▸ Understand what is meant by a calling and a called program.
▸ Know the syntax of the CALL verb.
▸ Know what is required to exchange data between two programs.
▸ Know the difference between a static and a dynamic program.

29.1 Introduction

Frequently in a business application there will be programming procedures that are common to many programs. As a simple example, consider an application using a data base with customer names and addresses. One program may prepare invoice forms; another may generate shipping forms. If these two forms are similar, the lines of code that generate the address lines may be the same in each program. We might decide, therefore, to make a subprogram to generate the address lines and have each program call this subprogram. This would save us the trouble of writing the code twice. More importantly, should we redesign the forms, we need modify only the subprogram.

If the task we wish to code is complex, we may wish to divide it into a series of programs each of which performs a subset of the tasks. This would greatly facilitate coding and testing the modules. It would also allow a group of programmers to work as a team with each programmer working on a separate part of the project.

In other cases, we may wish a COBOL program to call a subprogram written in another language such as Pascal or C.

In the diagrams below we illustrate the three ways of keeping the calling and called program on the computer disk. The programming examples are trivial but demonstrate how one program (PROG-A) may invoke another with a CALL statement and how the called program (PROG-B) returns control to the calling program with a EXIT PROGRAM statement. The three arrangements are:

1) To keep the code for A and B in separate source files.
2) To keep the code in one source file with two separate programs.
3) To nest the called program within a main program.

Method 1 is of more general use in that PROG-B may be called by programs in addition to PROG-A. Method 2 has some merit when you wish to "package" an application containing a number of programs into one file for ease of distribution. We will briefly examine the third method (nested programs) later in the chapter.

Method 1: Separate source files

```
          Source file for PROG-A

IDENTIFICATION DIVISION.
PROGRAM-ID.        PROG-A.
PROCEDURE DIVISION.
MAIN-PARA.
    DISPLAY "Start of PROG-A"
    CALL PROG-B
    DISPLAY "End of PROG-A"
    STOP RUN.
```

```
          Source file for PROG-B

IDENTIFICATION DIVISION.
PROGRAM-ID.        PROG-B.
PROCEDURE DIVISION.
MAIN-PARA.
    DISPLAY "Running  PROG-B"
    EXIT PROGRAM.
```

Method 2: One concatenated source file

Method 3: One source file with nesting

```
  Source file for PROG-A and PROG-B
               not nested

IDENTIFICATION DIVISION.
PROGRAM-ID.        PROG-A.
PROCEDURE DIVISION.
MAIN-PARA.
    DISPLAY "Start of PROG-A"
    CALL PROG-B
    DISPLAY "End of PROG-A"
    STOP RUN.
END PROGRAM PROG-A.

IDENTIFICATION DIVISION.
PROGRAM-ID.        PROG-B.
PROCEDURE DIVISION.
MAIN-PARA.
    DISPLAY "Running  PROG-B"
    EXIT PROGRAM.
END PROGRAM PROG-B.
```

```
  Source file for PROG-A and PROG-B
                 nested

IDENTIFICATION DIVISION.
PROGRAM-ID.        PROG-A.
PROCEDURE DIVISION.
MAIN-PARA.
    DISPLAY "Start of PROG-A"
    CALL PROG-B
    DISPLAY "End of PROG-A"
    STOP RUN.

IDENTIFICATION DIVISION.
PROGRAM-ID.        PROG-B.
PROCEDURE DIVISION.
MAIN-PARA.
    DISPLAY "Running  PROG-B"
    EXIT PROGRAM.
END PROGRAM PROG-B.

END PROGRAM PROG-A.
```

Note the use of the CALL verb and the fact that B ends with EXIT PROGRAM rather than STOP RUN. Also note the use of the END PROGRAM headers in Methods 2 and 3. In the second example PROG-A is ended with END PROGRAM PROG-A before the Identification Division of PROG-B, so we have concatenation. In Method 3, PROG-B is ended before PROG-A, so we have nesting.

29.2 The CALL Verb

The CALL statement is used to pass control from one program to another in the same run-time unit. We shall discuss run-time units at the end of the chapter. Our major interest in this chapter is to see how one COBOL program can interact with another COBOL program. We briefly look at calling non-COBOL subprograms at the end of the chapter.

The ANSI COBOL format of the CALL verb for COBOL to COBOL interprogram communication is shown below. We have slightly simplified the discussion by omitting reference to passing file-name data.

```
CALL  { identifier-1 }  [ USING { [ BY REFERENCE ] (identifier-2 )...  } ... ]
      { literal-1    }         { BY CONTENT (identifier-2 )...         }
      [ ON OVERFLOW imperative-sentence-1 ]
      [ END-CALL ]
```

literal-1
identifier-1

This data item names the *called* program. When a COBOL subprogram is called, the data item has a value matching the name of the subprogram as specified in its PROGRAM-ID entry.

Example in which a literal is used: CALL "SUBPROGX"...

Example in which an identifier is used:
```
    03 SUBPROGRAM-1    PIC X(10) VALUE "SUBPROGX".
    ......
    CALL MY-SUBPROGRAM-NAME...
```

identifier-2

Names of the data item(s) passed to the called program. The ellipse indicates that more than one data item may be used.

The order of these data items is important. When a COBOL program is called, there must be a positional correspondence between the data item in the calling program's CALL USING statement and those in the called program's PROCEDURE DIVISION USING phrase. In addition, the data items must be defined in the LINKAGE SECTION of the called program. See Sample Program 2 below.

This is one way of exchanging data between two programs; the other is to use the EXTERNAL clause in the data description.

REFERENCE   This is the default method of passing a parameter, and is the method generally used when one COBOL program calls another COBOL program.

When a parameter is passed by *reference*, the data item in the calling program and the corresponding data item in the called program appears to be one and the same. Thus if one program changes the value of the item, the other has access to the new value.

CONTENT   When a data item is passed by CONTENT, the called program receives a copy of the data item's value. This value may be changed in the calling program but such a change will not affect the value in the calling program. As an extension to ANSI COBOL, many compilers allow the use of literal parameters. For example:
```
BY CONTENT 110.25 "BOOK PRICE"
```

OVERFLOW   An OVERFLOW condition occurs when the system fails to activate the called program. This applies only when the CALL uses identifier-1 not literal-1.

Some rules affecting identifier-2, and comments on the use of BY REFERENCE and BY CONTENT are discussed in Sample Program 2.

29.2.1 Nested calls

A called program (a subprogram) may itself call another subprogram. This is referred to as a *nested call* — do not confuse this with *nested programs* that are discussed later in the chapter. Nested calls in Micro Focus COBOL require the compiler directive NESTCALL. Nested calls in the Educational version of RM/COBOL-85 are supported only in nested programs.

A called program may not call, either directly or indirectly, the program that called it nor may it call itself. That is to say, recursive calls are not legal. In this manner, the rules for nesting subprograms are similar to those for nesting perform paragraphs. Micro Focus COBOL does permit recursive CALLS but this is beyond the scope of this book.

29.3 Sample Program 1

No data is passed between the two programs in this example. The main program is executing; it gets to the CALL statement and control passes to the subprogram; this displays a message; the subprogram returns control to the main program with the EXIT PROGRAM statement; the main program then executes its next statement following the CALL. This program is in file CHAP29-1.CBL; concatenation is used to facilitate distribution.

The output from this example will be:
```
About to call subprogram
This message comes from the subprogram
Returned from subprogram
```

```
1     IDENTIFICATION DIVISION.
2     PROGRAM-ID.          CHAP24-1A.
3     PROCEDURE DIVISION.
4     CALLING-PARA.
5        DISPLAY "About to call subprogram"
6        CALL "CHAP29-1B"
7        DISPLAY "Returned from subprogram"
8        STOP RUN.
9     END PROGRAM CHAP29-1A.
10
11    IDENTIFICATION DIVISION.
12    PROGRAM-ID. CHAP29-1B.
13    PROCEDURE DIVISION.
14    MAIN-PARA.
15       DISPLAY "This message comes from the subprogram"
16       EXIT PROGRAM.
17    END PROGRAM CHAP29-1B.
```

Other than in exceptional circumstances, it is a mistake to code a STOP RUN statement in a subprogram since this will terminate the entire run-time unit; i.e. the main program and the subprogram.

29.4 Sample Program 2

In the next example the main program passes numeric values to the subprogram. The subprogram determines which is the larger of the first two and returns the two numbers in order of value, together with the sum of the two numbers. These programs may be found on the disk in file CHAP29-2.

```
1     IDENTIFICATION DIVISION.
2     PROGRAM-ID.          CHAP29-2A.
3     DATA DIVISION.
4     WORKING-STORAGE SECTION.
5     01 TEST-DATA.
6        03 TEST-WHEN     PIC X(10).
7        03 FILLER        PIC X(17) VALUE " First number  = ".
8        03 TEST-ONE      PIC 99.
9        03 FILLER        PIC X(17) VALUE " Second number = ".
10       03 TEST-TWO      PIC 99.
11       03 FILLER        PIC X(6)  VALUE " Sum = "
12       03 TEST-SUM      PIC 999   VALUE ZERO.
13
14    PROCEDURE DIVISION.
15    CALLING-PARA.
16       DISPLAY "Give first number  "  NO ADVANCING
17       ACCEPT TEST-ONE
18       DISPLAY "Give second number "  NO ADVANCING
19       ACCEPT TEST-ONE
20       MOVE "BEFORE" TO TEST-WHEN      DISPLAY TEST-DATA
```

```
21          CALL "CHAP29-2B" USING TEST-ONE TEST-TWO TEST-SUM
22          MOVE "AFTER"  TO TEST-WHEN     DISPLAY TEST-DATA
23          STOP RUN.
24     END PROGRAM CHAP29-2A.

 1     IDENTIFICATION DIVISION.
 2     PROGRAM-ID.          CHAP29-2B.
 3     DATA DIVISION.
 4     WORKING-STORAGE SECTION.
 5     01 NEW-DATA.
 6          03 FILLER      PIC X(10) VALUE "SUBPROGRAM".
 7          03 FILLER      PIC X(17) VALUE " Larger =   ".
 8          03 NEW-ONE     PIC 99.
 9          03 FILLER      PIC X(17) VALUE " Smaller = ".
10          03 NEW-TWO     PIC 99.
11          03 FILLER      PIC X(6)  VALUE " Sum = ".
12          03 NEW-SUM     PIC 999   VALUE ZERO.
13     LINKAGE SECTION.
14     01 SUB-ONE          PIC 99.
15     01 SUB-TWO          PIC 99.
16     01 SUB-SUM          PIC 999.
17
18     PROCEDURE DIVISION USING SUB-ONE SUB-TWO SUB-SUM.
19     MAIN-PARA.
20          IF SUB-ONE > SUB-TWO
21               THEN    MOVE SUB-ONE TO NEW-ONE
22               MOVE SUM-TWO TO NEW-TWO
23          ELSE    MOVE SUB-TWO TO NEW-ONE
24               MOVE SUB-ONE TO NEW-TWO
25               MOVE NEW-ONE TO SUB-ONE
26               MOVE NEW-TWO TO SUB-TWO
27          END-IF
28          ADD SUB-ONE TO SUB-TWO GIVING SUB-SUM NEW-SUM
29          DISPLAY NEW-DATA
30          EXIT PROGRAM.
31     END PROGRAM CHAP29-2B.
```

A sample output from this run-unit:
```
Give first number  12
Give second number 20
BEFORE     First number = 12 Second number = 20 Sum = 000
SUBPROGRAM Larger =      20 Smaller =       12 Sum = 032
AFTER      First number = 20 Second number = 12 Sum = 032
```

29.5 Notes on CALL USING

1) The data items in the USING phase of the CALL statement should be at the 01 or 77 level, or be elementary items.

2) When the calling program passes parameters to the called program, the called program

contains a LINKAGE SECTION following the WORKING-STORAGE SECTION, and its PROCEDURE DIVISION contains the USING phrase.

3) The parameters passed need not have the same names in the two programs. The correspondence between parameters in the two programs is determined by the order of the data items in the USING phrase in the CALL statement in the main program, and in the PROCEDURE DIVISION in the subprogram.

```
CALL USING                    TEST-ONE  TEST-TWO  TEST-SUM
PROCEDURE DIVISION USING      SUB-ONE   SUB-TWO   SUB-SUM
```

The data items TEST-ONE and SUB-ONE correspond since they are first in their respective USING phrases, etc.

4) In the LINKAGE SECTION the three parameters are defined at the 01 level. This is the simplest way to ensure the data items are on word boundaries. The order of data items within this section is unimportant.

The rules concerning the correspondence between the data-description-entries for an identifier in the called and the calling program differ slightly depending on the use of BY REFERENCE or BY CONTENT. The simplest thing to do is to use the same PICTURE and USAGE clause in both descriptions.

The VALUE clause (other than for an 88 level item) is not allowed in the LINKAGE SECTION.

5) When a parameter is passed BY CONTENT, there are separate memory storage areas for the item referenced in the calling and in the called program. The called program may change the value in its own (subprogram) storage area but not in that of the calling (main) program.

Let us replace the CALL statement in Sample Program 2 by:

```
CALL "SUBPROGRAM" USING BY CONTENT TEST-ONE TEST-TWO TEST-SUM
```

Now the subprogram will not change the values of TEST-ONE, TEST-TWO and TEST-SUM. The output will be:

```
Give first number  12
Give second number 20
BEFORE     First number =  12 Second number = 20 Sum = 000
SUBPROGRAM Larger =        20 Smaller =       12 Sum = 032
AFTER      First number =  12 Second number = 20 Sum = 000
```

A BY REFERENCE or BY CONTENT phrase applies to all identifiers following it until another phrase is defined. To pass TEST-ONE and TEST-SUM by reference, and TEST-TWO by content we would use:

```
CALL "SUBPROGRAM" USING BY REFERENCE TEST-ONE
                  BY CONTENT TEST-TWO BY REFERENCE TEST-SUM
```

The first BY REFERENCE is optional since this is the default.

29.6 Initial State of a Program

When a program is called for the first time in a run-unit it is said to be in its *initial state*. A program in its initial state when: (1) identifiers containing the VALUE clause have values specified by that clause, (2) all files are closed, and (3) control mechanism for PERFORM statements are set to their initial values.

Some of these conditions may be altered when a program is executed. If it is a subprogram then, when it is called subsequent to the first time, its values will be the same as they were when the program was last exited. The programmer may need to reinitialize some variables each time a subprogram is called.

A program that does not begin in its initial state after the first execution is sometimes called a *static program* — its state at the start of each execution is that in which it was left at the end of the previous execution When a subprogram is *dynamic* it is in its initial state every time that it begins execution.

29.6.1 The IS INITIAL clause

A program may be declared to be dynamic by including the IS <u>INITIAL</u> PROGRAM clause in the PROGRAM-ID. For example:

```
        PROGRAM-ID.  SUBPROG   IS INITIAL PROGRAM.
or      PROGRAM-ID.  SUBPROG   INITIAL.
```

Consider a called program with the following code:

```
        03 FILE-FLAG   PIC X   VALUE "N".
           88 EOF   VALUE "Y".
        ....
        OPEN INPUT MY-FILE
        READ MY-FILE AT END SET EOF TO TRUE END-READ
        PERFORM UNTIL EOF
            process the file record
            READ MY-FILE AT END SET EOF TO TRUE END-READ
        END-PERFORM
        CLOSE MY-FILE
```

The first time this subprogram is called, the file is read until end-of-file is encountered. At this point FILE-FLAG is given a value of "Y". A subsequent call to this subprogram will cause no records to be processed; the EOF condition is already true so the PERFORM will pass control to END-PERFORM immediately.

One way to solve this problem is to add the statement: MOVE "N" TO FILE-FLAG prior to the first READ statement. Alternatively, we may include the INITIAL clause in the PROGRAM-ID entry.

```
        PROGRAM-ID.  PROG-X   IS INITIAL PROGRAM.
or      PROGRAM-ID.  PROG-X   INITIAL.
```

This method would be more convenient when several identifiers need to be reset.

29.6.2 The CANCEL verb

Another method of ensuring that a program is in its initial state next time it is called is to use the CANCEL statement after the CALL in the main program:

```
CALL "PROG-X".        or        CALL PROGRAM-NAME.
CANCEL "PROG-X".                CANCEL PROGRAM-NAME.
```

If you wish the program to be in the initial state always, use the IS INITIAL clause. If you wish it to be in the initial state sometimes then use the CANCEL statement as required.

29.7 The EXTERNAL Clause

```
             <data item picture-clause>  IS   EXTERNAL
```

When a data element is declared to be EXTERNAL, it is available to all other programs in the run-unit without the need to pass parameters.

Only record descriptions may be declared external. These are (i) a file description entry (FD) in FILE SECTION and (ii) 01 data-description-entries in WORKING-STORAGE SECTION. Items subordinate to an external item are also external. The name and length of an external record must be the same in the two (or more) programs using the record. External items may not contain the REDEFINES clause. Items subordinate to the external item may contain REDEFINES clauses. When a data item is declared to be external, neither that item nor any item subordinate to it may have a VALUE clause. This rule does not apply to the VALUE clause of condition-names (88 level items).

Data items and files declared as EXTERNAL are not affected by the INITIAL PROGRAM clause or by a CANCEL statement.

The next example performs the same operation as Sample Program 2, but uses the EXTERNAL clause. In this example we do not need the LINKAGE SECTION and the USING clause in the PROCEDURE DIVISION heading because we are using external data. Note that the EXTERNAL clause must appear in both programs.

Example to demonstrate use of EXTERNAL

```
IDENTIFICATION DIVISION.          IDENTIFICATION DIVISION.
PROGRAM-ID.  CHAP29-3A.           PROGRAM-ID. CHAP29-3B.
DATA DIVISION.                    DATA DIVISION.
WORKING-STORAGE SECTION.          WORKING-STORAGE SECTION.
01 TEST-DATA IS EXTERNAL.         01 TEST-DATA IS EXTERNAL.
   03 TEST-ONE    PIC 99.            03 TEST-ONE    PIC 99.
   03 TEST-TWO    PIC 99.            03 TEST-TWO    PIC 99.
   03 TEST-SUM    PIC 999.           03 TEST-SUM    PIC 999.
                                  01 HOLD-SMALL     PIC 99.
```

```
PROCEDURE DIVISION.                    PROCEDURE DIVISION.
MAIN-PARA.                             MAIN-PARA.
    DISPLAY "First number  > "           IF TEST-ONE < TEST-TWO
    ACCEPT TEST-ONE                        MOVE TEST-ONE TO HOLD-SMALL
    DISPLAY "Second number > "             MOVE TEST-TWO TO TEST-ONE
    ACCEPT TEST-ONE                        MOVE HOLD-SMALL TO TEST-ONE
    DISPLAY "(A) " TEST-ONE " "          END-IF
          TEST-TWO " " TEST-SUM        ADD TEST-ONE TO TEST-TWO
    CALL "CHAP29-3B"                                 GIVING TEST-SUM
    DISPLAY "(C) " TEST-ONE " "          DISPLAY "(B) " TEST-ONE " "
          TEST-TWO " " TEST-SUM                 TEST-TWO " " TEST-SUM
    STOP RUN.                            EXIT PROGRAM.
```

29.7.1 Two programs sharing a file

The EXTERNAL clause is very useful when we wish to share a file between a calling
program and a called program. In the example below, the subprogram has full access to the
file PRINTER because the file description is declared to be external in both programs.
Within the subprogram one may reference the file, its record and items within the record in
the same way as one would do in a paragraph within the main program. The subprogram may
also reference LINAGE-COUNTER of PRINTER. If there are several subprograms using
the same file, it is simpler to open and close the file in the main program.

Example to show how to share a file

```
IDENTIFICATION DIVISION.                IDENTIFICATION DIVISION.
PROGRAM-ID.  MAINPROG.                  PROGRAM-ID.  SUBPROG.
ENVIRONMENT DIVISION.                   ENVIRONMENT DIVISION.
INPUT-OUTPUT SECTION.                   INPUT-OUTPUT SECTION.
FILE-CONTROL.                           FILE-CONTROL.
 SELECT PRINTER                          SELECT PRINTER
    ASSIGN TO PRINTER.                      ASSIGN TO PRINTER.
....                                    ....
DATA DIVISION.                          DATA DIVISION.
FILE SECTION.                           FILE SECTION.
FD PRINTER LINAGE 66 EXTERNAL.          FD PRINTER LINAGE 66 EXTERNAL.
01 PRINT-REC.                           01 PRINT-REC.
      03 PRINT-ONE    PIC X(10).              03 PRINT-ONE    PIC X(10).
      03 PRINT-TWO    PIC X(30).              03 PRINT-TWO    PIC X(30).
      03 PRINT-THREE  PIC 999.                03 PRINT-THREE  PIC 999.

WORKING-STORAGE SECTION.                WORKING-STORAGE SECTION.
.....                                   .....
PROCEDURE DIVISION.                     PROCEDURE DIVISION.
    .....                                   .....
    OPEN OUTPUT PRINTER                     move data to print-rec
    move data to print-rec                  WRITE PRINT-REC AFTER 3
    WRITE PRINT-REC AFTER PAGE              .....
    .....
    CALL "SUBPROG"
    ......
    CLOSE PRINTER
    STOP RUN.
```

If two or more programs are using the same file one should use the COPY statement to ensure that the FD entry for the file is the same in each program — see Chapter 30.

29.8 Calling a Non-COBOL Program

Many implementations of COBOL enhance the ANSI Format-2 of the CALL verb to more readily facilitate calling non-COBOL programs. The GIVING phrase is a non-ANSI feature. What follows is a brief and incomplete overview. The reader should consult the vendor's COBOL manual for more details.

```
CALL {identifier-1}  [ USING {[ BY REFERENCE ] (identifier-2 )... } ]
     {literal-1   }           {BY CONTENT (identifier-2 )...     }...
     [ GIVING identifier-3 ]
     [ ON EXCEPTION imperative-sentence-1 ]
     [ NOT ON EXCEPTION imperative-sentence-2 ]
     [ END-CALL ]
```

The programmer must ensure that the passing mechanism (BY REFERENCE, CONTENT, etc.) in the COBOL program is compatible with the mechanism used by the language of the called program. It is also essential to match the type of each data item being passed. The table below shows some compatibilities. All COBOL numeric items must have USAGE COMP or USAGE BINARY, and they are either at level 01 (or 77) or they contain the SYNC clause in their data description.

COBOL	C	PASCAL	BASIC
X	char	CHAR	string
X(n)	char [n]	PACKED ARRAY [n] OF CHAR	string
S9 to S9(4)	signed shortint	SHORTINT	integer
S9(5) to S9(9)	signed int	INTEGER	integer
9 to 9(4)	unsigned shortint		

29.9 Nested Programs

When the task to be performed by your program is somewhat complex and there are parts of it which use certain data items and/or files while other parts use different data and/or files, then it could be advantageous to use the nesting technique. Nesting allow you to isolate data in the same way as do other structured languages like Pascal and C. The diagram below shows the source code and the schematic for a very simple nested program.

```
IDENTIFICATION DIVISION.
PROGRAM-ID.          PROG-A.
PROCEDURE DIVISION.
BEGIN-A.
    DISPLAY "A is outermost program"
    CALL "B"
    CALL "D"
    CALL "E"
    STOP RUN.

IDENTIFICATION DIVISION.
PROGRAM-ID.          PROG-B.
PROCEDURE DIVISION.
BEGIN-B.
    DISPLAY "B is nested in A"
    CALL "C"
    EXIT PROGRAM.

IDENTIFICATION DIVISION.
PROGRAM-ID.          PROG-C.
PROCEDURE DIVISION.
BEGIN-C.
    DISPLAY "C is nested in B"
    EXIT PROGRAM.
END PROGRAM C.

END PROGRAM B.

IDENTIFICATION DIVISION.
PROGRAM-ID.          PROG-D.
PROCEDURE DIVISION.
BEGIN-D.
    DISPLAY "D is nested in A"
    EXIT PROGRAM.
END PROGRAM D.

END PROGRAM A.


IDENTIFICATION DIVISION.
PROGRAM-ID.          PROG-E.
PROCEDURE DIVISION.
BEGIN-E.
    DISPLAY
      "E is a concatenated program"
    EXIT PROGRAM.
END PROGRAM E.
```

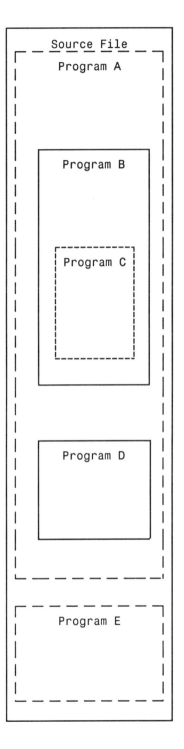

With this simple example we may introduce some terminology:

Program A is the *parent* of programs B and D. Correspondingly, B and D are the *children* of A.

Program C is a *grandchild* of program A.

Programs B and D are *siblings*.

Programs B and D are *nested* directly within A; i.e. B and D are directly contained within A. Program C is nested in B; it is indirectly contained within A.

Program E is a *concatenated* program; it is not nested in A. Program E is said to be a separately compiled program.

29.9.1 The COMMON clause

When the COMMON clause is not used, the rules for which programs can be called by another are:

1) A program can call any of its children. (A may call C and D, B may call C).
2) A program may not call one of its grandchildren or their descendants (A may not call C).
3) A program may not call one of its siblings. (B may not call D, nor D call B).
4) Any program can call a separately compiled program. (A, B, C and D may call E).

The COMMON clause, which changes these rules, is used on the PROGRAM-ID entry:

```
PROGRAM-ID.  PROG-C  IS COMMON PROGRAM.
```

The words IS and PROGRAM in this clause are optional.

The rules above state that a nested program may be called only by its parent — C may be called only by B. When the COMMON clause is specified by a nested program it may be called by its parent, a sibling or a descendent of a sibling. However, a program may not call itself directly or indirectly; that is to say recursion is not allowed.

If we make program C a COMMON program then it may be called by programs A and D in addition to its parent program B. A program may specify both the COMMON and the INITIAL clause using one of:

```
PROGRAM-ID.  program-name   IS COMMON INITIAL PROGRAM.
PROGRAM-ID.  program-name   IS INITIAL COMMON PROGRAM.
```

29.9.2 The scope of data items and files: the GLOBAL clause

By default, data items and files declared in one program are private to that program and are not accessible by parent, children or sibling programs. The use of the GLOBAL clause makes data items and files accessible to any program nested within the program that declares the data item or file as global; that is to say a global item may be accessed by any descendent of the program that declares the item as global.

In the program shown below, ITEM-X is declared global by the program PROG-A so all the nested programs (PROG-B, PROG-C and PROG-D) have access to it. Note that ITEM-X is not declared in programs PROG-C and PROG-D hence the global item is used. It is declared in PROG-B so the local item is used. The output from this program would be:

```
Program A Global ITEM-X
Program B Local ITEM-X
Program C Global ITEM-X
Program D Global ITEM-X
```

```
1     IDENTIFICATION DIVISION.
2     PROGRAM-ID.          PROG-A.
3     DATA DIVISION.
4     WORKING-STORAGE SECTION.
5     01 ITEM-X PIC X(20) VALUE "Global ITEM-X"  GLOBAL.
6     PROCEDURE DIVISION.
7     BEGIN-A.
8         DISPLAY "Program A " ITEM-X
9         CALL "PROG-B"
10        CALL "PROG-D".
11
12    IDENTIFICATION DIVISION.
13    PROGRAM-ID.          PROG-B.
14    DATA DIVISION.
15    WORKING-STORAGE SECTION.
16    01 ITEM-X PIC X(20) VALUE "Local ITEM-X".
17    PROCEDURE DIVISION.
18    BEGIN-B.
19        DISPLAY "Program B " ITEM-X
20        CALL "PROG-C".
21
22    IDENTIFICATION DIVISION.
23    PROGRAM-ID.          PROG-C.
24    PROCEDURE DIVISION.
25    BEGIN-C.
26        DISPLAY "Program C " ITEM-X.
27    END PROGRAM PROG-C.
28
29    END PROGRAM PROG-B.
30
31    IDENTIFICATION DIVISION.
32    PROGRAM-ID.          PROG-D.
33    PROCEDURE DIVISION.
34    BEGIN-D.
35        DISPLAY "Program D " ITEM-X.
36    END PROGRAM PROG-D.
37
38    END PROGRAM PROG-A.
```

The rules for the GLOBAL clause are:

1) It may be used only at the 01 level for data items.

   For example:
   ```
   01 THIS-GROUP    IS GLOBAL.
      02 ELEMENT-A PIC XX.
      02 ELEMENT-B PIC 99.
         88 LARGE-VALUES 50 THRU 99.
   ```

   This makes THIS-GROUP, its subordinate data items and the condition name, global items. The word IS is optional in the clause.

2) If a data item is global, its name must be unique in the DATA DIVISION in which it is declared.

3) It may not be used in the LINKAGE SECTION.

4) To make a file global, the clause is used with the FD (file description):
   ```
   FD PRINT-FILE    GLOBAL.
   ```
   When a file is declared to be global, its record(s) and the subordinate data items are also global.

29.10 Review Questions

1. What are the advantages in using subprograms?

2. What is a nested call?

3. Most programs have FILE and WORKING STORAGE sections. What additional section is needed in a called program? Name a clause that cannot be used in the data-description-entries in that section.

4. Why do we use EXIT PROGRAM and not STOP RUN for the normal termination of a called program?

5. Which is true?
    a) The calling and called programs must use the same names for the identifiers passed as parameters.
    b) Identifiers are exchanged according to their positions in the CALL statement and LINKAGE SECTION.
    c) Identifiers are exchanged according to their positions in the CALL statement and the USING phrase.

30
The COPY Statement

Objectives

▸ Be competent in the use of a nonreplacing CALL statement.

Consider a business application that has a few hundred programs and a dozen or so files or databases. Each program will need to describe the record structure of every file it accesses. The programmer would like to avoid the task of typing the record description of every file when a new program is coded.

One approach would be to put these descriptions into one or more files. Then the programmer could import the required file into the source code using an editor command. This could certainly save a great deal of typing. It would also remove the possibility of typo errors. However, what would happen if we needed to change a file description? We would need to alter the file containing the description, delete the description from the source file of every program which used the description and import the new description. Finally, we would need to recompile each program.

Fortunately, there is a better way — use the COPY statement. Again the file descriptions are put into files but we do not use the editor to import them into the source file. Rather we use a COBOL statement such as COPY MYCOPY in the place where we need the file description. The copying of the lines in MYCOPY is not done with the editor but by the compiler. This makes it dynamic. If a change is needed, we merely change MYCOPY and then recompile the programs.

```
COPY text-name  [ { OFF }  library-name ]
                 [ { IN  }               ]
      [ REPLACING { replace-option }... ]
```

The REPLACING option allows identifiers, words and strings of text in the copy file to be changed as it is copied into the source file by the compiler.

text-name   The name of the file containing the text to be copied into the source
                program. A literal or an alphanumeric identifier may be used. In

RM/COBOL-85, if *text-name* has no file extension, a file with the extension .CBL is assumed. Micro Focus COBOL looks first for a file with the .CBL extension, then for one with .CPY and, finally, for a file with no extension in its name. The lines in the file are coded as if it were a COBOL source file.

library-name The name of the directory where the file *text-name* is stored. This is not needed if the file is in the default directory, or the full path is included in *text-name.*

NOTE: Do not compile the copy file *text-name*. If you do, it will generate errors since it is unlikely to be a complete program.

In the following examples the file to be copied is called MYCOPY; it is in the directory C:\COPYDIR.

```
          Source file                        Copy file

FILE SECTION.                       FD TESTFILE.
COPY MYCOPY IN "C:\COPYLIB".        01 TEST-RECORD.
                                        02 TEST-NAME   PICTURE X(20).
                                        02 FILLER      PICTURE X(5).
                                        02 TEST-AMOUNT PICTURE 99.
```

When the source file is compiled, the compiler listing will contain:

```
FILE SECTION.
COPY MYCOPY IN "C:\COPYLIB".
01 TEST-RECORD.
    02 TEST-NAME    PICTURE X(20).
    02 FILLER       PICTURE X(5).
    02 TEST-AMOUNT  PICTURE 99.
```

The final example is a simple one using the REPLACING clause.

```
          Source file                        Compiler listing

FILE SECTION.                       FILE SECTION.
COPY MYCOPY IN "C:\COPYLIB"         COPY MYCOPY  IN  "C:\COPYLIB"
   REPLACING PICTURE BY PIC         REPLACING PICTURE BY PIC
            FILLER  BY TEST-A.               FILLER   BY TEST-A.
                                    01 TEST-RECORD.
                                        02 TEST-NAME   PIC X(20).
                                        02 TEST-A      PIC X(5).
                                        02 TEST-AMOUNT PIC 99.
```

Carefully note that each COPY statement ends with a period. The COPY statement is generally used in the DATA DIVISION but it may be used in any division. Thus one could use it in the PROCEDURE DIVISION to copy a statement or a paragraph.

31
COBOL Functions

Objectives

▸ Be competent in the use of those functions applicable to your programs.

31.1 Introduction

The 1989 Addendum to the COBOL 85 specifications defined 42 intrinsic functions. These provide the programmer with some very useful and simple ways of achieving results which would otherwise require extensive programming. RM/COBOL-85 version 5.2 does not support these functions.

In COBOL, a *function* behaves very much like an elementary identifier. The format of a *function-identifier* is:

```
        FUNCTION function-name ( parameter-1 [ parameter-2]...).
```

The functions which return alphanumeric values (see below) can be used in a MOVE statement: `MOVE FUNCTION UPPER-CASE (WORD-X) TO WORD-Y`. When we compare this with the syntax of the MOVE verb: `MOVE identifier-1 TO identifier-2` we see that the phrase `FUNCTION UPPER-CASE (WORD-X)` takes the place of identifier-1 in the syntax.

We may classify the functions by the category (see Chapter 8) of the data they return:
a) alphanumeric functions return alphanumeric data,
b) numeric functions return numeric data with an operational sign,
c) integer functions return integer values with an operational sign.

With some exceptions, an alphanumeric function may be used in a statement wherever an alphanumeric identifier is required. Since UPPER-CASE returns alphanumeric data we may use it, for example, in these statements:

```
        MOVE FUNCTION UPPER-CASE (WORD-X) TO WORD-Y
        WRITE PRINT-REC FROM FUNCTION UPPER-CASE (TEMP-REC)
```

Numeric functions may be used only in arithmetic expressions but cannot be referenced where an integer operand is required. Integer functions may be used only in arithmetic expressions and may be referenced wherever an signed integer operand is allowed. Micro Focus COBOL also allows numeric and integer functions to be the source in a MOVE statement. Example of ANSI standard usages of numeric and integer function:

```
IF FUNCTION SUM(A B C) > 0 ...
ADD FUNCTION FACTORIAL (5) TO ITEM-N.
```

We shall use the MOVE verb for alphanumeric functions and the COMPUTE verb for numeric and integer functions in the examples that follow.

31.2 Using the ALL Subscript with Tables

The figurative constant ALL may be used in functions as a table subscript. If we wished to sum all the elements in the table defined by: 02 X OCCURS 5 TIMES PIC 99 it would be bothersome to have to code :
```
    COMPUTE TOTAL-VALUE = FUNCTION SUM ( X(1) X(2) X(3) X(4) X(5) )
```
It would be more so if X occurred say 100 times. Fortunately, we can avoid this with the ALL subscript: `COMPUTE TOTAL-VALUE = FUNCTION SUM ( X(ALL) )`

We may use the ALL subscript with multidimensional tables. If X is defined by:
```
        02 X OCCURS 3 TIMES.
          03 Y OCCURS 2 TIMES PIC 99.
```
Example: `COMPUTE TOTAL-VALUE = FUNCTION SUM ( Y(ALL, 1) )`
Value returned: `Y(1,1) + Y(2,1) + Y(3,1)`
Example: `COMPUTE TOTAL-VALUE = FUNCTION SUM ( Y(ALL, ALL) )`
Value returned: `Y(1,1) + Y(1,2) + Y(2,1) + Y(2,2)+ Y(3,1) + Y(3,2).`

31.3 The String Functions

Function	Type	Value Returned
CHAR	Alphanumeric	The character in the specified position in the collation sequence
LENGTH	Integer	The number of character positions of the parameter
LOWER-CASE	Alphanumeric	The same parameter converted to lowercase letters
NUMVAL	Numeric	Numeric value of a simple string
NUMVAL-C	Numeric	Numeric value of a string with commas and/or currency sign
ORD	Integer	Ordinal position of the parameter in the collating sequence
REVERSE	Alphanumeric	The same parameter in reverse order
UPPER-CASE	Alphanumeric	The same parameter converted to uppercase letters

CHAR (parameter-1)   type: alphanumeric

Returns the character whose *ordinal position* in the collating sequence corresponds to parameter-1. Parameter-1 must be an identifier or numeric literal with a positive integer value not exceeding the number of positions in the collating sequence. The function ORD performs the converse of the CHAR function.

In the following examples we assume the collating sequence is ASCII.

```
02 N      PIC 999.
02 A      PIC X.

MOVE FUNCTION CHAR ( N )   TO  A
```

Value of N	Value returned by FUNCTION CHAR (N)
66	A
98	a
6	#

Note that since ASCII 00 is the first ordinal position, the ordinal positions of each character will be one greater than its ASCII code. Thus ASCII 65 is the character "A" so the ordinal position of "A" is 66. The COBOL function differs from similar functions in other languages in returning the character specified by the ordinal position rather than the ASCII code value. See Chapter 20 for a table of the ASCII character set.

LENGTH (parameter-1)   type: numeric

Returns the length in bytes of parameter-1. Parameter-1 may be a nonnumeric literal or an identifier (elementary, group or record).

```
COMPUTE N = FUNCTION LENGTH ( ITEM-A )
```

Description of ITEM-A	Value returned by FUNCTION LENGTH (ITEM-A)
`ITEM-A PIC X(10)`	10
`ITEM-A PIC 9(4).99`	7
`ITEM-A PIC 9(4)V99`	6
`ITEM-A OCCURS 5 TIMES PIC X(3)`	15
`ITEM-A OCCURS 1 TO 5 TIMES` `   DEPENDING ON LEN-ITEM PIC X(3)`	`3 times value of LEN-ITEM`

Note that if ITEM-A has PIC X(10) and value "ABC", the LENGTH function returns 10; it does not return the number of nonblank characters. See also "Size of picture" in Chapter 8.

LOWER-CASE (parameter-1)   type: alphanumeric
```
      MOVE FUNCTION LOWER-CASE (ITEM-A) TO ITEM-A
```
Returns parameter-1 with all the uppercase alphabetic characters (A through Z) replaced by lowercase characters (a through z.) The function UPPER-CASE performs the converse operation. Parameter-1 must be an alphanumeric or alphabetic identifier or literal.

NUMVAL (parameter-1)   type: numeric
  Returns the numeric value represented by the text in parameter-1. Parameter-1 must be
  a nonnumeric literal or an alphanumeric identifier whose contents has one of the formats
  shown in Figure 31-1.

```
02 MY-STRING PIC X(10) VALUE "   0.345".
02 MY-NUM    PIC S9(4)V9(4).
COMPUTE MY-NUM = FUNCTION NUMVAL ( MY-STRING )
```

Figure 31-1 Formats for the parameter used with NUMVAL

In Figure 31-1: **space** is a string of zero or more spaces and **digit** is a string of 1 to 18 digits.

NUMVAL-C (parameter-1){parameter-2}   type: numeric
  Returns the numeric value represented by the text in parameter-1. Parameter-1 must be
  a nonnumeric literal or an alphanumeric identifier whose contents has one of the formats
  shown in Figure 31-2. This function differs from NUMVAL in that parameter-1 may
  contain a comma and/or a currency sign. The optional parameter-2 is an alphanumeric
  item specifying the currency symbol.

```
02 MY-STRING PIC X(10) VALUE " $1,234.45".
02 MY-NUM    PIC 9(5)V99.
COMPUTE MY-NUM = FUNCTION NUMVAL ( MY-STRING )
```

Figure 31-2 Formats for the parameter used with NUMVAL-C

In Figure 31-2: **space** is a string of zero or more spaces and **digit** is a string of 1 to 18 digits.

ORD (parameter-1)   type: integer
  Returns the ordinal position of a character in the collating sequence. Parameter-1 must
  be an alphabetic or alphanumeric identifier or a literal, one character long. The function
  CHAR performs the converse of the ORD function; see above.

In the following examples we assume the collating sequence is ASCII.

```
02 N      PIC 999.
02 A      PIC X.
COMPUTE N = FUNCTION ORD ( A )
```

Value of A	Value returned by FUNCTION ORD (A)
A	066
a	098

REVERSE (parameter-1)   type: alphanumeric
```
   MOVE FUNCTION REVERSE (ITEM-A) TO ITEM-B
```
Returns the value of parameter-1 with the characters in reverse order. The length of the returned string is the same as the length of parameter-1. This means that any trailing spaces in the sending item become leading spaces in the receiving item. Parameter-1 must be an alphabetic or alphanumeric identifier or a literal at least one character long.

UPPER-CASE (parameter-1)   type: alphanumeric
```
   MOVE FUNCTION UPPER-CASE (ITEM-A) TO ITEM-B
```
Returns parameter-1 with all the lowercase alphabetic characters (a to z) replaced by uppercase characters (A to Z). The function LOWER-CASE performs the converse operation. Parameter-1 must be an alphanumeric or alphabetic identifier or literal.

31.4 The General Functions

Function	Type	Value Returned
MAX	Depends on parameters	Maximum value of all parameters
MIN	Depends on parameters	Minimum value of all parameters
ORD-MAX	Integer	Ordinal position of maximum parameter
ORD-MIN	Integer	Ordinal position of minimum parameter

MAX ({parameter-1}...)   type: variable
Returns the maximum value of all the parameters. The type of this function depends on the category of the parameters:

Parameter type	Function type
Alphabetic	Alphabetic
Alphanumeric	Alphanumeric
All parameters integer	Integer
Numeric (some may be integer)	Numeric

If there are two or more parameters they must all be of the same class.

We shall use literals in some examples for convenience; clearly the function is normally used with identifiers.

Example: `DISPLAY FUNCTION MAX ( "A" "B" "m" "Z")`
Value returned: "m", since that letter is higher in the ASCII collating sequence.

Example: `COMPUTE N = FUNCTION MAX ( 1 25 53 37)`
Value returned: 53, since this is the maximum value of the parameters.

Example: `COMPUTE N = FUNCTION MAX ( ELEMENT (ALL) )`
Value returned: the maximum item in the table called ELEMENT.

MIN ({parameter-1}...)   type: variable
Returns the minimum value of all the parameters. The type of this function depends on the category of the parameters as detailed above for MAX.

Example: `DISPLAY FUNCTION MIN ("K" "A" "B" "m" "Z")`
Value returned: "A" since, in the ASCII collating sequence, "A" is lower than the other characters in this example.

Example: `COMPUTE N = FUNCTION MIN ( ELEMENT (ALL) )`
Value returned: the value of the minimum item in the table called ELEMENT.

ORD-MAX ({parameter-1}...)   type: integer
Returns the ordinal position of the data item, in a series of data items, that has the greatest value. The function ORD-MIN performs the converse. If there are two or more parameters, they must all be of the same class.

```
02 TABLE-N   OCCURS 6 TIMES PIC 99.
```

Let the values in the table be: subscript: 1   2   3   4   5   6
                                    value: 17 22 33 15 33 17

```
COMPUTE N = ORD-MAX( TABLE-N (ALL) )
```

This will return the value 3 since TABLE-N (3) has the greatest value. Note that TABLE-N (5) has the same value; the function returns the ordinal position of the first item when two or more have the same value.

ORD-MIN ({parameter-1}...)   type: integer
Returns the ordinal position of the data item, in a series of data items, that has the lowest value. The function ORD-MAX performs the converse. If there are two or more parameters, they must all be of the same class.

```
02 TABLE-A   OCCURS 4 TIMES PIC 99.
```

Let the values in the table be:
         subscript: 1   2   3   4
         value: SMITH   JONES   EVANS   FLOYD

Example: COMPUTE N = ORD-MIN (TABLE-A (ALL), "AALTO")
Value returned: 5; the function examines 5 items (TABLE-A(1), TABLE-A(2),
                 TABLE-A(3), TABLE-A(4) and "AALTO") and the fifth item has
                 the lowest value.

Example: COMPUTE N = ORD-MIN (TABLE-A (ALL), "ZEBRA")
Value returned: 3, because TABLE-N (3) has the lowest value.

31.5 The Date Functions

Function	Type	Value Returned
CURRENT-DATE	Alphanumeric	Current date and time and difference from GMT
DATE-OF-INTEGER	Integer	Standard date equivalent (YYYYMMDD) of integer date
DAY-OF-INTEGER	Integer	Julian date equivalence (YYYYDDD) of integer date
INTEGER-OF-DATE	Integer	Integer date equivalence of standard date (YYYYMMDD)
INTEGER-OF-DAY	Integer	Integer date equivalence of Julian date (YYYYDDD)
WHEN-COMPILED	Alphanumeric	Date and time program was compiled

CURRENT-DATE   type: alphanumeric
    Returns a 21-character string that represents the date, time of day, and the number of
    hours that local time differs from Greenwich Mean Time. The description of this is given
    in Figure 30-3.

Example:
```
    01 THE-CURRENT-DATE.
        03 C-DATE.
            05 C-YEAR        PIC 9(4).
            05 C-MONTH       PIC 99.
            05 C-DAY         PIC 99.
        03 C-TIME.
            05 C-HOUR        PIC 99.
            05 C-MINUTE      PIC 99.
            05 C-HUNDRED     PIC 99.
        03 C-GMT.
            05 C-GMT-DIFF    PIC X.
            05 C-GMT-HOUR    PIC 99.
            05 C-GMT-MINUTE  PIC 99.
```

```
MOVE FUNCTION CURRENT-TIME TO THE-CURRENT-TIME
DISPLAY "Year is: " , C-YEAR " Month is: ", C-MONTH
```

Result: Year is: 1995 Month is: 09

Figure 30-3 String returned by CURRENT-DATE

Positions   Data Values
1-4   The current year in the Gregorian calendar.
5-6   The current month of the year; values 01 to 12.
7-8   The current day of the month; values 01 to 31.
9-10   The number of hours past midnight; values 00 to 23.
11-12   The number of minutes past the hour; values 00 to 59.
13-14   The number of seconds past the minute; values 00 to 59.
15-16   The number of hundredths of a seconds past the second; values 00 to 99.
17   A plus sign (+) indicates local time is the same as or ahead of GMT.
          A negative sign (-) indicates local time is behind GMT.
          A "0" is returned if the system cannot provide this information.
          Consult your operating system to find how to set this value.
18-19   How many hours local time differs from GMT.
          If position 17 is "0" position 18 will be "0"
20-21   How many minutes local time differs from GMT.

The metric convention for representing a date in numeric form is represented by YYMMDD. January 25 1993 is written as 930125. This convention, which is used by the ACCEPT statement — see Chapter 16 — has the advantage that dates can readily be sorted.

As we approach the year 2000 the YYMMDD convention becomes unworkable because, for example, 000125 (Jan 25th 2000) is a smaller number than 991231 (Dec 31st 1999). COBOL has defined for itself the *standard* conventions as YYYYMMDD — using 4 digits for the year.

None of the date conventions (YYMMDD, YYYYMMDD, MMDDYY OR DDMMYY) are satisfactory for performing calculations. For example if today is 19931020 and a bill was due on 19930831, is it 45 days or more overdue?

There are two date formats which address the issue of how to format a date in a manner which allows calculations. The first is the Julian form in which a date has the format YYYYDDD. In this system 1993006 is the sixth day of 1993.

An alternative format is to chose a day in history as "day zero" and number all dates by the number of days since then. This is the *integer* date format. In COBOL, the integer form of a date is the number of days that have passed since December 31st 1600 in the Gregorian calendar. The date 1 January 1601 is 0000001 ("day one") using this convention. Readers familiar with PC spreadsheets such as Lotus and Excel will recall these applications have a similar integer date format but use 1 January 1900 as "day one".

DATE-OF-INTEGER (parameter-1)　　　type: integer
　Converts a date from an integer form to the standard form — YYYYMMDD.
　Parameter-1 must be a positive integer.

DAY-OF-INTEGER (parameter-1)　　　type: integer
　Converts a date from an integer form to the Julian form — YYYYDDD. Parameter-1
　must be a positive integer.

INTEGER-OF-DATE (parameter-1)　　　type: integer
　Converts the date from standard form (YYYYMMDD) to the integer date form.
　Parameter-1 must be a valid date in the form YYYYMMDD with YYYY greater than
　1600.

INTEGER-OF-DAY (parameter-1)　　　type: integer
　Converts the date from Julian form (YYYYDDD) to the integer date form. Parameter-1
　must be a valid date in the form YYYYDDD with YYYY greater than 1600 and DDD
　less than 365 (366 for leap years).

Example:　　In this example we will use the data item THE-CURRENT-DATE as described
　　　　　　above in the discussion of the CURRENT-DATE function. We will also use:

```
02 JULIAN-DATE.           PIC 9(6).
02 REDEFINES JULIAN-DATE.
   05 J-YEAR              PIC 9999.
   05 J-DAY               PIC 999.
02 NEW-DATE               PIC 9(8).
02 REDEFINES NEW-DATE.
   05 N-YY                PIC 9999.
   05 N-MM                PIC 99.
   05 N-DD                PIC 99.

02 STANDARD-DATE          PIC 9(8).
02 REDEFINES STANDARD-DATE.
   05 S-YY                PIC 9999.
   05 S-MM                PIC 99.
   05 S-DD                PIC 99.
02 NUMBER-DATE            PIC 9(9).
02 DISPLAY-DATE           PIC 9999/99/99.

MOVE FUNCTION CURRENT-DATE TO THE-CURRENT-DATE
MOVE C-DATE TO STANDARD-DATE
MOVE STANDARD-DATE TO DISPLAY-DATE
DISPLAY "Today is : " DISPLAY-DATE
COMPUTE NUMBER-DATE = FUNCTION INTEGER-OF-DATE(STANDARD-DATE)
ADD 45 TO NUMBER-DATE
COMPUTE STANDARD-DATE = FUNCTION DATE-OF-INTEGER (NUMBER-DATE))
MOVE STANDARD-DATE TO DISPLAY-DATE
DISPLAY "The date 45 days from today will be : " DISPLAY-DATE
```

WHEN-COMPILED   type: alphanumeric
Returns the date and time when the program was compiled. This function returns a string with the same structure as the CURRENT-DATE function — see Fig. 31-3.

WHEN-COMPILED may be used in the same way as the CURRENT-DATE function to provide information on when the program was compiled rather than on the current date and time.

31.6 The Arithmetic Functions

Function	Type	Value Returned
INTEGER	Integer	The greatest integer not greater than the given parameter
INTEGER-PART	Integer	The integer part of the parameter
LOG	Numeric	The natural logarithm of the parameter
LOG10	Numeric	The logarithm to base 10 of the parameter
MOD	Integer	Modulo of two parameters
RANDOM	Numeric	Pseudo-random number
REM	Numeric	Remainder after division
SQRT	Numeric	Square root of the parameter
SUM	Integer or Numeric	Sum of the parameters

INTEGER (parameter-1)   type: integer
Returns the greatest integer value that is less than or equal to the parameter. That is to say, the parameter is rounded to the nearest integer.   Parameter-1 must be of class numeric.

INTEGER-PART (parameter-1)   type: integer
Returns the integer part of the parameter. That is to say, the parameter is truncated. Parameter-1 must be of class numeric.

```
Example:    02 NUM-REAL      PIC S99V99.
            02 NUM-INT       PIC S99V99.

   (a)    COMPUTE NUM-INT = FUNCTION INTEGER (NUM-REAL)
   (b)    COMPUTE NUM-INT = FUNCTION INTEGER-PART (NUM-REAL)
```

Value of INT-REAL	Value returned by (a)	Value returned by (b)
12.94	+12.00	12.00
-12.94	-13.00	-12.00
+01.50	+01.00	+01.00
-01.50	-02.00	-01.00

LOG (parameter-1)   type: numeric
LOG10 (parameter-1)   type: numeric
These functions return the natural (log to the base e) and the Napierian logarithm (log to base 10), respectively, of the supplied parameter. In both cases, parameter-1 must be class numeric and greater than zero.

Example:
```
COMPUTE MY-LOG ROUNDED = FUNCTION LOG (50)
             ON SIZE ERROR MOVE 0.0 TO MY-LOG
        END-COMPUTE.
```

MOD (parameter-1 parameter-2)   type: numeric
Returns an integer value that is (parameter-1 MOD parameter-2). Both parameters must be integer, parameter-2 must be non-zero.
By definition: $X \bmod Y = X - (Y \times INT(X/Y))$

Examples: Statement   Value Returned

Statement	Value Returned
COMPUTE X = FUNCTION MOD (0, 5)	0
COMPUTE X = FUNCTION MOD (11, 5)	1
COMPUTE X = FUNCTION MOD (-11, 5)	4
COMPUTE X = FUNCTION MOD (11, -5)	-4
COMPUTE X = FUNCTION MOD (-11, -5)	-1

RANDOM [(parameter-1)]   type: numeric
Returns a pseudo-random number for a rectangular distribution. The value is greater than or equal to zero and less than 1. Parameter-1 is called the seed. If used, it must be a positive integer; the upper limit depends on the CPU but is always at least 32767. When a seed is used the subsequent sequence of random numbers produced is always the same.

Usage:
```
COMPUTE RAN-NUM = FUNCTION RANDOM (10)
```

To generate an integer value in the range A to B, inclusive, the programmer may use:
```
COMPUTE MY-VALUE = FUNCTION INTEGER ((RAN-NUM * (B - X + 1)) . + X)
```

REM (parameter-1 parameter-2)   type: numeric
Returns the remainder of parameter-1 divided by parameter-2. The two parameters must be class numeric; parameter-2 must be non-zero.

SQRT (parameter-1)   type: numeric
Returns the square-root of parameter-1. Parameter-1 must be numeric with either a zero or positive value.

SUM ({parameter-1}...)   type: numeric or integer
Returns the sum of all the parameters. The parameter must be class numeric. When all parameters are integer the value returned is integer.
When the parameter is numeric, or a mix of integer and numeric, a numeric result is returned.

```
Example:    02 ITEM-X    OCCURS 10 TIMES    PIC 999.
            02 ITEM-N PIC 99.99.
            COMPUTE MY-SUM = FUNCTION SUM ( ITEM-X (ALL) )
            COMPUTE MY-SUM = FUNCTION SUM ( ITEM-X(ALL) ITEM-N)
```

31.7 The Statistical Functions

Function	Type	Value Returned
FACTORIAL	Integer	Factorial of an integer value
MEAN	Numeric	Arithmetic mean of the parameters
MEDIAN	Numeric	Median value of the parameters
MIDRANGE	Numeric	Mean of the smallest and largest of the parameters
RANGE	Integer or Numeric	Value of the largest parameter minus the smallest parameter
STANDARD-DEVIATION	Numeric	Standard deviation of the parameters
VARIANCE	Numeric	Variance of the parameter

FACTORIAL (parameter-1)   type: integer
Returns the factorial of the parameter (N!). Parameter-1 must be a positive integer in the range 0 to 19. Since factorial 20 contains more than 18 digits (the number of digits COBOL uses), the upper limit for the parameter is 19.

MEAN ({parameter-1}...)   type: numeric
Returns the arithmetic mean value of the parameters. The parameters must be class numeric.

Usage: COMPUTE MY-SUM = FUNCTION MEAN (ITEM-X (ALL))

MEDIAN ({parameter-1}...)   type: numeric
Returns the median of the parameters. If there is an odd number of parameters, the value returned is the parameter with a value such that at least half the parameters have values equal to, or less than, the returned value and at least half have values greater than, or equal to the returned value. If the number of parameters is even, the returned value is the arithmetic mean of the two middle-valued parameters. All the parameters must be of class numeric.

Example: COMPUTE MY-MIDD = FUNCTION MEDIAN (9 7 1 85 35)
Value returned: 9

MIDRANGE ({parameter-1}...)   type: numeric
    Returns a value that is the arithmetic mean (average) of the minimum and maximum parameters. All the parameters must be of class numeric.

RANGE ({parameter-1}...)   type: numeric
    Returns a value that is the difference between the maximum and the minimum parameters. All the parameters must be of class numeric.

STANDARD-DEVIATION ({parameter-1} ...) type: numeric
    Returns the standard deviation of the parameters. All parameters must be of class numeric.

    The standard deviation is computed in three steps:
        1) Compute the average of the parameters: $\bar{x} = \sum x_i/n$
        2) Compute the variance: $\sigma^2 = \sum(x_i - \bar{x})^2 /n$
        3) Compute the standard deviation: $\sigma = \sqrt{\sigma^2}$

```
Example:    COMPUTE STD-VAR  =
                      FUNCTION STANDARD-DEVIATION (1, 7, 9, 23, 85)
```
    Value returned: +125.00.

VARIANCE ({parameter-1} ...)   type: numeric
    Returns the variance of the parameters. Variance is defined as the square of the standard deviation. See STANDARD-DEVIATION above for more details.

```
Example:    COMPUTE THE-VAR =
                      FUNCTION VARIANCE (1, 7, 9, 23, 85)
```
    Value returned: + 952.00.

31.8 The Financial Functions

Function	Type	Value Returned
ANNUITY	Numeric	Ratio of an annuity paid for a specified number of periods at a specified interest rate, to an initial investment of one
PRESENT-VALUE	Numeric	Present value of a series of future period-end amounts at a specified interest rate

ANNUITY (parameter-1 parameter-2)   type: numeric
    Returns a value that approximates the amount of a periodic payment for a number of periods at a given interest rate for an ordinary annuity whose present value is $1.00. An "ordinary annuity" is an annuity where the payments are made at the end of each period.

    Parameter-1 is the interest rate per period; it must be numeric value equal to or greater than zero. Parameter-2 is the number of periods; it must be a positive integer.

$$annuity = \frac{interest\text{-}rate}{(1 - (1+interest\text{-}rate))^{-number\text{-}of\text{-}periods}}$$

If parameter-1 (interest rate) is zero the function returns 1/ (parameter-2)

Example: COMPUTE MONTH-RATE ROUNDED = YEAR-RATE / 12.00
COMPUTE MY-ANNUITY ROUNDED =
FUNCTION ANNUITY (MONTH-RATE MONTH-COUNT)

Value returned: +0.0314 for an annuity with 36 monthly payments when the annual interest rate is 8% (0.08)

PRESENT-VALUE (parameter-1 {parameter-2}...)   type: numeric
Returns the present value of an ordinary annuity at a fixed interest rate.
Parameter-1 is the interest rate per period; it must be numeric value greater than -1.
Parameter-2 specifies the amount of the payment(s); it must be a positive integer.

$$present\text{-}value = \sum_{i=1}^{n} \frac{payment(i)}{(1 + interest\text{-}rate)^{i}}$$

Where *n* is the number of payments, i.e. the number of times parameter-2 occurs.

Example: COMPUTE MY-VALUE =
FUNCTION PRESENT-VALUE (INT PAY-1 PAY-2 PAY-3)

Value returned: +2.7233, if the interest rate (INT) is set at 5% (0.05) and each payment at 1.00. There are three payment-2 arguments, hence *n* = 3.

31.9 The Trigonometric Functions

Function	Type	Value Returned
COS	Numeric	Cosine of an angle measured in radians
SIN	Numeric	Sine of an angle measured in radians
TAN	Numeric	Tangent of an angle measured in radians
ACOS	Numeric	Arccosine, in radians, of a numeric value
ASIN	Numeric	Arcsine, in radians, of a numeric value
ATAN	Numeric	Arctangent, in radians, of a numeric value

Since there are 2π radians and 360 degrees in a complete circle, it follows that 2π radians = 360 degrees or π radians = 180 degrees. Hence to convert degrees to radians we divide by $180/\pi$ (or 57.2958) and to covert radians to degrees we multiply by 57.2958.

All the trigonometric functions are of type numeric and each requires one numeric parameter.

Example: COMPUTE COS-OF-ANGLE = FUNCTION COS (ANGLE)
Value returned: 0.7071, if ANGLE = 0.7854 radians (approximately 45 degrees)

Example: COMPUTE THE-ANGLE =
                FUNCTION ACOS (COS-OF-ANGLE) * 57.2958
Value returned: 45 in units of degrees, if COS-OF-ANGLE = 0.7071

Example: COMPUTE PI = FUNCTION ATAN (1) * 4.0
Value returned: 3.14159 … — the value of π.

32
I-O Exceptions

Objectives

▸ Know how to determine and interpret a FILE STATUS value.
▸ Understand the use of DECLARATIVES to trap I-O errors.

32.1 Introduction

This chapter discusses I-O exception conditions ("errors") which may occur with input-output verbs such as OPEN, CLOSE, READ, WRITE, REWRITE, etc.

Unless we make provisions in our program to handle I-O exceptions they will cause the program to abort ("crash"). We are then confronted with a cryptic error message. For example, if we attempt to write to a file that has not been opened the message will read something like: Program aborted. I-O error number 48. We can look up error 48 in Table 32-1 to find the cause.

There are two methods that allow the program to end more gracefully. The first method uses the FILE STATUS clause in the SELECT entry whilst the second makes use of DECLARATIVES.

32.2 File Status

Each I-O operation causes the computer to generate a File Status value. To have access to this value, the SELECT entry in the FILE-CONTROL paragraph must contain a FILE STATUS clause and the identifier used in this clause must appear within the WORKING-STORAGE SECTION as a 2-byte alphanumeric item. For example:

```
FILE-CONTROL.
    SELECT TESTFILE ASSIGN TO "MYFILE.DAT"
        ORGANIZATION IS …
        FILE STATUS TEST-FILE-STATUS.
    ...
WORKING-STORAGE SECTION.
01 WORK-ITEMS.
        02 TEST-FILE-STATUS        PIC XX.
```

The meanings of the possible values of the File Status identifier are shown in Table 32-1. Note that codes beginning with "0" indicate the I-O process was successful but unless the code is "00" there may have been a nonfatal exception.

Compare codes 05 and 35. When a SELECT clause contains the OPTIONAL clause, the programmer is indicating that this file may be present at run-time or it may not be. If it is not present, a code of 05 is returned by the OPEN statement. However, if the file is not present and OPTIONAL was omitted from the SELECT clause, a nonsuccessful code of 35 is returned.

Table 32-1 Codes for File Status

Value	File Organization	Meaning
00	all	Successful execution
02	indexed	Duplicate key detected
04	all	READ: record length inconsistent with record
05	sequential	OPEN: OPTIONAL file not present, created
07	sequential	CLOSE/OPEN: tape phrase used with a non-tape file
10	sequential	End-of-file condition
14	relative	Record number too large
21	indexed	Sequence error
22	indexed/relative	WRITE/REWRITE: duplicate
23	indexed/relative	Invalid key, record does not exist
24	indexed/relative	WRITE: file is full
30	all	Permanent error, no other information. See Note A
34	sequential	WRITE: beyond file boundary. See Note B
35	all	OPEN: non-OPTIONAL file not present
37	all	Invalid mode for file medium (e.g. READ a printer)
38	all	OPEN: file is closed with lock
39	all	OPEN: file attributes conflict
41	all	OPEN: file already open
42	all	CLOSE: file not open
43	all	REWRITE: not preceded by READ
44	all	WRITE/REWRITE: boundary violation, record wrong
46	all	READ: pointer passed end-of-file marker
47	all	READ/START: file not open for input
48	all	WRITE: file not open for output
49	all	REWRITE/DELETE: file not open for I-O

NOTE A: Error 30 is generally an operating system problem, e.g. disk drive door open, floppy not in drive, printer not switched on, etc. An RM/COBOL-85 program may give this error when running from Windows if the AUTOEXEC.BAT file does not include SHARE.EXE.

NOTE B: The Educational version of RM/COBOL-85 is limited to 1000 records when writing to a sequential file, or 100 records when the file is opened with EXTEND or is an indexed or relative file.

With appropriate coding, one may test the File Status code after any I-O operation: OPEN, CLOSE, READ, WRITE, START or DELETE. From Table 32-1 we can see that some codes are possible with all types of files; others are specific to sequential, or indexed/relative files.

Example 1: The programmer wishes to test if an OPTIONAL file was present after an OPEN statement. If it is present, the file records will be read in the PROCESS-TESTFILE paragraph.

```
OPEN INPUT TESTFILE
EVALUATE  TEST-FILE-STATUS
   WHEN   "00"  DISPLAY "TESTFILE is present"
                PERFORM PROCESS-TESTFILE
   WHEN   "05"  DISPLAY "TESTFILE not present"
   WHEN   "35"  DISPLAY "Program error - no OPTIONAL clause"
   WHEN   "41"  DISPLAY "Program error - TESTFILE already open"
   WHEN   OTHER DISPLAY "Other error"
                DISPLAY "File status value is " TEST-FILE-STATUS
END-EVALUATE.
```

The reader may wish to consider this program's file-closing strategy. If the file was not present a CLOSE statement will fail.

Example 2: In some systems, a file has a specified amount of disk space reserved for it. Once this limit is reached, any attempt to write more records to the file will be unsuccessful.

```
* TESTFILE has been opened in OUTPUT or EXTEND mode
      WRITE TEST-REC
      IF TEST-FILE-STATUS = "34"
         DISPLAY "TESTFILE is full"
      END-IF
```

Example 3: Perhaps a harried programmer forgot to OPEN a file before executing a READ statement, but he/she is not sure which file is giving the problem. This type of code could help debug the program.

```
READ TESTFILE
    AT END SET EOF TO TRUE
END-READ
IF TEST-FILE-STATUS = "47"
    DISPLAY "TESTFILE not opened for input"
END-IF.
```

32.3 File Attributes

When a program attempts to open an existing file, that program must use *file attributes* that match the attributes specified when the file was first created. To understand this exception we need to know what is mean by "file attribute". The attributes of a file specify:

a) File organization (SEQUENTIAL, RELATIVE or INDEXED).
b) Record format (fixed or variable length records).
c) Physical record size (length of record).
d) File size (number of records in the file).
e) Position in the record description of the identifiers used as keys, both primary and alternate, in an indexed file.

Thus if MYFILE was created in one program with ORGANIZATION INDEXED, it would be erroneous for another program to refer to MYFILE with an ORGANIZATION RELATIVE clause. Similarly, if THISFILE was created with a primary and an alternate key, all programs that process this file must declare the same keys even if the program does not make use of one of the keys.

32.4 Using DECLARATIVES

DECLARATIVES are sets of statements that appear immediately after the PROCEDURE DIVISION heading in the program. One form of declarative procedure is used to trap I-O exceptions, another with debugging operations. We shall be concerned only with the former.

In the sample code given in section 32.2, we were able to test all values of the file status identifier. Declaratives are used for exception, or error, trapping. Therefore one cannot use declarative procedures to find values of the file status that begin with a zero because these values are returned by "successful" statements. The syntax of a declarative procedure has the format:

```
DECLARATIVES·
    {section-name SECTION·
    USE  statement·
        [paragraph-name·
            [sentence]... ]...}...
END DECLARATIVES·
```

The following is an outline of a COBOL program with EXCEPTION declarative.

```
PROCEDURE DIVISION.
DECLARATIVES.
section-name-1 SECTION
    USE AFTER {EXCEPTION / ERROR } PROCEDURE ON
              {INPUT / OUTPUT / I-O / EXTEND / file-name-1}.
para-name-a.
      :
para-name-b.
      :
section-name-2 SECTION.
    USE AFTER etc.
    para-name-u.
      :
    para-name-v.
      :
END DECLARATIVES.              <Declarative end here>

section-name-3 SECTION.        <The "normal" part of the Procedure
begins here>
FIRST-PARAGRAPH.
```

Before we see how to use a declarative, note the following:

a) The words EXCEPTION and ERROR are synonymous — you may use either.
b) The programmer must supply section-names.
c) The phrases DECLARATIVES and END-DECLARATIVES, the section headings ending with the word SECTION and the USE statement must all end with periods. Periods are, of course, required after paragraph names and within paragraphs in the normal way.
d) No statement within a Declarative section may refer to a nondeclarative procedure. It may reference a procedure in another declarative section by use of a PERFORM statement.
e) Within the nondeclarative part of the program, the only way in which a declarative procedure may be referenced is through a PERFORM statement.

Consider a statement such as: `USE AFTER EXCEPTION ON TESTFILE.`
We may think of this as saying: If there is an I-O exception condition affecting TESTFILE when this program is running, then perform the procedures that follow.

Similarly, a statement such as `USE AFTER EXCEPTION ON INPUT` causes the procedures in that section to be perform if an exception occurs with any file that is OPEN for input.

Some fairly obvious rules apply:

1) A given filename may appear only once in the Declarative Section of a program.

2) The INPUT, OUTPUT, I-O, and EXTEND phrases can be specified in only one USE statement. Thus we could, for example, have one USE... ON INPUT statement, and one USE... ON OUTPUT statement.

3) If file-name-1 appears in a USE statement, no other USE statement will be considered applying to it. Suppose we have in SECTION-A a USE ... ON TESTFILE, and in SECTION-B a USE ... ON INPUT. If an exception occurs with TESTFILE, only the procedures in SECTION-A become operative even if TESTFILE has been opened for INPUT.

Example 4: The use of Declaratives.

```
1    IDENTIFICATION DIVISION.
2    PROGRAM-ID.      FILETEST.
3    ENVIRONMENT DIVISION.
4    INPUT-OUTPUT SECTION.
5    FILE-CONTROL.
6        SELECT DATAFILE
7            ASSIGN TO DISK "ABC123.DAT"
8            ORGANIZATION LINE SEQUENTIAL.
9        SELECT OPTIONAL TESTFILE
10           ASSIGN TO DISK "TEST.DAT"
11           ORGANIZATION LINE SEQUENTIAL
12           FILE STATUS IS TEST-FILE-STATUS.
13   DATA DIVISION.
14   FILE SECTION.
15   FD DATAFILE.
16   01 DATA-REC    PIC X(80).
17   FD TESTFILE.
18   01 TEST-REC    PIC X(80).
19   WORKING-STORAGE SECTION.
20   01 WORK-ITEMS.
21       02 TEST-FILE-STATUS        PIC XX.
22       02 FILE-FLAG               PIC X    VALUE "N".
23          88 EOF         VALUE "Y".
24
25   PROCEDURE DIVISION.
26   DECLARATIVES.
27
28   TESTFILE-PROBLEM SECTION.
29      USE AFTER EXCEPTION PROCEDURE ON TESTFILE.
30   TESTFILE-PARA.
31      EVALUATE TEST-FILE-STATUS
32          WHEN   "35"
33               DISPLAY "TESTFILE: no OPTIONAL clause"
34          WHEN   OTHER
35               DISPLAY "TESTFILE: status is " TEST-FILE-STATUS
36      END-EVALUATE
37      DISPLAY "Program stopped by declarative"
38      STOP RUN.
39
40   DATAFILE-PROBLEM SECTION.
41      USE AFTER ERROR PROCEDURE ON DATAFILE.
42   NEWFILE-PARA.
43      DISPLAY "There is a problem with DATAFILE"
```

```
44          DISPLAY "Program stopped by declarative"
45          STOP RUN.
46      END DECLARATIVES.
47
48      MAIN-PROCEDURE SECTION.
49      MAIN-PARA.
50          OPEN INPUT  DATAFILE
51               EXTEND TESTFILE
52          PERFORM FILE-COPY-PARA
53          STOP RUN.
54      FILE-COPY-PARA.
55          READ DATAFILE AT END SET EOF TO TRUE END-READ
56          PERFORM UNTIL EOF
57              WRITE TEST-REC FROM DATA-REC
58              READ DATAFILE AT END SET EOF TO TRUE END-READ
59          END-PERFORM.
```

Note that TEST.DAT is opened in EXTEND mode. Provided the input ABC123.DAT exists, this program will run successfully even if the output file TEST.DAT does not. This is because TEST.DAT was specified as OPTIONAL. Had the OPTIONAL clause been omitted, the declarative procedure for TESTFILE would trap the error; the program would display "TESTFILE: no OPTIONAL clause" and it would then terminate.

A
COBOL Reserved Words

Flagged words are not ANSI reserved words but are reserved words as follows:
'r' RM/COBOL-85, '*' Micro Focus COBOL, '|' both implementations.

ACCEPT	* BACKGROUND-	* COMP-0
ACCESS	COLOUR		COMP-1
ACTUAL	* BACKWARD	* COMP-2
ADD		BEEP		COMP-3
* ADDRESS	BEFORE		COMP-4
ADVANCING		BELL	* COMP-5
AFTER	BINARY	r COMP-6
ALL	BLANK	* COMP-X
ALPHABET		BLINK	COMPUTATIONAL
ALPHABETIC	BLOCK	* COMPUTATIONAL-0
ALPHABETIC-LOWER	BOTTOM		COMPUTATIONAL-1
ALPHABETIC-UPPER	BY	* COMPUTATIONAL-2
ALPHANUMERIC			COMPUTATIONAL-3
ALPHANUMERIC	CALL		COMPUTATIONAL-4
-EDITED	CANCEL	* COMPUTATIONAL-5
ALSO	CD	r COMPUTATIONAL-6
ALTER	CF	* COMPUTATIONAL-X
ALTERNATE	CH	COMPUTE
AND	* CHAIN	CONFIGURATION
ANY	* CHANGED	* CONSOLE
* APPLY	CHARACTER	CONTAINS
ARE	CHARACTERS	CONTENT
AREA	CLASS	CONTINUE
AREAS	CLOCK-UNITS	CONTROL
ASCENDING	CLOSE	CONTROLS
ASSIGN	COBOL		CONVERT
AT	CODE		CONVERTING
AUTHOR	CODE-SET	COPY
	AUTO	r COL	CORR
* AUTO-SKIP	COLLATING	CORRESPONDING
	AUTOMATIC	COLUMN	COUNT
	COMMA	* CRT
r BACKGROUND	COMMON	* CRT-UNDER
	BACKGROUND-	COMMUNICATION	CURRENCY
COLOR	COMP		CURSOR

* CYCLE

DATA
DATE
DATE-COMPILED
DATE-WRITTEN
DAY
DAY-OF-WEEK
DE
DEBUG-CONTENTS
DEBUG-ITEM
DEBUG-LINE
DEBUG-NAME
DEBUG-SUB-1
DEBUG-SUB-2
DEBUG-SUB-3
DEBUGGING
DECIMAL-POINT
DECLARATIVES
DELETE
DELIMITED
DELIMITER
DEPENDING
DESCENDING
DESTINATION
DETAIL
DISABLE
* DISK
DISPLAY
DIVIDE
DIVISION
DOWN
DUPLICATES
DYNAMIC

* ECHO
EGI
* EJECT
ELSE
EMI
* EMPTY-CHECK
ENABLE
END
| END-ACCEPT
END-ADD
END-CALL
* END-CHAIN
END-COMPUTE
END-DELETE
* END-DISPLAY
END-DIVIDE

END-EVALUATE
END-IF
END-MULTIPLY
END-OF-PAGE
END-PERFORM
END-READ
END-RECEIVE
END-RETURN
END-REWRITE
END-SEARCH
END-START
END-STRING
END-SUBTRACT
END-UNSTRING
END-WRITE
ENTER
* ENTRY
ENVIRONMENT
| EOL
EOP
| EOS
EQUAL
* EQUALS
| ERASE
ERROR
ESCAPE
ESI
EVALUATE
EVERY
* EXCEEDS
EXCEPTION
* EXCESS-3
| EXCLUSIVE
* EXEC
* EXECUTE
* EXHIBIT
EXIT
EXTEND
EXTERNAL

FALSE
FD
FILE
FILE-CONTROL
* FILE-ID
FILLER
FINAL
FIRST
| FIXED
FOOTING
FOR

r FOREGROUND
| FOREGROUND-
COLOR
* FOREGROUND-
COLOUR
FROM
| FULL
FUNCTION

GENERATE
GIVING
GLOBAL
GO
| GOBACK
GREATER
* GRID
GROUP

HEADING
| HIGH
| HIGHLIGHT
HIGH-VALUE
HIGH-VALUES

| ID
IDENTIFICATION
IF
IN
INDEX
INDEXED
INDICATE
INITIAL
INITIALIZE
INITIATE
INPUT
INPUT-OUTPUT
INSPECT
INSTALLATION
INTO
INVALID
I-O
I-O-CONTROL
IS

* JAPANESE
JUST
JUSTIFIED

* KEPT
KEY
* KEYBOARD

LABEL	NUMERIC-EDITED	RD
LAST		READ
LEADING	OBJECT-COMPUTER	* READY
LEFT	OCCURS	RECEIVE
* LEFT-JUSTIFY	OF	RECORD
* LEFTLINE	OFF	I RECORDING
LENGTH	OMITTED	RECORDS
* LENGTH-CHECK	ON	REDEFINES
LESS	OPEN	REEL
LIMIT	OPTIONAL	REFERENCE
LIMITS	OR	REFERENCES
LINAGE	ORDER	RELATIVE
LINAGE-COUNTER	ORGANIZATION	RELEASE
LINE	OTHER	REMAINDER
LINE-COUNTER	OUTPUT	r REMARKS
LINES	OVERFLOW	REMOVAL
LINKAGE	* OVERLINE	RENAMES
* LOCAL-STORAGE		REPLACE
LOCK	PACKED-DECIMAL	REPLACING
* LOCKING	PADDING	REPORT
r LOW	PAGE	REPORTING
LOW-VALUE	PAGE-COUNTER	REPORTS
LOW-VALUES	* PARAGRAPH	I REQUIRED
* LOWER	PERFORM	RERUN
I LOWLIGHT	PF	RESERVE
	PH	RESET
I MANUAL	PIC	RETURN
MEMORY	PICTURE	I RETURN-CODE
MERGE	PLUS	* RETURNING
MESSAGE	POINTER	r REVERSE
MODE	POSITION	I REVERSE-VIDEO
MODULES	POSITIVE	REVERSED
MOVE	I PREVIOUS	REWIND
MULTIPLE	* PRINTER	REWRITE
MULTIPLY	* PRINTER-1	RF
	PRINTING	RH
* NAME	PROCEDURE	RIGHT
* NAMED	PROCEDURES	* RIGHT-JUSTIFY
* NATIONAL	PROCEED	* ROLLBACK
* NATIONAL-EDITED	PROGRAM	ROUNDED
NATIVE	PROGRAM-ID	RUN
* NCHAR	I PROMPT	
NEGATIVE	* PROTECTED	SAME
NEXT	PURGE	I SCREEN
NO		SD
* NO-ECHO	QUEUE	SEARCH
NOT	QUOTE	SECTION
* NULL	QUOTES	I SECURE
* NULLS		SECURITY
NUMBER	RANDOM	SEGMENT
NUMERIC	* RANGE	SEGMENT-LIMIT

SELECT	SYMBOLIC	UNTIL
SEND	SYNC	UP
SENTENCE	SYNCHRONIZED	I UPDATE
SEPARATE		UPON
SEQUENCE	r TAB	* UPPER
SEQUENTIAL	TABLE	USAGE
SET	TALLYING	USE
SIGN	TAPE	* USER
SIZE	TERMINAL	USING
* SKIP1	TERMINATE	
* SKIP2	TEST	VALUE
* SKIP3	TEXT	VALUES
SORT	THAN	I VARIABLE
SORT-MERGE	THEN	VARYING
* SORT-RETURN	THROUGH	
SOURCE	THRU	* WAIT
SOURCE-	TIME	WHEN
COMPUTER	* TIME-OUT	* WHEN-COMPILED
SPACE	* TIMEOUT	WITH
* SPACE-FILL	TIMES	WORDS
SPACES	* TITLE	WORKING-STORAGE
SPECIAL-NAMES	TO	WRITE
STANDARD	TOP	
STANDARD-1	* TRACE	ZERO
STANDARD-2	TRAILING	* ZERO-FILL
START	* TRAILING-SIGN	ZEROES
STATUS	TRUE	ZEROS
STOP	TYPE	
STRING		
SUB-QUEUE-1	I UNDERLINE	
SUB-QUEUE-2	* UNEQUAL	Special Characters:
SUB-QUEUE-3	UNIT	
SUBTRACT	I UNLOCK	+ * / ** < > = :
SUM	UNSTRING	. , ; ( ) " ` ' :
SUPPRESS		

B
Defining Alphabets

This appendix discusses the use of the SPECIAL-NAMES entry that defines an alphabet.

The first example is useful when we wish upper and lower case letters to be treated the same.

```
SPECIAL-NAMES.
    ALPHABET ALPHA-UPPER IS
        1 THRU 65,  'A' ALSO 'a', 'B' ALSO 'b', 'C' ALSO 'c',
                    'D' ALSO 'd', 'E' ALSO 'e', 'F' ALSO 'f',
                    'G' ALSO 'g', 'H' ALSO 'h', 'I' ALSO 'i',
                    'J' ALSO 'j', 'K' ALSO 'k', 'L' ALSO 'l',
                    'M' ALSO 'm', 'N' ALSO 'n', 'O' ALSO 'o',
                    'P' ALSO 'p', 'Q' ALSO 'q', 'R' ALSO 'r',
                    'S' ALSO 's', 'T' ALSO 't', 'U' ALSO 'u',
                    'V' ALSO 'v', 'W' ALSO 'w', 'X' ALSO 'x',
                    'Y' ALSO 'y', 'Z' ALSO 'z',
        92 THRU 97, 124 THRU 128.
```

Note that in defining an alphabet, we use the *ordinal* position of each character not the ASCII (or EBCDIC) *value*.

If we wish each lower case letter to be treated as if it were an uppercase letter throughout the program, our CONFIGURATION SECTION would contain the entry:

```
OBJECT COMPUTER.
  MS-DOS  PROGRAM COLLATING SEQUENCE IS ALPHA-UPPER.
```

With this collating sequence, the relational comparisons of alphanumeric items will be altered. For example, an item with a value of "a" will be equal to, not larger than, another item with a value of "A". An item whose first character is "a" will be smaller than one whose first character is "B".

Should we need the collating sequence to apply only when we are sorting (or merging) a file, we would omit the PROGRAM COLLATING clause. The SORT statement would have the form:

```
SORT SORT-FILE   ASCENDING KEY SORT-NAME
        COLLATING SEQUENCE IS ALPHA-UPPER …
```

We may also use this alphabet to copy one file to another while converting lower case letters to upper case. Suppose the data (lowercase or a mixture of upper/lowercase) is in LOWER-FILE, and we wish UPPER-FILE to contain the converted data. We need to modify the File Description of UPPER-FILE to read:

```
FD UPPER-FILE  CODE-SET IS ALPHA-UPPER.
```

Then when we use a statement such as WRITE UPPER-REC FROM LOWER-REC, the new file will receive the converted data. The conversion occurs with the WRITE statement. Within the program, data in UPPER-REC will appear unconverted.

If this is not satisfactory, we could reverse the treatment. First, we will define an alphabet:

```
ALPHABET LOWER-TO-UPPER IS
  1 THRU 65, 'A' THRU 'Z',
      92 THRU 97, 'A' THRU 'Z', 124 THRU 128.
```

Then we will specify this as the CODE-SET for the input file.

```
FD LOWER-FILE  CODE-SET IS LOWER-TO-UPPER.
```

Now the READ statement will convert all lowercase letters to uppercase. Note that because this alphabet defines each letter twice, it would be an illegal alphabet for a file opened for output (OUTPUT, EXTEND or I-O), or for a COLLATING SEQUENCE. Standard ANSI COBOL does not allow the user to define an alphabet in which there is character duplication; the RM/COBOL-85 compiler allows it as an extension to the standard.

Suppose you receive a file from an IBM mainframe. The data will be stored not in ASCII but in EBCDIC code. To convert this data to ASCII, we copy this file (EBCDIC-FILE) to a new file (ASCII-FILE). We would define an alphabet such as:

```
ALPHABET IS EBCDIC-ALPHA IS EBCDIC.
```

Our input file would be defined thus:

```
FD EBCDIC-FILE   CODE-SET IS EBCDIC-ALPHA.
```

C
Programming Strategies

C.1 Introduction

1. Writing computer programs can be very enjoyable. There is a sense of accomplishment when a program performs to its specifications. However, for the beginner it can also be frustrating. The student whose program still has dozens of compiler errors or generates incorrect output when the deadline for handing in the assignment is fast approaching, truly knows the meaning of frustration. The ideas set out in this appendix may help you to avoid this sinking feeling.

The stages for program development are:

1) Defining the problem. For the student programmer this means that you should fully understand the program specifications.
2) Algorithm development. Do this *before* you start to code.
3) Coding and compiling the program. This step is repeated until the program compiles error-free.
4) Testing. If your program performs calculations, try it with a range of possible input values and check the results with a calculator. You may need to return to step 3.
5) Maintenance. Business programs frequently need to be altered with changes in the company's methods of operation, government regulations, etc. Maintenance is not normally required for a student's program but you should write your program in such a way that it is easy to maintain.

C.2 Algorithms

Once you understand the program specifications, break the problem into its major components. A program which must generate a report using the data in a file will have two major components:

1   Read all the file records
2   Print the report.

This forms the basis for a *structured plan*. We can now concentrate on each part separately. This divide-and-conquer method is similar to preparing the outline for any essay. How detailed you make the structured plan is a matter of personal choice. You may wish to be very detailed for your first few programs. We might expand the first stage in our plan to:

1	Read all the files records
1.1	open the file
1.2	read the first record
1.3	perform until end of file
1.4	process the record
1.5	read the next record
1.6	end-perform
1.7	close file

You will see that some of this looks somewhat like COBOL. This is what is meant by *pseudocode* — we write the plan in a mixture of English and COBOL.

At this stage we have not troubled ourselves with the details of what we do with each record; we rather cryptically wrote "process the record" as step 1.4. We have broken step 1 into its major parts. If we get bogged down with step 1.4 at this point we may forget to complete all the major steps in stage 1.

The next stage in developing the plan will be to write steps to specify in detail the actions required for step 1.4; these will be called 1.4.1, 1.4.2, etc.

Once you have the major steps defined, it is time to think about data structures. In the report program we are considering, the records of the input file will be pre-determined. However, you need to decide how the data extracted from the file will be stored. Suppose the input file contained data on the number of shipments a company sent to three different airports called LAX, LHR, ZHR on certain dates, and we need to report the total for each destination.

```
950228    LAX    100
950228    ZHR    050
950301    LHR    150
```

We will need three identifiers to keep track of the three totals. It is good practice to list your data items at the top of the structured plan. If we need a report detailing the total shipments to each destination in each month of the year then we may consider using a table.

C.3 Stub Paragraphs

Do not fall into the trap of coding the entire program and then compiling it. For the example we are considering, we could start by coding only the lines needed for step 1. The main paragraph of our program could contain the lines:

```
MAIN-PARA.
 .....
 PERFORM READ-FILE
 PERFORM WRITE-REPORT
 ....
```

At this stage the code for WRITE-REPORT may read:

```
REPORT-PARA.
  DISPLAY "Write report code next".
```

This would be a *stub paragraph*. We can delay coding the lines to write the report until we have the first stage working correctly. How will we know it is working correctly? We may wish to change WRITE-PARA so that it displays the results on the screen.

```
REPORT-PARA.
  display "LAX count " lax-count
  display "LHR count " lax-count
  display "ZHR count " zhr-count
  DISPLAY "Write report code next".
```

This will let us know that something is being counted but are the values correct? If we are able to view the input file, we may read the first few records and manually compute the result for, say, 10 records. If we had a line in the READ-FILE paragraph such as PERFORM UNTIL EOF, we could temporarily change this to PERFORM 10 TIMES. Then the displayed output may be compared with the manual calculation.

C.4 Debugging a Program

We have a program which compiles error-free but gives the wrong output. What can we do? Micro Focus COBOL and RM/COBOL-85 both provide extensive debugging features. The simplest of these is the STEP mode. This allows you to run the program line-by-line and see how the program behaves. Another method is to add DISPLAY statements in the program.

There are many traps into which even the experienced programmer can fall. These include:

(a) Errors with conditional statements. Your program is writing a series of lines to the printer. The program specifications require an X in the field OUT-COMMENT if the value of ITEM-X is greater than 100.

```
1 PERFORM ....
2   move various items to the fields in OUT-REC
3   MOVE ITEM-X TO OUT-X
4   IF OUT-X > 100    MOVE "X" TO OUT-COMMENT·    END-IF
5   WRITE PRINT-REC FROM OUT-REC
6 END-PERFORM
```

Have you spotted the error? Once a value of ITEM-X greater than 100 is found, the X will be printed in the next and all subsequent lines of the output. We could add ELSE MOVE SPACES TO OUT-COMMENT. A better way is to add INITIALIZE OUT-REC before line 2.

MORAL: Initialize output records always, you may add a conditional statement later.

b) Forgetting to add a scope-terminator. What is wrong with this code?

```
READ-PARA.
2 READ DATA-REC AT END SET EOF TO TRUE
3 PERFORM UNTIL EOF
4   PERFORM PROCESS-RECORD
5   READ DATA-REC AT END SET EOF TO TRUE END-READ
6 END-PERFORM.
```

As it stands this code means execute lines 3 through 6 when the AT END condition is true — obviously not what was meant. Only the first record is read and the paragraph ends! In line 2 there should be an END-READ.

MORAL: Be sure to complete all conditional phrases with the appropriate scope-terminator.

There may be logic errors that you find yourself making over and over again. You may spend hours debugging your program only to find the problem is one of your personal foibles. Keep a list, hopefully a short one, of the logic errors you find yourself making. Refer to it when a program gives you trouble.

It is often difficult to find a logic error in a program no matter how carefully you study the code. How often do we read what we expect to see rather than what is actually there? Explaining the program to a patient friend (hopefully one who is computer, but not necessarily COBOL, literate) can make you think more clearly. Such "sounding board friends" can be worth their weight in gold!

D
Answers to Starred Questions

Chapter 2

2* Divisions are divided into *sections*, which, in turn, are divided into *paragraphs*.

3* The word PROGRAM-ID is a *reserved word*. The word PROG-X is a *user defined word*.

4* Paragraphs in the procedure division are composed of *sentences*, which, in turn, are composed *of statements*.

Chapter 3

2* The *asterisk* (*) character is used to denote a comment; it must be in column 7.

3* Statements must begin in Area *B*.

4* The last word in a paragraph must be followed by a *period*.

5* Underlined words are required, the others may be omitted without changing the operation.

6* False: in general the result of the calculation will be different with or without ROUNDED.

8* The braces indicate that either an identifier or a literal must be coded at this point.

Chapter 4

3* The program-name should be the same as the name of the source file, without the extension.

Chapter 5

4* a. OPEN INPUT INFILE.

Chapter 6

1* When a program uses a file, the file record must be described in the *FILE* SECTION. The program must also contain a *SELECT entry* in the Environment Division.

3* a. ITEM-A, c. 9COUNT (not recommended — begins with a digit).

4* a. `Hello, world` b. `"Hello, world"`.

Chapter 7

4* An elementary item is one that is not further subdivided. Generally it will have a PICTURE clause.

5* To improve the readability of the code. It does *not* affect a COBOL program.

6* Z-REC is a record item because it declared at the 01 level. It is also an elementary item since it is not subdivided. J-ALPHA is a group item.

7* TAX-RATE IN X-REC or TAX-RATE OF X-REC.

8*
```
01  X-REC.
    02  X-NAME      PIC X(8).
    02  X-NUMBER    PIC 99.
```

If we were sure there was a space between the name and number in each record, we could code
```
01  X-REC.
    02  X-NAME      PIC X(7).
    02  FILLER      PIC X.
    02  X-NUMBER    PIC 99.
```

Chapter 8

6* The value 4.0, since we have no S character in the picture.

7* The literal 1050SF. If we wanted `10.50 SF` we should move the elementary items.

Chapter 9

2* a)
```
    02  ITEM-A    PIC XXX    VALUE ABC. (needs "ABC")
```
d)
```
    02  ITEM-D                VALUE 1234.
        03  ITEM-D1   PIC 99.
        03  ITEM-D2   PIC 99.
        03  ITEM-D3   PIC 99     VALUE 25.
```
An elementary item may not have a VALUE when its group has one.

e) 02 ITEM-E   PIC X(4)   VALUE "ABCDE". (literal too long).

Chapter 10

1* b) 02 B-ONE   PIC X(4).
       02 B-TWO   PIC X(4).
       02 B-THREE PIC 9(4) REDEFINES B-ONE.
       (redefining item must appear as soon as possible after the redefined item).

    c) 02 C-ONE   PIC X(5).
       02 C-TWO   PIC X(4) REDEFINES C-ONE.
       (redefining item is too small).

    e) 02 E-ONE   PIC 9(4).
       02 E-TWO   PIC X(4) REDEFINES E-ONE   VALUE SPACES.
       (redefining item may not have VALUE clause).

Chapter 11

1* 01 SEASON-TABLE   VALUE "WinterSpringSummerFall".
       02 SEASON OCCURS 4 TIMES   PIC X(6).

2* 01 FARE-TABLE.
       02 FARE-ROW OCCURS 100 TIMES.
          03 FARE-CITY   PIC X(20).
          03 FARE-MILES PIC 999.
          03 FARE-FARE   PIC 99V99.

Chapter 13

1* The literal displayed would be ABC   000.
    To get the desired editing move elementary items before displaying the group.

Chapter 15

3* An IF statement may be used as an imperative statement provided it ends with the scope terminator END-IF.

4*   PARA-ONE   *missing period*
            MOVE ZERO TO ITEM-N
            MOVE SPACES TO ITEM-A   *missing period*
        PARA-TWO   *missing period*
            DISPLAY "Value of Item-A is   " ITEM-A
            STOP RUN.

Chapter 16

3* A single format-1 DISPLAY statement may be used to display *a number of identifiers and/or literals.*

4* The enhanced "field oriented" DISPLAY verb in your implementation, may be used to display: in Micro Focus COBOL *one identifier or one literal*; in RM/COBOL-85 *a number of identifiers and/or literals.*

5* The user's reply will overwrite the prompt!

6* A. Micro Focus COBOL: `DISPLAY ITEM-A FOREGROUND 3` *missing WITH.*
   B. RM/COBOL-85: `DISPLAY ITEM-A CONTROL "FCOLOR = GREEN REVERSE"` *missing comma in the CONTROL literal.*

8* False. Any named screen-data-name may be displayed or accepted.

Chapter 17

1* The literal displayed will be `Weekly Rep 0.00`. We need to make both items larger.

2* The most likely cause is that the identifier A-ONE was not an elementary item.

3* ```
INITIALIZE X-REC
    REPLACING NUMERIC-EDITED BY ZERO   NUMERIC BY 100.
```


## Chapter 18

2* a) SET TAB-X UP BY 2
   b) In Micro Focus COBOL: DISPLAY TAB-X is acceptable.
      In RM/COBOL-85: TAB-X must be moved to a numeric or numeric-edited identifier, which is then displayed.
   c) Never! We cannot use an index-name in a MOVE statement. The statement SET TAB-X TO ITEM-N would be valid if ITEM-N had a value in the range 1 - 10.

3* ```
01 CITY-TABLE.
     02 CITY-INFO OCCURS 50 TIMES INDEXED BY CX.
         03 CITY-CODE    PIC X(3).
         03 CITY-NAME    PIC X(20).
```
   Set CX to 1
   Perform until all records read
       Read a record
       Move AIRPORT-CODE to CITY-CODE (CX)
       Move AIRPORT-NAME to CITY-NAME (CX)
       Set CX up by 1
   End perform.

```
4*  01  SALES-TABLE.
        02  SALES-YEAR              OCCURS 10 INDEXED BY SALES-Y.
            03  SALES-OUTLET        OCCURS 5 INDEXED BY SALES-S.
                05  SALES-MONTH     OCCURS 12 INDEXED BY SALES-M.
                    07  SALES-PROD  OCCURS 2 INDEXED BY SALE-P
                                    PIC 9(6)V99.
```

Chapter 19

```
3*  MULTIPLY 3 BY Y GIVING X
    ADD 7.0 TO X
    DIVIDE X BY K
```

```
5*  DIVIDE LENGTH BY 12 GIVING FEET REMAINDER INCHES
```
The identifier FEET should have PIC 999.

```
6*  COMPUTE D = ( B ** 2 - 4 * A * C ) ** 0.5
  or  COMPUTE D = ( B * B - 4 * A * C ) ** 0.5
```
If $4ac > b^2$, the quantity $b^2 - 4ac$ would be negative causing the COMPUTE statement to abort the program unless ON SIZE ERROR had been included.

Chapter 20

```
2*  SELECT X-FILE ASSIGN TO DISK "F:\BOOK\DATA\PROG-20.DAT"
    ORGANIZATION LINE SEQUENTIAL
```

Chapter 21

```
1*  a)  IF TOTAL-COUNT GREATER THAN ZERO
            DIVIDE A-COUNT BY TOTAL-COUNT GIVING FRACTION
        ELSE
            MOVE ZERO TO FRACTION
        END-IF
```

```
    b)  DIVIDE A-COUNT BY TOTAL-COUNT GIVING FRACTION
            ON SIZE ERROR MOVE ZERO TO FRACTION
        END-DIVIDE
```

```
4*  MOVE SPACES TO ITEM-A
    PERFORM UNTIL ITEM-A IS NUMERIC
        DISPLAY " Enter a two-digit number" NO ADVANCING
        ACCEPT ITEM-A
        IF ITEM-A NUMERIC MOVE ITEM-A TO ITEM-N END-IF
    END-PERFORM.
```

```
5*  02  ITEM-N       PIC 99.
            88  VALID-N   VALUE 5 THRU 15.

    MOVE ZERO TO ITEM-N
```

```
PERFORM UNTIL VALID-N
    DISPLAY " Enter a two-digit number" NO ADVANCING
    ACCEPT ITEM-A
    IF ITEM-A NUMERIC MOVE ITEM-A TO ITEM-N END-IF
END-PERFORM.
```

Chapter 22

```
1* PERFORM VARYING MSX FROM 1 BY 1 UNTIL MSX > 12
        SET OUT-MSX TO MSX
        MOVE MONTHLY-SALES (MSX) TO OUT-SALES
        DISPLAY OUT-REC
    END-PERFORM
```

Where OUT-REC is defined by :
```
01 OUT-REC.
    02              PIC X(16) VALUE "Sales for Month".
    02 OUT-MSX      PIC Z9.
    02              PIC X(8)  VALUE SPACES.
    02 OUT-SALES    PIC ZZZ9.
```

```
2* SET EVEN-X TO 1
    PERFORM VARYING LOOP-COUNTER FROM 2 BY 2 UNTIL LOOP-COUNTER > 20
        MOVE LOOP-COUNTER TO EVEN-VALUE (EVEN-X)
        SET EVEN-X UP BY 1
    END-PERFORM
```

```
3* PERFORM WITH TEST AFTER UNTIL ITEM-N >= 25
        ADD 5 TO ITEM-N
    END-PERFORM
```

Chapter 23

```
1* IF MONTH < 4
        DISPLAY "First Quarter"
        IF MONTH = 1    DISPLAY "First Month of Quarter" END-IF
        ELSE    IF MONTH < 7
                    DISPLAY "Second Quarter"
                    IF MONTH = 4 DISPLAY "First Month of Quarter" END-IF
                END-IF
        ELSE    IF MONTH < 10
                    DISPLAY "Third Quarter"
                    IF MONTH = 7 DISPLAY "First Month of Quarter" END-IF
                END-IF
        ELSE
                DISPLAY "Fourth Quarter"
                IF MONTH = 10    DISPLAY "First Month of Quarter" END-IF
        END-IF.
```

2* The output from A in each case would be "X = 5" and "All done".
The output from B with the period would "All done". Without the period it would be
"X = 5" and "All done".

3*
```
EVALUATE MONTH
     WHEN    1 THRU 3      DISPLAY "First Quarter"
     WHEN    4 THRU 6      DISPLAY "Second Quarter"
     WHEN    7 THRU 9      DISPLAY "Third Quarter"
     WHEN    10 THRU 12    DISPLAY "Fourth Quarter"
END-EVALUATE
EVALUATE TRUE
     WHEN MONTH = 1 OR 4 OR 7 OR 10
                           DISPLAY "First month of Quarter"
END-EVALUATE
```

Provided we knew that the value of Month did not exceed 12, the fourth WHEN phrase
in the first statement could read: WHEN OTHER …

4*
```
EVALUATE    ITEM-1        ALSO ITEM-2   ALSO ITEM-3
     WHEN    -20 THRU 0    ALSO "COLD"   ALSO 0    DISPLAY "Valid"
     WHEN    1 THRU 20     ALSO "WARM"   ALSO 1    DISPLAY "Valid"
     WHEN    21 THRU 40    ALSO "HOT"    ALSO ANY  DISPLAY "Valid"
     WHEN    OTHER                                 DISPLAY "Invalid"
END-EVALUATE.
```

Chapter 25

1*
```
SORT SORT-FILE
     DESCENDING KEY    SORT-BALANCE
     ASCENDING KEY     SORT-NAME
     USING DATAFILE GIVING DATAFILE
```

3*
```
MAIN-PARA.
     DISPLAY "Enter City of Customers to list" NO ADVANCING
     ACCEPT TEST-CITY
     SORT SORT-FILE
         ASCENDING KEY SORT-NAME
         USING DATA-FILE
         OUTPUT PROCEDURE IS DISPLAY-PARA.
DISPLAY-PARA.
   IF SORT-CITY = TEST-CITY
       DISPLAY SORT-NAME
   END-IF.
```

Chapter 26

2* It is most likely that, since you did not need to use the alternate key, you omitted the
ALTERNATE KEY IS CUST-LAST-NAME clause.

4* When an indexed file is processed with ACCESS MODE DYNAMIC, the READ statement must include the key word NEXT, as in READ file-name NEXT...

Chapter 27

5* This function will work without synonyms. It is not efficient. Consider the two sequential codes AZ and BA; the former will give 0026, the latter 0101. Thus there will be 75 unused record key values between AZ/BA, BZ/CA, etc.

Chapter 28

3* Code a) is the more appropriate. If we use b) we will lose the second word in such place names as Bramford Speke, Medicine Hat, Alice Springs, etc.

Index